BROTHERS IN BATTLE, BEST OF FRIENDS

BROTHERS IN BATTLE, BEST OF FRIENDS

Two WWII Paratroopers from the
Original Band of Brothers Tell Their Story

WILLIAM "WILD BILL" GUARNERE AND
EDWARD "BABE" HEFFRON

with Robyn Post

Foreword by Tom Hanks

CALIBER

Dutton Caliber
An imprint of Penguin Random House LLC
375 Hudson Street
New York, New York 10014

Copyright © 2007 by William Guarnere and Edward Heffron
Front cover photo © Time Life Pictures/Getty Images
Front and back cover photos of the authors courtesy of the authors

DUTTON CALIBER is a registered trademark and the D colophon is a trademark of Penguin Random House LLC.

THE LIBRARY OF CONGRESS HAS CATALOGUED THE HARDCOVER EDITION AS FOLLOWS:
Brothers in battle, best of friends : two WWII paratroopers from the original band of brothers tell their story / by William "Wild Bill" Guarnere and Edward "Babe" Heffron with Robyn Post.
  p. cm.
Includes bibliographical references and index.
ISBN 978-0-425-21728-3
1. Guarnere, William.   2. Heffron, Edward.   3. United States. Army. Airborne Division, 101st Easy Company—History.   4. United States. Army. Airborne Division, 101st—Biography.   5. United States Army—Parachute troops—Biography.   6. World War, 1939–1945—Personal narratives. American.   7. World War, 1939–1945—Regimental histories—United States.   8. World War, 1939–1945—Campaigns—Western Front.   9. Soldiers—United States—Biography.   I. Heffron, Edward.   II. Post, Robyn.   III. Band of brothers (Television program : 2001)   IV. Title.
  D769.346101st.G83   2007
  940.54'12730922—dc 22
  [B]   2007021056

PUBLISHING HISTORY
Berkley Caliber hardcover edition / October 2007
Berkley Caliber trade paperback edition / October 2008
First Dutton Caliber trade paperback edition: 2017
Dutton Caliber trade paperback ISBN: 978-0-425-22436-6

Cover design by Richard Hasselberger
Book design by Tiffany Estreicher

Printed in the United States of America

17th Printing

For
Henry Guarnere
and the kids who never came home

CONTENTS

FOREWORD

Too often, war on film becomes a glamorous action movie. The horrors of battle look thrilling as heroes defy odds and cheat death. The bullets are blanks, the explosions are special effects, and the costumed actors wear made-up wounds in an art-directed fiction that is improbably "cool."

Before the characters see combat, war can look like a long camping trip. Young men get into the best physical shape of their lives, make friends and laugh at every opportunity, then perform daring acts like jumping out of airplanes. Their camaraderie is the stuff of being young, being proud, and being a part of a great adventure. In the movies, the battle is when things get exciting. In real war, it's when young men kill other young men.

The European Theater of World War II is particularly attractive, as London, Paris, and the Austrian Alps are some of the locales. The D-day invasion of Normandy had an understandable geography. The Battle of the Bulge was a pure drama with a surrounding, desperate enemy. Victory in Europe was definitive, marked by the time and the place and the party that followed. And everyone knows the alliance of Good Guys won the Good War.

In the HBO miniseries *Band of Brothers,* we producers held an ace up our filmmaking sleeve that helped span the divide between what actually happened and how it appeared on the screen—that was the book, a marvelous piece of history told by Stephen Ambrose, a great scholar and a dazzling storyteller. The details came straight from the mouths of the characters—and what characters they are.

Easy Company of the 506th Regiment of the 101st Airborne was a collection of fascinating men. Some of them were taciturn, others hilarious. Some were country boys, others came from the biggest of cities. Most of America's faiths were represented, including atheism. Some were accomplished ladies' men, others so shy they passed the war with their virginity intact. Each of them faced the coming struggles with a priceless advantage—each other.

To single out one or two of these Screaming Eagles as the Most Super-Duper Paratrooper or the Best Source for a free beer on VE day would be a fool's errand. But to fail to single out Bill Guarnere and Babe Heffron would overlook a grand entertainment and a stirring inspiration.

"Wild Bill" and Babe. Even their names beg the telling of their tale, like great ball players from the 1920s, or legendary lawmen— or outlaws—of the Old West. They are the guys who grew up just blocks from each other in Philadelphia, yet never met until they were in England. Babe, you see, *walked* a certain way, with a combination of a confident stride and a cocky bounce so Bill knew, just *knew,* this replacement trooper had to be from Philly. Guarnere was a veteran of the jump into Normandy and had already survived the killing, the misery, and the miles of bloody territory that would have to be taken before the war would end and he could go home. Heffron, newly assigned to Easy Company, was soon to fight in Operation Market Garden and barely survive the Battle of the Bulge. They were young, strong, oversexed, and over there—just the kind of heroes that history makes out of two guys from Philadelphia.

The true measure of what Bill and Babe experienced in the war—what they lost and suffered, what challenges they faced and conquered—could never be fully re-created in a miniseries for television, even in a thousand hours. The best we filmmakers could aim for was capturing a true portrait of *who* they were.

While shooting the fifth episode of *Band of Brothers*, the production was on the massive back lot, once an abandoned aerospace plant north of London, which we turned into Normandy, Holland, Belgium, Germany, and even Camp Toccoa, Georgia. Two units were filming simultaneously, with actors moving between episodes—from one false battlefield to another—often on the same day.

Frank John Hughes, who played Wild Bill Guarnere, had a special duty that required his wearing his uniform/costume off the set. Looking exactly like an American paratrooper of 1944, complete with his set of jump wings, his pant legs bloused into his Corcoran boots, and a Screaming Eagle patch on his shoulder, Hughes reported to Heathrow Airport.* VIP guests were due in from the United States, and he was to escort them to the movie set.

With a crisp salute at ramrod attention, the actor greeted Wild Bill Guarnere and Babe Heffron upon their return to England.

* In uniform, Hughes attracted many looks of admiration, especially from women.

When the two veterans arrived at our version of Holland, word of their presence spread like wildfire, as if Elvis Presley and the Beatles were on the lot. Shooting stopped, the production offices emptied, and the cast and crew began flocking to the back lot on foot, in vintage army jeeps, on scooters and bikes. Everyone wanted to see the men themselves, the troopers whose stories we were telling, two of the band of brothers who jumped into hell on earth in order to save the world.

Bill Guarnere and Babe Heffron were old men by then. Fifty-six years earlier, Bill had lost one of his legs somewhere in the woods outside of the village of Foy in Belgium. Babe was still reeling from the long flight and the jet lag. Both of them were gracious, gregarious, and needed a beer. And there, on only three legs, stood the paradox of our series *Band of Brothers*—the war was not glamorous but the men of Easy Company were, and still are.

Tom Hanks

PREFACE

On assignment for *Philadelphia* magazine in the spring of 2001, I went to meet Bill Guarnere and Babe Heffron, World War II veterans who would later be portrayed in the HBO miniseries *Band of Brothers*, produced by Steven Spielberg and Tom Hanks. Babe is the father of one of my dearest friends. Bill is her godfather.

We met at Bill's house, a humble war shrine with American flags and eagles everywhere. "Yowwwwza!" Bill yelled when he saw his buddy, Babe. "Yoooooooooo!" echoed Babe. They were as fired up as young enlistees, their youth preserved in their friendship. Bill imitated Bogart; Babe looked and sounded like Ralph Kramden. They bantered like an old-time comedy duo (Bill: "Babe never liked my jokes." Babe: "Bill ain't as funny as he thinks. When he thinks he's funny, he isn't. When he *is* funny, he don't know it!"). Babe poured himself a Baileys Irish Cream, and settled into the brown recliner that's become his chair. Bill plopped on the couch and patted the seat next to him. "Sit down, honey," he said sweetly. "What do you want to know?" We dug out piles of photos and letters from the war, while Bill puffed away on Pall Malls, and the two of them reminisced about war buddies. "Sing that song you used to sing with Joe Toye," Bill urged, and Babe belted out a rendition of "I'll Be Seeing You" worthy of Broadway. (He sang "Bridget O'Flynn" in the miniseries' companion documentary *We Stand Alone Together: The Men of Easy Company*.)

The men had first met during the war, when both were part of an Army experiment to collect teenage boys across America, turn them into hardened warriors, and pit them against the vicious Nazi machine that was swiftly overtaking Europe. They'd be the Army's first paratroopers, trained to incapacitate foes while surrounded behind enemy lines. The boys of the 506th Parachute Infantry Regiment would be the first to stay together from basic training to combat, making them so cohesive and efficient, they would be unmatched on the battlefield. One group of men, known as Easy Company, stood out above the rest. Led by a masochistic commander they bonded to hate, Easy became one of the toughest, most physically fit, closest-knit group of soldiers the Army ever produced. In June 1943, their regiment was attached to the 101st Airborne, the Screaming Eagles, for what the 101st's commander called a "rendezvous with destiny." They stormed through Normandy on D-day, liberated Holland in Operation Market Garden, defended Bastogne at the Battle of the Bulge, captured Hitler's Eagle's Nest in Berchtesgaden, and liberated a concentration camp in Landsberg, Germany. Easy Company incapacitated German troops who outnumbered them in the biggest, bloodiest war ever fought.

Bill was a platoon sergeant in Easy Company over forty-eight men. His commander, Dick Winters, called him a natural killer; his men called him "Wild Bill." Babe joined Easy Company after the Normandy invasion, and became a machine gunner and private first class under Bill's command. The two grew up blocks apart in South Philadelphia, yet never met until they were united by an enemy three thousand miles from home. The men were an unlikely pair—Babe was guided by his Irish Catholic upbringing and played by the rules; Bill was fearless and spontaneous, and lived by his own rules—but they became fast friends and fought side by side all over northern Europe. When they reconnected in their hometown after the war, they were bonded in a way no civilian could ever fathom.

Today, their friendship is extraordinary. In sixty-three years, the men haven't gone a day without a phone call between them. They finish each other's sentences, laugh alike, and have adopted each other's sayings, like "Don't irrigate me." They talk in an old dialect reminiscent of the Bowery Boys and everyone the war generation grew up with. They say "foist" for first, and "thoid" for third, and call people scallywags. To a question they often exclaim, "Why, soitainly!" They're tough and unstoppable, and ready to go "fist city" with the unpatriotic.

I made one mistake that first day: I called the men heroes. "We are *not* heroes!" Bill said adamantly. "The kids who never came home are the heroes!" They believe they only did what their country asked of them, like millions of other men and women all over the world. They came from humble beginnings in South Philadelphia, raised in an era when you simply did what needed to be done for family, for community, for your country.

Despite what they say, these men *are* heroes. They risked their young lives, fighting fearlessly for the world's freedom. We must never forget the heavy price all of our combat veterans have paid. Some paid the ultimate price, while others bear the daily burden of having lived through the horror, with their haunting memories or permanent wounds.

When my piece "Veteran's Day" was published in *Philadelphia* magazine, it caught the attention of Scott Miller, a very clever literary agent and former Philadelphian, who thought Bill and Babe's war stories and profound friendship were worthy of a book. He brought the idea to the Berkley Publishing Group, and this incredible project was born.

Bill and Babe agreed to share their most personal stories "for the kids who never came home." This wasn't easy for them. I interviewed them about a hundred times between 2001 and 2006. Sometimes the stories flowed like water, but more often, I had to poke and prod and wring out details. In either case, I was completely humbled by their honesty and openness in talking about some very tough subjects. Time has clouded their memories a bit, but the men recall events from sixty-three years ago like they happened yesterday, and help each other fill in missing details.

In each chapter, Bill and Babe take turns telling their story, one often beginning where the other left off. The frequency of the back-and-forth mirrors their proximity during different parts of their wartime and postwar lives. For example, Babe was not in Normandy, so that chapter is Bill's alone. The same goes for Babe in Germany. In "Bastogne," and "Back to the Places We Fought," for example, they're nearly side by side, so the exchange is constant down the page, with Bill's stories always in italics. The stories, voices, grammar, and lexicon are all theirs. The sequence is mine in that stories and observations were rearranged to follow the sequence of events as they occurred, based on the men's recollections and historical accounts of Easy Company's campaign. Two invaluable resources were *Band of Brothers* by Stephen Ambrose, and *Beyond Band of Brothers* by Maj. Dick Winters. Using the latter, with the men's permission, I incorporated any time and place references they could not recollect, to make it easier for readers to follow.

Bill's war experiences begin with the "Army experiment" at Camp Toccoa, Georgia. Babe's begin with an artillery outfit at Fort Eustis, Virginia. Where Bill's training was part of the adventure, Babe's is just a necessary prelude. He joined Bill and Easy Company as a replacement after the men returned from Normandy and remained with the company until war's end.

Bill and Babe hope this book teaches the true meaning and importance of freedom, and what it means to fight for it. I'm extremely honored and grateful to have been part of this worthy task, and I thank Bill and Babe with all my heart for their courage, bravery, honesty, and generosity. I will forever be inspired by them, and by their story.

Robyn Post

Introduction

BILL

When you're a paratrooper, you're the elite of the Army, you're always on the front lines. You know you're going to pay the price. Then you had the German army. They were fighting the war for years. By World War II, they had it perfected, they had the best weapons in the world. We were no match for German artillery. Those Germans were technologically advanced for being a small country. They had the best fighters in the world, the *Fallschirmjäger*, German paratroopers, and the SS—Nazis, even the Germans were scared of them. They were fearless, raised as boys to live and die for Hitler. Germany was prepared, and America was sound asleep. We didn't make the plans for it, kid.

Our company, our entire division, the 101st Airborne, was on the front lines of every major battle in the European Theater, without enough men, weapons, artillery, ammunition, supplies, and proper clothing. Easy Company had a reputation—because of our captains, Herbert Sobel and Dick Winters—as the toughest and best. Since the Army lacked manpower, we were always sent in to take up the slack. As trained as we were, as good as we were, it was chaos, death was all around, you knew any minute could be your last. We froze, we starved, we were covered in filth, we were exhausted, we lost good kids every day, we saw things people don't see in ten lifetimes. When we thought we were beaten down as far as we could go, we were kept on the front lines. I never expected to survive a day, let alone the whole war.

We lost a lot of men, but we inflicted more casualties on the Germans than they inflicted on us. In Bastogne, they had three times the men and three times the firepower. I have no idea how we done it. I still can't believe we won the war.

The most haunting part by far was Bastogne. But when I think about the war, I don't think about the battle, I think about the men. I look at an American flag today, and I see the faces of the men I fought with, the ones who lived and the ones who died.

We were eighteen, nineteen years old when we went in. We knew we wanted to be the best and fight beside the best. Be in the Airborne. Be paratroopers. The uniform alone showed the world you were different and special. You put on those silver wings, bloused up your pants, and you were it. Training was brutal, but we were with guys from all over the country. You faced the challenges together. We spent every minute together from basic training to jump training to combat. We were a family, way before we hit the battlefield. We could predict each other's every move. We were like a machine. Ready for anything. We figured we'll get to Europe, knock off the Germans real quick, and come home for Christmas. We had no idea, kid. *No* idea.

BABE

The day I joined Easy Company, the commander, Dick Winters, sent me to see Bill Guarnere, 2nd Platoon sergeant, a fellow South Philly kid. Bill was one of Easy Company's most respected leaders. He was gruff, and wisecracking, and he had a reputation. The guys called him Wild Bill. He was a tough SOB, and strict, but he took good care of the men. They just returned from fierce combat in Normandy, and newcomers like me had to prove themselves to fit in. Bill and I talked about home and got to be friends, even though he was a sergeant and I was a private, and you never socialized outside your rank.

After the war, I took a walk down to Bill's neighborhood and found him shooting dice on the street. We've been almost inseparable for sixty years since. We've talked on the phone every day, we've had breakfast or lunch together every week, we've worked together, traveled together, we take care of each other. My daughter recently asked me, "Dad, what are you gonna do if something happens to Uncle Bill?" She didn't say Uncle Jack or Uncle Jimmy, my blood brothers. She said "Uncle Bill." Bill and I made a pact that if anything happens to the other one, we'll go out and get stinkin' drunk. I can't explain our friendship, but you can't explain the bonds you have with the men you fight beside in combat either. For a veteran, that's the only good that comes from war. That, and knowing what you fought for was worth the sacrifice.

I never told anyone about my war experiences, not even my family, even though not a day went by that it wasn't on my mind. When the book *Band of Brothers*, and then the HBO movie, came out, it opened up old wounds. Some of the memories were painful, and it was hard to relive them. But the fond memories are of your war buddies. I'm grateful to have been among the men of Easy Company, men of the highest caliber. I'd put them up against anyone in the military.

I want people to know we're not heroes. We did our duty, just like the sixteen million others who fought in the war. Everyone, including the families, sacrificed in some way. The kids who didn't come home are the heroes. They're the ones who gave their lives. Their parents are the heroes, because they gave a child. But if our story can bring more attention to what it means to fight for freedom, then it's worth telling. A Dutchman in Holland said to me and Bill when we liberated Eindhoven, "Can you define freedom?" He said, "You can't. You don't know what freedom is until you lose it." I never forgot that. He knew what it was to lose it because he'd lived under German occupation for five years, and like another Dutchman told us, "that wasn't living."

Sometimes over a beer, Bill and I talk about the war. We go back every couple years to visit the graves of our war buddies in Normandy, Holland, and Belgium, and visit people we liberated who've kept in touch with us over the years. Every June we think of D-day, every September we think of Holland, every December we think of Bastogne. That was Belgium's coldest winter on record, and we spent it outside in the ground. To this day, every time we see snow, we say to each other, "Thank God we're not in a foxhole and no one is trying to kill us."

I went back to Aldbourne, England, right after the war and returned to the village where I first joined Easy Company, where we ate, slept, and trained. As I walked on our old training field, the strangest thing happened. I could hear plain as day the men counting cadence, double-timing, rifle bolts being pulled back, the guys shouting and kidding each other. I even heard the voices of the kids who never came back. I heard them clearly. I told Bill about it, and he thought I was crazy. He told me I had a screw loose. Then we went back to Aldbourne the following year, and he said, "Babe, remember what you told me about what you heard in Aldbourne? It happened to me, too." I wasn't surprised. The memories of the war almost never leave your mind.

What you don't know going in is that when you come out, you will be scarred for life. Whether you were in for a week, a month, or a year—even if you come home without a scratch—you are never, ever going to be the same. When I went in, I was eighteen. I thought it was all glory and you win lots of medals. You think you're going to be the guy. Then you find out that the cost is very great. Especially when you don't see the kids you were with when you went in. Living with it can be hell. It's like the devil presides in you. I knew what I signed up for, yes, and I would do it again. But the reality of war—words can't begin to describe it.

1

★

GROOMED FOR WAR ON THE STREETS OF SOUTH PHILLY

BILL

In South Philadelphia, you didn't survive unless you learned the tricks of the streets. Food was scarce, money was scarce. Everything you got you worked for, or you stole; nobody gave you nothing. I thought stealing was a normal thing to do. I learned later it was wrong, but back then we did it to eat, to survive. Everyone was in the same boat. You were always in survival mode. You lived for today and tomorrow. I had six brothers and three sisters. I was the baby of ten. Think of trying to feed ten kids today. Back then it was a hundred times harder. Have you ever had an empty stomach for three or four days? We weren't starving, but we went hungry a lot.

Being the baby came in handy. We had ten kids at the dinner table, some older than twenty, and I'm five or six. Nobody touched nothing till Pop sat down and said the prayer and Mom gave the okay. And boy, you never said, "I don't like this." They'd throw you out of the kitchen. You didn't eat. There would be two donuts left from the night before—two donuts, ten kids. Mom would walk to the light switch and say, "Okay, boys and girls, you ready?" When the lights went out, if you got your hands on that food, it was yours. I stuck my hand in the dish, I got nine forks stabbing me! I thought, I'll fix these rat finks. When the lights went back on, I cried. They'd say, "Oh, the poor baby," and they'd give me some. I always got more than everybody else. I got wise real early in life.

Even as a baby, you were geared to work and to try to earn a penny. Every day I worked—helped Mom clean, did windows, swept streets. For that your parents fed and clothed you. You did it for neighbors, too. You didn't have to be asked. You noticed something was wrong, you went over there and did it. They handed you an apple or a penny and you were happy.

There was only one car in our whole neighborhood. No one had telephones. Anytime you got a phone call, you ran to the corner store to Jew Meyers's and took the call. That's what we called the store! It wasn't discrimination back then. It was a term of endearment. There were all nationalities in your neighborhood and you took care of each other. We were a well-oiled machine, the Irish, the Italians, the Polish, and the Jews. All very nice people. You called Italians dagos, you called the Polish Pollacks—it was like a nickname, and everyone had nicknames. There was none of this stuff you hear today. Today, you'll get arrested if you call someone a dago, or call someone Jew Meyer.

I was a resourceful kid. Up the street there were five or six auto repair garages, and I would go to Melrose Diner and fill up a stainless steel thermos that held about ten cups of coffee; it cost me twelve or fifteen cents. I'd take cups with me and sell coffee to people at the garage for a nickel a cup. I'd make a quarter, and give it to Mom, and she'd get so excited. She'd go play the numbers with it, and hope to double it. Times were tough. Even at the garage, sometimes they said, "Get out of here, kid!"

We played a lot of sports; it kept your mind off what you didn't have. If you bought a ball for five cents, and it broke in half, you played half-ball. If you didn't have a football, you got newspapers and wet them and layered them up until you had a football, you put tape around it and you played. We played kick the can. We took big wooden crates like you find in back of the markets, took the wheels off baby coaches and attached them under the box, and we'd make racing cars. Or we made roller coasters with flat wood and parts of roller skates. Sounds silly, but it makes you resourceful in life. You're always thinking about how simple things can be used. We didn't go to college like the kids today. Today they push buttons and a machine tells you what to do.

Sometimes I tagged along with my brother Henry, and hung out with the older kids. He was closest to my age in my family; he was four years older. We played sports, gambled, chased girls. He was a baseball nut. He played baseball and collected baseball cards and sports clippings from the paper. He had a big collection, knew every player on every team.

Babe says he hung out in Laundromats. We never heard of hanging out in Laundromats. We hung outside on the corner. We'd bring a table out, sit under the lights, play cards all night in the street. Or we'd play craps. Broads didn't play craps.

There was a lot of fighting in the streets. You had the kids who were good street fighters. But when you got done, most of the time you shook hands. Everybody fought with each other. That was street life.

My pop was Joe the tailor. He worked out of our house at Chadwick and McKean. Pop was a tough old bird, came to the United States from Italy in 1891. Spoke broken English. Mom was born here, but she talked Italian, and every time they talked Italian it meant somebody was in trouble.

When I was five or six, I'd watch the men gamble, drink, play cards, play numbers and bocci ball in the street. It was a den of iniquity where I grew up! There were no cars around, and if there was a car in the street, they'd take the bocci ball and break it right through the windshield. In bocci, you shoot the ball with a mallet to get it close to the beanie ball. Sometimes someone would hit the ball right into the sewer. So they called me: "Billyyyyyy!" I'd run over, my pop would grab one leg, someone else grabbed the other, they dunked me down the sewer to get that ball! Oy, veh. I smelled like a rat. Then they fixed you up and gave you a glass of wine. I'm telling you, kid, I was only five or six years old! Then they said, "You smoke?" I said, "No." They gave me two cigars. I'm drinking wine and smoking two cigars. That stopped you from smoking real fast. You turned green, red, purple. These were Italian cigars! Other times two players' balls would get close. They'd call me and say, "Hey, Billy, measure with your fingers." I'd look at my father's ball, then my uncle's ball, and they'd both look at me, like *Pick mine or I'll kill you.* I made a few calls and they beat the shillelagh out of me after they checked. After that,

I learned. I'd make the call and smack the balls away. Then they gave me a glass of wine. I got exposed to booze at a very young age. I was a good kid—devilish, but a good kid.

Mom's name was Augusta. An absolute angel. I spent a lot of time with Mom. We'd make ravioli together. Ever hear of Sophie Tucker? Before movies came out, they had vaudeville. Sophie Tucker was a big, fat mama, short and plump. She sang and smoked. Mom was like Sophie Tucker. Those days there was no worrying about clothes, how you looked, how you dressed, how fat you were, how skinny you were. Nobody could care less.

I went to junior high and worked for Pop at the same time. Ooh, I was a devil. Here's a story: Now Pop can't get none of the older brothers to be a tailor. Along comes Billy the baby. This is the last resort he has. He thinks to himself, *I'm gonna make a tailor out of Billy.* He's got me picking up the iron, sewing, doing everything by hand. I'm killing myself. I must weigh about ninety pounds soaking wet. I'm thinking, *This ain't for me!* But you can't say no to Pop. Sometimes you get some smartness in your head, see. So I walked up to Passyunk Avenue, to stores that sold clothing and asked what prices were for tailoring. So I told them I charged a nickel. I'd undercut the other people at the beginning to get the work. After school, I picked people's pants up and brought them to Pop, he fixed them in an hour, I ran them back. Pop forgot all about me working in the store!

The summer of 1938, Mom signed me up for Citizens Military Training Camp (CMTC) in Fort Meade, Maryland. You went four summers and then you could become an officer in the Army. They taught you military skills. To get me in, Mom lied and said I was seventeen. I was only fifteen. Henry and Earnest went to CCC, Civilian Conservation Corps. Times were tough, and the camp meant food, clothing, and someone to take care of you. It kept you out of trouble. It was the first time I'd ever been out of my neighborhood, but I adapted real fast. Even then, my leadership abilities came right out. We learned Army basics, but the camp didn't have much—maybe two trucks, one gun, a couple mops and brooms. We had to share. Even as a kid I could see we weren't prepared for war. We did mostly garrison duty, cleaning windows, dusting. We did close-order drills, learned some soldiering, learned to shoot guns. I went three summers until they closed it in 1941 when we entered the war.

The day Pearl Harbor was bombed, I was at 17th and McKean playing craps in the street. One of the guys on our block was stationed in Pearl Harbor, so news got around real fast. With the war coming, I quit high school and went to work in a defense factory called Baldwin Locomotive, making Sherman tanks. I figured the hell with graduation. No one in my family graduated high school. They quit and went to work. But Mom was not happy. She begged me, "You're the last one, Billy, please, you gotta graduate." She kept after me. So I asked to work midnight to eight for four or five months. I went to school in the day, worked all night. Got my diploma in 1941. Made Mom the happiest gal in the world.

The spring of 1942, me, Dino, and Eddie from the neighborhood went to volunteer. I was exempt from the draft because of my job. But everyone was going. You looked like a fool if you didn't go. Get me in the action, Jackson! I was going to enlist in the Marines—they're known as the best of the military, but at the recruiting station I saw a big poster, it said, "All New! Paratroopers." I went to see what it was all about, and I enlisted. The paratroopers were all volunteer. The elite of the Army. If you're going to combat, you want to fight with the best. You're accepting something no one else wanted to do. It was new, untested, people thought you would get killed fast. If you volunteer for that, you're half nuts. Same if you join the submarines—that's the elite of the Navy—they were just as crazy. The ones who make it through are the toughest, the best, the ones you want to fight beside and trust your life to. I knew I could pass the training because I was in great physical shape. I played a lot of football and basketball and was good at it.

Dino and Eddie enlisted in the paratroopers, too, but they didn't make it; they went into the Army as infantry. The neighborhood kids went all over—the Marines, Army, Navy—everyone went their separate ways.

Most of my brothers were older and married, so only the three youngest were going to war: me, Henry, and Earnest. Earnest joined the Navy; he was the first of us to go, sent to the Pacific. Later he was in the merchant marines and was torpedoed in the Pacific. He was missing for six months and wound up in a leper colony. He served in the Army, the Canadian army, the Black Watch—they wear Scottish kilts—and the Coast Guard. How he did it, I don't know. He went under different names, different serial numbers. Earnest was all over the place. A true soldier of fortune. I wish I knew his stories. He was never around, never went to school, couldn't read or write, but he was smart about life. Henry was sent to Africa and then Monte Cassino, Italy. He was a medic in the 1st Armored Division of the 47th Armored Medical Battalion. Henry and I wrote letters back and forth, but he couldn't say where he was because of Army regulations. I was accepted into the Airborne and was being sent for training to Camp Toombs, Georgia, in July.

I hated to leave my girl, Frannie. I met her on the corner when she was thirteen years old and I was sixteen. A beauty. I fell in love with her like I never knew what a broad was. I knew I would marry her. She was nuttier than me, a spitfire, didn't take no guff from nobody. I liked that about her. I gave her a fifty-dollar diamond ring before I left. Where did I get fifty dollars? I have no idea. She gave me a photo of herself in a grass Hawaiian skirt to carry with me. She promised she'd be waiting for me.

Before the three of us left, Mom said, "You behave yourselves, you be good boys." Pop cried and said, "Watch what you do." He wasn't worldly. He had no concept of the war. The old people didn't understand. They didn't know what happened in their own neighborhood, let alone outside Philadelphia or the United States. Pop knew nothing of Pearl Harbor. He couldn't have imagined where we were going, or that one of us wouldn't be coming back.

BABE

Growing up poor in South Philly built up my stamina. So did the Sisters of the Immaculate Heart of Mary. I was born in a small row house in an alley in South Philadelphia. Christened Edward James Heffron, I was the third of five children in an Irish family. Our house was three stories, one room on each floor. We called those houses "Father, Son, and Holy Ghost." If someone asked you where you lived, you said, "up the gut." That meant the alley. None of us on Wilder Street had any money.

My street was like the League of Nations, people of all nationalities, and we all got along well. The neighbors would chip in for backyard beer parties. Extra money meant we could have a bottle of whiskey. My family came from strong Irish stock and we were reared to work hard for whatever we wanted in life. I think this is where I learned the philosophy I live by: If you work hard, do what's right, if you're good to people, then it will all come back to you in the end. I've had very good fortune that way.

My father, Joseph, was a prison guard. The neighbors would come by and ask him to take cigarettes or books to friends and relatives in the prison. He had a weakness for betting on the ponies and, in his later years, could always be found on the couch, Camel in hand, perusing racing forms. Dad wasn't an emotional or affectionate person. He never gave any of us a hug. A kiss was out of the question. When my brothers and I came home after the war, he shook our hands and said, "Glad you're back." We knew we were loved. Dad just couldn't bring himself to show it.

The greatest gift ever given me was my mother, Anne. She was a fiery redhead with big blue eyes that could look right through you. She always knew when one of us was fibbing. She was the most loving, caring woman I've ever known. There were plenty of nights we had little or no food on the table and Christmases with nothing under the tree. Mom made it not so bad to have an empty stomach or be forgotten by Santa Claus.

My parents had five children from 1921 to 1936: Joseph, James, me, John (we called him Jack or Jake), and Anna Margaret. We went to Sacred Heart Catholic School from first to eighth grades and went to Mass every Sunday.

There was a sense of community and loyalty in those days. Even with the cops. When I was about twelve, my cousin Jim asked me to buy him a "loosie," a cigarette they sold individually for a penny. My cousin told me, "You can light it and take a couple of drags, but don't steam it up." So I did. Just then, a cop walked up behind me, took me and the cigarette to the station house two doors away. There was another cop there I knew. He said, "I know all of these kids. They're good kids. This kid's dad ain't going to like this." They sent a police car down to the Lyric Theater at Second and Morris to get my father. When I got home I got the belt and was kept in the house for two weeks.

We hung out on street corners, or in the local candy store, or the Laundromat. My friends and I ranged in ages from eleven to fourteen. Everyone had nicknames. I got my nickname, Babe, when I was an infant. My older brother, Jimmy, heard my mother call me the baby and he tried to say "baby" and said "babe" instead. Jimmy's nickname is Shad, just like the fish because his mouth is always open, shouting and hollering. There was also Skip-a-Beat Nelson; he had a heart condition. Rubber-nose Morris could push his nose all over his face. Anthony "the Brain" Cianfrani became the most educated of all of us. One of my oldest and dearest friends is Tony "Save you for Wednesday" Cirigilo. He got that name in grade school auditioning for the choir. He sang a few bars of "Ave Maria," and the nun said, "That's okay, Tony, we'll save you for Wednesday."

We hung out inside Laundromats so the nuns wouldn't see us and put us to work. That's where we put together our first football team, and called it Damp Wash, A.C. As we got older, we'd replace older men on the Corsac team. That's Latin for "sacred heart," part of our parish church's name.

We played rough football on the cinders at Heron Prep. A black eye or broken bone wasn't unusual, but one day, my hand and my fingers contracted to the wrist, and curled under, and I was in excruciating pain from my wrist all the way up my arm. I couldn't open my hand. I had to walk away for a few minutes. It kept happening whenever I used my hands too much, and always to both hands at once. I didn't know then, but it would stay with me for decades. I never told anyone. My mother would have made me stop playing football, and I didn't like that idea! If you wanted to be one of the guys, you took your pain, and that was it. I used to sit in the parlor and my mother would come in and see the pain on my face, and she'd say, "Babe, your back bothering you again?" I'd say, "Yeah." A backache was common. But you never went to a doctor in those days. There was no money, and there was no charity then; if anyone tells you there was, they are full of hooey. Once or twice a year a doctor would visit the school, and they just looked at you and gave you a clean bill of health.

Most of the neighborhood kids went to Catholic school. The nuns were strict, but they weren't as hard on the girls. The boys would be extra good on Fridays because if we weren't, the nuns would make us clean the convent after school and make us come back on Saturday! We thought cleaning was a girl's job. But you didn't complain to your parents. If the nuns said you misbehaved, that was good enough for them. And if they found out you got a beating from a nun, they figured you deserved it, so you got another beating!

The neighborhood had its share of problems, too. On Christmas Eve 1936, the local grocer, Mr. Katz, was killed in a robbery. Mr. Katz was a wonderful man who ran a book, which meant that if a housewife didn't have the money to pay, she could take the groceries she needed and pay him when she could. The entire neighborhood was lost in grief.

My parents couldn't continue to afford to send us to Catholic school, so for high school I was sent to South Philadelphia High; we called it Southern. It was like I had been released from prison! But I dropped out during my third year to help the family with money. It was during the Depression, and my old man had to go months at a time without pay because his employer, the city of Philadelphia, was broke. Betting on the horse races became one of my hobbies, and I started taking numbers on the streets, going from house to house to see if anyone wanted any "action." They picked three numbers and if they hit, they gave you 10 percent of their winnings. Some days I made as much as three dollars, a lot of money considering that many men were making eighteen to twenty dollars a week. I gave everything to my mother.

To make money, the neighbors on Wilder Street held a crap game every Sunday morning, right after Mass. The guy who ran the game would post a lookout on each corner. Each housewife would make sure the front door was unlocked, so if the cops came by, you could run home to sanctuary.

The kids would watch the adults play or find their own fun on Sundays. My friend "the Brain" got an idea to rent a room above a garage, and a group of us got together—fixed the electric, the plumbing, the floors—and made ourselves a dance hall called the Shindig. For a ten cents admission fee, anyone could come to the Shindig, and we got a full house on Sundays.

We were all there on the afternoon of December 7, 1941. I left the dance hall to get a soda at the candy store at 2nd and Wharton. A Jewish fella we called Old Man Marker owned it with his brother— good guys, they took care of us kids. I asked for a Pepsi, the new soda then, and Old Man Marker said, "You better enjoy that one. Did you hear the news?" He said, "The Japanese bombed Pearl Harbor." I said, "Where the hell's Pearl Harbor?" He said "You'll find out. We're all gonna have to go." I went back upstairs and everyone was dancing and laughing and having a good time, and I shut the jukebox off.

Everyone started hollering. I said, "I got some bad news. The Japanese just bombed Pearl Harbor." Of course nobody knew where it was, but I told them it was somewhere in the Pacific. The girls started to cry and were hugging the fellas they were going with.

My brothers and I and a bunch of the guys went straight from the dance hall to Chestnut Street to enlist. The place was mobbed. The line went from 2nd Street to Chestnut to Market, and at seven p.m., a guy came out and said they had their quota, come back tomorrow. The next day, we decided to tell our parents first, and let them have their say. About one o'clock in the morning my father called the four of us downstairs. Maybe he didn't want my mother to hear what he had to say. He told us that we had to fight for our country and for the freedom of those less fortunate than ourselves. He made it clear he wouldn't accept a slacker for a son and that he was expecting us to do our part. He fought in World War I when he was seventeen, so he knew what he was asking of us. I thought about the problem I was having with my hands, and knew I'd have a problem in combat. But I knew the Army doctors wouldn't find it, and when I enlisted in the Army, I didn't tell them. I wasn't about to stay home.

My mother took it pretty bad. With all four sons marching off to war, she cried often. She took each of us aside and gave us rosaries and scapula to wear, so we would be watched over. I put mine on and never took them off. My father would fill up with emotion, and just when we thought he might cry, he would walk away. For Mom's sake, we made sure not to enlist at the same time.

All the talk in the neighborhood was about who was going where. My best buddy Cianfrani joined the Airborne to be a paratrooper, just for the thrill of it. He told me all about the paratroopers—they were all volunteer, the best of the Army, they jumped out of airplanes, and they were paid pretty well. If you're athletically inclined, that's the kind of outfit you wanted to be in. I seen a couple paratroopers on leave in the neighborhood, and they looked great. I figured if I go in the Army, that's what I want to be. When Cianfrani went off to Camp Blanding, Florida, for training, I wanted to go, too.

I enlisted in the Airborne the following August, just after my oldest brother, Joe, was drafted into the Army. Jimmy and Jake signed up for duty in the Navy. Jimmy was on a destroy and rescue, chasing submarines and convoys. Jake served on the *San Jacinto*, the same ship where George Bush Sr. was a pilot when he got shot down in the Pacific. Joe, who was in the 83rd Infantry Division in training down south, ended up being medically discharged. He'd had his share of troubles at home—he had twin boys and one died, and then while he was in training, his wife gave birth to twin girls. It happened that just before deploying overseas, they found he had two perforated eardrums and discharged him.

I waited months to be called for duty, and when I finally got called in November, I was sandblasting cruisers that were being converted into aircraft carriers at New York Ship, in Camden, New Jersey. The company liked my work, and I never told them I enlisted. One afternoon the boss handed me a 2B slip. A 2B slip meant you were exempt from the war, because your job assisted the war effort. I tore it up immediately and told the boss that I wasn't going to shrink from my duty to my country. If my brothers, neighbors, and friends were all going, I wasn't about to stay behind.

2

---★---

EARNING THOSE COVETED JUMP WINGS

BILL

July 1942 to September 1943

I boarded a train at 30th Street Station in Philadelphia with three other kids from Pennsylvania. It was July 1942. We were headed to Camp Toombs, Georgia. What a hell of a name that was for kids getting ready for combat! It was an old training base named after a Confederate general. After we got there, the commander of the 506th Parachute Infantry Regiment, Colonel Robert Sink, renamed it Camp Toccoa.

The place was a sloppy mess, all muddy, red clay. The barracks and buildings were under construction, dirt and mud everywhere. We slept in tents on cots and when it rained your cot floated away. But where do you think you're going, to a resort? Roughing it ain't the word for what it was. There were bugs, mosquitoes, rats, mice, everything. It's out in the woods. But the war was on. And the generation that came there, we didn't have nothing to start with. Times were hard. If you got a slice of bread or an apple, you were thankful. Now if you came from a rich family and went to Toccoa, you'd go nuts.

I was assigned to the 506th PIR, which was an Army experiment. Usually you got into a paratrooper regiment in jump school at Fort Benning. Kids came from basic training camps all over, qualified for their wings, got into a regiment, and got split up by the time they got to combat. They might not know anyone they were fighting with. The 506th was the first regiment to be together for basic training, jump training, combat training, and combat. Same units, same men, qualifying together, and staying together from start to finish. By the time we were done, we'd know each other's thoughts. They took ordinary kids and were going to turn us into the best soldiers the Army ever had.

The 506th had three battalions, plus headquarters. Each battalion had three companies plus a headquarters company. 1st Battalion had Companies A, B, and C; 2nd Battalion had D, E, F. They had names, like Able, Baker, Dog. I was assigned to E Company, or Easy Company, 2nd Battalion, 2nd Platoon. The company had three forty-eight-man platoons plus headquarters. My platoon sergeant was Dick Winters, from Pennsylvania; our commanding officer was Cap. Herbert Sobel, from Chicago.

Kids from all over filtered in. I got there early, but kids were still coming in September. I can still see their faces now. Their eyes were bigger than the moon. When you got a bunch of teenage boys from all over the country, one is dumber than the next. Not stupid, just in awe of everything. It's all new. I had more life experience than most of them, from growing up on the streets and from the CMTC.

Those three summers in the garrison army taught me the ins and outs. When I got among these kids I stood out like a sore thumb, but I never told them about my Army experience. I kept my eyes and ears open and my mouth shut. That's what I learned growing up in South Philly. You want to get educated? You observe, but you don't say a word.

We had three cadre men from the regular Army teaching us. We had drill instruction, learned commands, salutes, line formations, learned how to fall in and fall out, turn, about-face, as a unit. We got it down pretty quick, but they try and instill fear in you when you're new. These guys were the same guys I was with in the CMTC, and I wasn't taking any guff from them. My first day there, I got into a fight. I asserted myself early. If they trained you properly, no problems, but when they tried to pull things not right, I took them in the back of the barracks for a fight. I didn't care who they were. I was out of line, but back then you could get away with it. Today, the world is too politically correct for its own good. You wind up in jail for exercising your rights, standing up to people who are no good. I took anyone on. People got to know me right away because I was very fiery.

I made friends real easy. The kids that didn't know what was up or down thought, *Hey, this guy knows more than I know,* and they learned from me. I would help the kids myself, on the side. The rest of the guys, I watched. I sized them up, learning real fast who I could trust, who I couldn't, who was good, who was a goldbricker. I had good intuition about people, I was good at remembering things and collecting info in my head—names, backgrounds, stories. I got along with everyone, but if anyone did anything bad, I spoke up. Everyone saw I wasn't a pushover, and I knew a thing or two, so they kind of respected me right away. Like one of the sergeants would say,

"We're starting an E Company fund, buy this or that, and donate to the fund." I knew the fund was in their own pocket. So I'd say, "Hey, you're not going to pull that on us." Sometimes I got into fights over it. I could have wound up in jail, but we never had any trouble.

Camp Toccoa was only about one thing: weeding out the weaklings. Our training schedule was brutal, and the training was brutal—all physical conditioning, led by Captain Sobel. Sobel didn't look like an officer. He was kind of awkward, and all he did was scream. He was high-strung, ranted and raved, criticized everything, a mean son of a bitch. He'd punish you for the hell of it. He was a chickenshit. Any GI knows what chickenshit is. A tyrant, takes authority to an extreme, the type that would get their ass kicked if the situation was reversed!

Every day we did calisthenics, push-ups, pull-ups, a timed obstacle course. We climbed walls, through tubes, jumped hurdles. And we did it over and over until we could barely stand up. Every day we ran up Currahee, a three-mile-high mountain at Toccoa. Currahee is Cherokee for "stands alone." That was the 506th motto—"We stand alone together." We started out walking up Currahee, and Captain Sobel would increase the speed a little every day, and about a week in, we were running the six miles up and down it. We ran shirtless in our little blue shorts and white socks and boots, did cadence, sang songs, cursed Sobel under our breath, huffed and puffed, some guys puked, some dropped, but you better keep going. If you couldn't take it, you were out. Men who were in good shape didn't make it. I never thought I'd make it, either. One day Sobel sent us up Currahee after a big spaghetti dinner. He tricked us, told us no runs that night. We were in the middle of eating, he blew the whistle and out we went. We were cursing, we wanted to kill him. On our way up, everyone threw their guts up. We were so sick. He said, "Keep running; you drop out, you're done." Sobel pushed you to the limit, beyond what you thought your body could take. But you *made* your body do it if you wanted to be in the paratroopers, that's all. The man was training us to be killers. The thing that kept me going was that Sobel was right up in front doing it with you. He ran like a duck. We called him the Black Swan. We also called him other names I won't mention. I thought, *If he can do it, I can do it.* Every day, men were ousted from the company, new ones brought in. You couldn't keep up, you were out. You made one tiny mistake, *out.* The guys that stayed there with you, you respected them for making it past Sobel.

Whatever my first impressions of the individual guys were, I kept to myself. But I tried to get to know more about them. In the beginning we were a bunch of blabbermouths. Told each other our life stories. This one's from Texas. That one's from California. He's married, he has a girl back home. Most of the guys were from Ohio, Pennsylvania, California, and New York. I liked Carwood Lipton right away, I could see he was a good, smart kid, very conscientious, used his brain. Joe Toye, he was tough as nails, looked out for the others. Chuck Grant, Ken Mercier, Salty Harris, all smart, took care of the other men. They ended up sergeants. They were all good. I liked Johnny Martin, too. He was a loner, he didn't get along with others, he was a force to be reckoned with, and he was a goldbrick (but not when it came to combat—he became sergeant of 1st Platoon). I thought he was as smart as me. He could get out of doing anything. He'd beg, borrow, and steal to get what he wanted. They called him the Scrounger. You needed a truck, he got you a truck. You need a tank, he'll get you a tank. You need eggs, he'll bring in the chickens. We became good friends right away. He got married that summer to a girl named Pat and I was his best man.

I watched the higher-ups, too. I didn't actually meet Colonel Sink. Nobody did. Only the officers met Sink. But I knew he was a good man. Everybody liked him. Honest, fair. We called him Bourbon Bob. He had the regiment from the beginning to the end. He turned down several offers to become a general. If he got promoted to general he'd have to leave the regiment, so he stayed with the 506th till the end. We called the regiment the Five-0-Sink. That tells you something about his dedication.

Maj. Robert Strayer, our battalion commander, was a smart man, because in order to be a good leader of a full battalion, you had to have good men under you. He had a knack for picking the best officers there, so it made his job much easier. All the best officers came to Easy Company, and most of the men in HQ company were former E Company men. We admired Strayer, because he got all the credit, while all the officers underneath him had all the brains. I could have done his job if I had men underneath me like Salve Matheson, Lewis Nixon, Dick Winters, Clarence Hester, Fred "Moose" Heyliger, all the best. So we respected Strayer for that. He didn't pick Captain Sobel. Now you're getting the ins and outs!

The two people that struck me most were Lieutenant Winters and Sobel. Winters was a good guy, led by example, you respected him, he took good care of the guys. But I was skeptical of his background. I went around calling him a Quaker—maybe with stronger language attached! He's not a Quaker, he's a Mennonite, but it was all the same to me because they're all against violence and war. I knew this because I came from Pennsylvania, where a lot of them live. So I didn't know what Winters was going to do when he got to combat, but I respected him in training, and we got along well.

Toccoa was about physical conditioning and combat basics. Most of the day, every day for five months, was physical conditioning. The rest of the time we learned how to use M1 rifles, bayonets, pistols, knives, grenades, machine guns, mortars, bazookas. It didn't matter if you planned to be using it, you learned about it. You had to be ready for anything. The rifles we had to know inside out; we took them apart and put them back together over and over.

We learned hand signals for combat, how to use phones and radios and wire up the communications in the field, how to read compasses and maps. We dug foxholes, trenches, learned to navigate the ground in all kinds of terrain—muddy, dry, flat, hilly, in the daylight, in the dark. We had night and overnight exercises to test us on the training. We got the basics on the Germans, too—their soldiers, guns, ammo, artillery, tanks. We didn't know all about what they were doing, just that they overran Europe, France, Belgium, Holland, Luxembourg, Austria, Poland, Russia, and they were going after England. That's all we knew. They were fighting for years. We know they were a little smarter than us. They had a much bigger army. We learned their army was advanced, their weapons were advanced, and everything they had would be superior to ours. So it was kill or be killed. The Army was training us to be killers. If you didn't like the training, *hit the pike*. We didn't want any goldbricks or sissies next to us in combat.

We trained harder than any other company. You already got the hardest training in the Army, you're a paratrooper, but Sobel doubled it. Everyone in Toccoa knew about Sobel and Easy Company. We got a reputation real fast. When the other companies were marching, Sobel took us running by. We didn't march by, we ran by. E Company did double-time by. If night marches were ten to twelve miles, Sobel added six more miles to that. All the other companies would be done, and we'd be out there running with gas masks on our heads. He found any way he could to make us more miserable. Heavier gear on our backs, no water. We would be doing a long forced march, and we'd be past the point of exhaustion, no water allowed, and after about two or three miles, guys would fall asleep walking, be out for maybe thirty to forty seconds, and that was like ten hours of sleep to us. Your body is done. If the guy in front of you fell asleep, he would drop his rifle, so you just poked him to wake him up. It happened all the time, we were so fatigued.

Instead of Thanksgiving dinner with the rest of the 506th, we were outside crawling on our bellies under barbed wire through pig guts, and being shot at with live ammo. Other companies crawled through mud, we crawled through pig innards, blood, guts, everything. What a sloppy mess. We were cursing, making all kinds of noise. If you stuck your head up, you got killed. Happy Thanksgiving. Holidays meant nothing.

The other companies all knew what we were dealing with. Sobel toughened us up, though. You never thought you could do it, but you did it. We wanted to kill him, but we just wanted our wings. You did exactly what he told you if you wanted the wings. If you wanted to be a paratrooper, you couldn't stand the thought of being put in an ordinary infantry unit. Hell no.

My leadership abilities came through right away. You can tell the leaders, they're at the front, they're observers, they're always looking out for the guys. The kids who are leaders make good choices, think quickly, have good instincts, figure things out for themselves; they don't wait to be told. They can read people and situations. If you lived on the streets, you done these things to survive. I got promoted to corporal pretty quick. It was just a promotion in stripes. I had two: one for private first class, and then corporal. The stripes went on both arms and showed your rank. Later at Camp Mackall, I was promoted to squad sergeant, leading the mortar squad. I never wanted to become a sergeant, it was just the way I was. Most of the men did not want to accept that kind of responsibility. They're smart. They know what it entails and they don't want no part of it.

It took time for the guys to get used to each other. We were eighteen-year-olds, we had to get out our aggressions. I got into a lot of fights. You called a kid from the South a rebel or a ridge runner. He called you a Yankee son of a bitch, and *bing-bang-boom*, you're cursing each other out. We were still fighting the Civil War. I called Liebgott "son of Abraham." So he was Jewish, so what? It was something to call him. If you were Italian, you got called a dago. It was kid stuff, that's all. Why certainly! Liebgott was a good friend of mine, but when I called him that, he got mad. He couldn't touch me. You couldn't touch anybody of higher rank. But nobody stayed mad for long. We had a boxing team, and me and Liebgott got into the ring with gloves on. There were boxing matches once or twice a month. I got the shit beat out of me, but I kicked some butts, too. I was like Rocky Marciano. You can be like a killer in the ring and like a pussycat outside the ring, you understand? But I thought, *This ain't for me, I'll get killed before I get into combat.* So I quit. We also had basketball, baseball, football teams, so you could be very physical. Made us tough. Brought out the best in us. We played against other companies. It was always E Company versus the whole damn world. We tried to be the best of the best, and we were good. We got beat sometimes. But while we were competing, we were bonding, too.

We all got real close; how could you not? At night we sat on our cots and talked, we cursed out Sobel, antagonized each other, sang songs, played craps and dice, talked about home. You got to know the next guy's mother, father, sister, brother, wife, sweetheart. That's how Frannie's sister got married. One of her brothers who was in the service took a fella home from New York with him on pass and met Frannie's sister. In Easy Company, only two guys were married— Frank Perconte and Johnny Martin. Most of the troopers were single. I had Frannie at home. She was seventeen. I was writing to her all the time, why certainly! I carried that picture of her in the Hawaiian skirt, the kind if you put a match to it, it will burn right up. Carried it all through the war, right in my musette bag, in my shirt, all over. I'm looking at it right now. All wrinkled up and bent. Johnny Martin used to say, "Look at that broad with the Hawaiian skirt." Everyone liked to look at her in the Hawaiian skirt.

We listened to the Andrews Sisters, Glenn Miller, all the big bands on the radio. Some kids had the radios on all night. The rest of us told them to shut up, put the lights out. There was noise all night. Sometimes we gambled all night. You learned who were the con men and cheaters. When you went broke, you learned real fast. We were so young, so hyped up, we didn't get too much sleep.

We trained hard all week and got passes on the weekends. But Sobel would find someone to make a fool out of and not give them a pass. Your tie wasn't tucked in right. It was. Your shoes weren't shined right. They were. Your sleeve wasn't buttoned. If he had it in for you, you were done. We had no control. He was devious. He kept me back a few times. When you got out, it was lucky. He got Tom Burgess one time. When you went out, you had to wear the uniform at all times. So Tom went dancing and took his jacket off, and Sobel walked in. He wouldn't let Tom take the jacket off for a month. Made him sleep with it, take a shower with it, everything. Day and night, Tom wore that jacket.

We went to tap rooms in Toccoa and drank beer. Half the kids didn't know what beer was. That was my first beer. That's right. Pop only gave me hard liquor! My first skidonies, too—I'm not touching that one with a ten-foot pole. I'll just say we grew up real fast at Toccoa. Sobel would be waiting for us back at the barracks, if you were one-half second late, you'd have latrine duty, be up all night digging thirty foxholes, and lose your next weekend pass.

Toward the end of our training, right before jump school, we did mock jumps off a thirty-five-foot tower, like jumping off a three-story building. We put on a parachute harness and jumped with pulleys and cables attached to us. It wasn't anything like a real jump, but it gave you some idea.

When we got done at Toccoa, they had the best of the best. Out of five thousand or so enlisted men, about fifteen hundred from the 506th qualified for jump school. There were good men who couldn't take this training, so you knew you done something good. We couldn't wait to get to Fort Benning because that's where you got your wings. Just before we left Toccoa, Colonel Sink read about the Japanese army establishing a record march—eighty-eight miles— and he wanted to beat it. He knew if anyone could do it, Sobel's company could. He knew we were trained well above the rest. So he chose 2nd Battalion to do the march, 118 miles from Toccoa, Georgia, to Atlanta, on our way to Benning. The 1st and 3rd Battalions took trains or trucks over. It was the beginning of December, cold, damp, and rainy. We marched for three days. Walked in the mud down side roads, through neighborhoods. We carried everything we owned on our backs—rifles, machine guns, mortars, all our equipment, everything on our backs. The guns were heavy, so we passed them back and forth, took turns carrying them so no one had all the burden. After we marched all day, we set up our pup tents, ate slop, slept on the wet ground, and we were freezing. Looking back, it was awful. We wanted to take our boots off, just to wiggle our toes after walking all day, but we didn't realize our feet swelled, and some of the guys couldn't get their boots back on. We learned everything the hard way. A lot of guys cut their boots to get their feet back in them, and left the laces loose. Everybody was in pain, our backs were killing us, our feet were killing us. We were exhausted, but we made it. When we got to the center of town, and walked down Peachtree Street, there was a big parade and a band. Suddenly your aches and pains left you. We were so proud. The march was historic, we made newspaper headlines, and it became known all over the world. We learned we could persevere through anything.

Fort Benning was straight jump training, and it was tougher than Toccoa. It's supposed to be a four-week course—A, B, C, D stages— but we were in such good shape, we skipped A phase, the physical training. It was the first time an entire regiment, three battalions and battalion headquarters, thousands of men, trained together and went on to jump training together to create nine parachute companies. We were a force to be reckoned with. Each man was like a heavyweight champ of the world boxer. We were way beyond the physical training Fort Benning offered. They asked us to run two miles, we went twenty miles. We outran everybody. Their training was nothing to us. They called us the walkie-talkie 506, as in "get walking," because we already knew our stuff, probably, too, because we walked there from Toccoa.

We had three phases—packing the parachutes, mock jumps from two-hundred-fifty-foot towers, and five jumps from a real aircraft. After that you qualified and got your wings. When we got to the last phase, jumping out of a plane, I had no idea what to expect. I'd never been on a plane before. You had to trust the pilot and not think. The guys were all joking and having a good time while we waited for the planes. I wasn't scared at all. Not until *after* I jumped. There were about two dozen of us in the plane, we got to fifteen-hundred feet, the green light came on, I was next in the stick, and I flung myself out the door. Then all my training went out the window. You're falling full speed and you have the urge to slow yourself down. You look down and see the ground coming at you at a hundred miles an hour and you're going *two* hundred miles an hour. I started running in the air. They're hollering at me from the ground, "Stop running! Stop running!" I'm running and flailing my arms, I almost broke my neck. It looks easy until you try it yourself. After that first jump, the second jump scared the hell out of me. I panicked again coming down, thought the chute wasn't going to open; I pulled the reserve chute. But instead of following the manual—you're supposed to pull the cord, hold it, and then throw it outward—I didn't throw it away from me, and it went down and opened between my legs. I had one chute over my shoulder and one chute between my legs. They both opened and were pulling me in different directions. I came down face forward, and they were watching all this from the ground, and I caught holy hell. I wasn't thinking. But I wanted those wings, I didn't care what I had to do to get them. I ignored the fear, just ignored it, never had a problem again. Courage isn't about fear, kid, it's about overcoming it. Everybody has fear.

Christmas Eve was our final jump, and we finally got those wings. December 26, 1942, we got our wings. Colonel Sink pinned them on us; it was the greatest day of my life. Every day for six months, all we wanted was to get those silver parachute wings. You put your wings on and you bloused your boots up. That was it. Everyone knew you were the best of the best. You were different from any other soldier. Those wings made you different, and you never took them off.

We all got a ten-day furlough, and before we left Colonel Sink told us to act like gentlemen. "You got your wings, you're Airborne men now, you're due back on such-and-such day." About a dozen guys didn't come back in time. They may have only been an hour late. There were a lot of transportation problems during the war. It didn't matter. Sink called an assembly that night and drummed those men right out of the paratroopers. After all that work, just sent them out. We were angry. But we learned real quick, no excuses. Whether they were real or not, no excuses. One kid who got bumped out was a good friend of mine, Gregory Rotella, from North Carolina. Wakes you up, you're only a kid. It separates reality from fantasy right there. When you learned lessons so harshly, you became a man real fast.

★ ★ ★

Spring 1943 we moved to Camp Mackall. It was a fort, and the military was actively working on all the forts, so it was much nicer than Toccoa. Nice barracks. We had more jump and weapons training there, but most of the training was on maneuvers. We jumped with more and more weight on us—weapons, supplies, ammo. We simulated combat jumps and practiced troop movements, offensive and defensive tactics. Training got harder and more complicated, more combat-oriented.

The platoons were broken down into three twelve-man rifle squads, with a machine gunner and assistant machine gunner, plus a six-man mortar squad to operate the platoon's 60mm mortar. I was promoted to sergeant of the mortar squad, and had Don Malarkey, Brad Freeman, Warren "Skip" Muck, Alex Penkala, and Ed Sabo in my squad. All good guys. Malarkey was a nice kid, very sentimental. He was from Oregon. Planned to go to college after the war. He could've paid for it with the money he won off me at craps. Muck and Penkala were real quiet, nice kids. Same with Freeman. Sabo was older than us, and he wasn't quiet at all. We had a good squad. Everyone dependable, smart, and good.

We got real good on the mortar. The mortar is a long tube, one person sets it down, then a shell goes down the tube, with increments—they're about the size of a fingernail, they cause the explosion and the thrust. The sergeant is key. He's watching the enemy and does fast reconnaissance. He tells you how to set it, what to use, how many increments to use. One increment will send it, say, twenty yards, two will send it forty yards—just examples. You can put four total. The sergeant gives range, tells you right, left. As the mortar squad sergeant, I had to be good at reconnaissance, because if it's not right, the minute you start shooting the mortar, shells will be on top of your head. You shoot the shells, hit the target, get the hell out of there.

Me and Malarkey were the best on the mortar. I could knock a fly out of the air. Malarkey was a great marksman. He was the best. When it came to being a good shot, you either had it or you didn't. In training we had competitions between the three platoons, and that's when we found out how good we were. Our platoon was the best. Third Platoon's mortar squad was second best. First Platoon wasn't up to the standard the company wanted. Before we went into combat, to even things out a little, Muck and Penkala were sent to 1st Platoon.

Johnny Martin became a sergeant in 1st Platoon, leading 1st Squad. Some of us had leadership abilities. They knew by who set examples through character and dependability. Sometimes they were wrong, but most of the time they were right. Some men were leaders, some followers. Some don't want responsibility. Jimmy Diel was promoted to 2nd platoon sergeant. Leo Boyle, who was in Johnny Martin's platoon, was promoted to sergeant. Boyle was the gas noncom in charge of all our gas training. We gave him the nickname Fearless Phosgene. You know what mustard gas is? Well, phosgene is just as bad as mustard gas. The Germans were planning to use it on the Allies, so we had a lot of training on it.

Once I got promoted I was able to con old Sobel. I got along with him very well, but I lied a lot, and he believed me. When he was giving out punishments, I would tell him his punishment wasn't bad enough. I'd say, "Give so-and-so to me and I'll do something worse." So he did. Then I'd go to the trooper and say, "Come here, you son of a bitch," and I would start cursing, saying "I'll fix you. You think Sobel's bad." And Sobel liked that. Then I would take the trooper aside and say, "Get friggin' lost, don't tell nobody. If Sobel asks, tell him I made you dig sixteen foxholes, instead of fourteen, or march twenty miles instead of ten." Sobel thought I was worse than him. He was nuts and I knew it and they knew it. I got away with a lot of stuff with Sobel.

In Toccoa Sobel told us, "You're gonna sleep with your gun. Twenty-four hours a day, your gun will be with you; you'll sleep with it, eat with it, make it your wife. Leave your gun for a minute and you're gonna be sorry." You even had to know the number on your gun by heart. So in Mackall, one night we were out doing maneuvers, sleeping in the woods, and he snuck around with the 1st sergeant, William Evans. At night, you post guards to watch the guns all night. Every two hours, someone else goes on watch duty so someone is watching all night while the rest of you are sleeping. Sobel snuck around one night and stole all the guns from the sleeping guys, like a thief in the night. Next morning, we fall out for formation, and we all have our guns. He says, "What the hell's going on?" He started hollering at us. We all gave our numbers and they were right, and he couldn't figure out what the hell was going on. Turns out he'd gone out and grabbed F Company's guns, and ooh, were they mad. But their men caught holy hell. Really Sobel done good, because if F Company did that in combat the guys would all be dead. Understand? The method was right, but the people he did it to was wrong.

Outside of physical training, when it came to field maneuvers, we saw that Sobel didn't know what to do under any circumstances. He had no clue. No common sense. I don't think he had the mentality for actual combat. He made all kinds of mistakes, stupid mistakes, that were so big you can't keep them a secret. He relied on Evans to tell him what to do. Everybody knew. In combat simulations, he would make noise and holler when we were supposed to be hiding; he was nervous and jumpy, he would overreact. He'd get lost, get disoriented, couldn't read a map. We saw this, and we thought, *You can't make those mistakes in combat.* And this ain't just one of the men, which would be bad, too—this guy's commanding a whole company. He makes one mistake, we're all dead. Nobody could say or do anything about it—officers will never, ever down each other—but everyone from Sink down to Winters knew about Sobel. There were about a hundred-forty-eight of us, and a hundred-forty-seven talked about "accidentally" killing Sobel as soon as we got into combat.

We started playing tricks on him. In training maneuvers, we had a mock battle. I was an umpire. The umpire declares people dead or winners in the battle. The idea is to get together afterward and see what mistakes are made and fix them. I made Sobel a casualty in our mock battle. Put him in the wrong place where he gets shot or killed. The medics were practicing, doing mock surgery, bandaging, moving people out. But we said give him a real incision—they had to practice, right? They gave him an anesthetic, put him to sleep, made a real incision like they were really operating, and bandaged him up. He was mad as hell, but nobody would confess.

Maneuvers got more intense. The entire 506th moved out to live outside for a month all over Kentucky and Tennessee for mock battles. They were big ones, very authentic. They never used live ammo. The only time they did was with the pig guts mess at Toccoa. They divided us, the Red Team versus the Blue Team, to simulate fighting the enemy. We were always on the move. We lived in foxholes and tents, dug trenches for latrines, fought in forests, rivers, mountains. You're out in the country. When we dug trenches for latrines, I was thinking, *What the hell am I doing here? I should be home playing craps on the street with my buddies.* What we ate on maneuvers made you want to go home, too. Beef with gravy—"shit on a shingle" we called it, or Spam. *Echhh.* Can't eat either one of them now. Makes me ill to even think about it. *Echhh!*

The maneuvers were more for the officers and higher echelon— the lieutenants, captains, majors, generals—to see what they were doing under combat conditions, how they were moving troops, reacting, whether they used the right tactics or not. When it's over, everyone meets up to talk about what was done right and wrong. We did it over and over and over again, rectifying mistakes, doing things better. We kept on doing it and discussing it, until we knew instinctively what the next guy's moves would be, and we worked as a team. By the time we were done, we knew it in our sleep.

In June, we got attached to the 101st Airborne Division, the Screaming Eagles. They were formed August 1942. They had the 502nd as their only parachute regiment. Then they added the 506th and the 501st. We didn't know what the 101st was about. We were hoping to go to the 82nd because they were going overseas real fast. The 82nd Airborne was well established. They were a damn good outfit. They were in Africa, and they fought on D-day and up in Holland and Bastogne, too.

When we became part of the Screaming Eagles, we put on our eagle patches, and we were so proud. Our division general was Maj. Gen. Bill Lee. He's the one who said, "We have no history, but we have a rendezvous with destiny." He never made it to combat. He had a heart attack before we left.

We got ten-day furloughs home, so we knew it was almost time to go overseas. I hitchhiked home and hitchhiked back. Back then, if you were in uniform, you could get anywhere you needed to go. When we got back, we took trains to Camp Shanks, on the Hudson River outside New York City. The night before we left for England, the whiskey was flowing and everybody got drunk. Some of the boys weren't used to whiskey and got sick. In the morning, they were hungover. I was used to the stuff; I was fine.

The Donut Dollies were there to see us off with coffee and donuts. That's what we called them. They were the Red Cross girls, wore a white uniform with a red cross on their shoulder. Every time we had maneuvers, every time we moved, we saw them at the depot. One of the prettiest and nicest was Helen Briggsy. She was a little older than us; she was from Washington, D.C., and after the war, she came to all our reunions.

When we were boarding our ship, the SS *Samaria*—this was a limey ship, we called it the Spindly Scowl—at the dock right next to us, the big French ship *Normandy* was capsized in the harbor. This big monster ship, the size of the *Queen Mary*, turned over on its side at the pier! We looked at that ship, and looked at our tiny little ship, and thought, *Jesus Christ, what a trip this is going to be!* Nobody was ever on a boat before in their life, let alone getting on a ship like that and going on the ocean. That woke us up real fast. We got on the boat single file, and this was the entire division, thousands of men crowded onto this little ship. I raced over by the dock where you could buy stuff before you got on the boat and bought boxes of butternut candies. They were chocolate and caramel, like a Milky Way without the nougat. I bought about two or three hundred of them. There's no method to what you do at a time like that. You're like crazy. But I could have made money with those candies. I was giving them out like I was Santa Claus.

When you boarded, you gave them your name, they gave you a serial number. You could barely move; we were packed in like sardines. I think everyone was scared. We were going into the unknown. We looked out at the Statue of Liberty and saluted her as we went past. I remember thinking, *This is it, I'm leaving America, going off to war.* I hoped we got over there, got it over with, got out alive, and got home.

The Navy escorted us over to watch for submarines. Thank God for the Navy. It was scary going over, being out there on the ocean with nothing around for thousands of miles. When we got to the ocean, the boat started going up and down, everyone turned green and started puking. I thought, *What the hell am I doing out here on this ocean? Jesus Christ!* I was cursing everybody, everybody was cursing. It was so bad, I tied my bag and everything else to the deck of the ship and never went down below. Sobel got us doing calisthenics every day. We gambled, too. It got our mind off the rancid boat. The boat stunk, we stunk, the food stunk. Limey food. We weren't used to it. I could puke just thinking about it. *Ecccchh.* But ten days later, we made it to Liverpool, England.

When we got off the boat, they told us not to wear anything that would identify us as Airborne so the Germans wouldn't be alerted. We had to take the eagles off our shoulders, take off our boots. After all that, the Germans still welcomed us. Over German radio, they said, "Welcome, the 101st Airborne." They knew we were coming, but they didn't know our plans.

We set up camp in Aldbourne. We were right in the middle of a little village, living among the civilians in horse stables. We had to have lectures in English etiquette; they told us we better behave ourselves.

We got right into training six days a week. It was September, and it rained almost every day; you never saw the sun in England. It was gray and wet, and we did field training and forced marches in the mud. We concentrated on training for combat conditions. We made jumps with all our gear, we slept in foxholes, ate K rations, attacked in woods, fields, attacked bunkers. We created a made-up village and launched an offensive. Just like in combat, sometimes everyone got separated and you were out there two or three days by yourself. When we got back, we went over what we did, the mistakes we made, and worked on fixing them.

When we were settled in, one of first things we did was find the two pubs in town—the Blue Boar and the Crown. They had hot beer.

No cold beer. They filled a big barrel of beer and put a red-hot poker in it. It would sizzle and smoke as the poker went in, and heat up the beer. We thought they were nuts, but that was all they had. Johnny Martin got a whole bucket of hot beer and drank it. He got drunk as a skunk. Puked his guts up. It took us a month to get used to that hot beer. But I wouldn't drink it now—hell no!

We ate fish and chips and we got used to it. We had no choice. If it wasn't fish and chips, then it was powdered, dehydrated, or pickled. Even the eggs were pickled.

There was a little joint, a nice little corner bakery, and First Sergeant Evans used to drive up there with his three-wheel motorcycle. We all used to go there for lardy cakes; they were very popular. Flat cakes made of pig lard, dough, sugar, and fruit, and they were dripping with grease. I wouldn't eat one now. They would kill you. But we were in peasant country, lots of pig farms, so we ate lardy cake.

Combat was getting closer, and I took it upon myself to learn every gun that I could get my hands on. Taking initiative is part of what makes a person a little better. No one tells you to do it, but you do it. I studied the guns, took them apart, put them together, fired them, made a lot of mistakes, did what I could to get to know them intimately. I found out how they loaded, how they sounded, what kind of glitches they had. I did this everywhere I was. If I saw a new gun, I grabbed it and figured out what made it tick. I was very nosy. I wanted to know everything I might encounter. I could drive a tank. I knew how because I was building tanks in Chester, Pennsylvania, before the war. Thank Christ I never had to do it. I could fire artillery pieces—not perfectly, but I knew in case I had to use them I could do it. I drove trucks. I drove Jeeps. I tried to be versatile. I didn't say a word to nobody. I just did it. If I told them, they'd have me all over the damn place. So I played dumb like a fox. Keep your mouth shut, never volunteer. You got to learn that real fast. When you first come in everybody volunteers. Once you volunteer, you think, *What the hell did I do that for?* I said to myself, *Keep your mouth shut, you dummy. You don't know what the hell they're going to throw at you.* It's usually the worst thing in the world. Never volunteer. Turn your back and run the other way. Say you didn't hear it.

I was ready for anything—ready for the broads, too. I did a lot of practicing over there. I had broads all over the place, in the haystacks, in the pup tents. Sometimes I had them in the barracks where the sergeants stayed. In the morning, I would hide them in the storage area—it was like an attic—and tell them to be quiet until after the inspections. The guys called me Hanky Panky Louie.

Me and Chuck Grant would get into trouble a lot. We would drink and get mischievous. One time we stole bicycles, and the bobbies (policemen) chased us. We threw the bikes away and took off, and the bobbies caught us and made us pay for them. I got thrown in jail a couple times, too. They'd throw me in one door, and I'd go out the other. A whole mob would follow me out the door. I sprang everybody! Oh man, I was a devil.

The stables in Aldbourne were good hiding places. Guys would hide in them to get out of night training. Some of us were more devilish than others. You're doing things you done 4,999 times. Repetitious and a pain in the neck. When it came time to do something we didn't want to, some of the guys, myself included, we'd get lost on purpose to miss something. We'd lie. Say we got lost. You had to be careful. We couldn't all do it at the same time. One day I was in talking to Sobel, and Popeye Wynn came in. He just showed up after being lost for a day or two. He went out on night problems and said he couldn't see—he got lost in the dark. So Sobel screamed, "You got to learn to see at night!" Popeye said, "How the hell can you *learn* to see? It's pitch black!" And Sobel ranted and raved. Poor Popeye. I knew what he done. He goofed off. I said to Sobel, "I'll take care of Popeye." Of course, I let him go. Everybody done their share of goldbricking. You take your gun apart nine thousand times, twenty-thousand times, you understand? Then the sergeant comes along and says, "Take it apart again." You think, *Oh Christ.* Repetition. Repetition. It gets old. *But* after all that, when the bullets start flying, it comes to you automatically. You don't have to think for a second. You just do it. That's good training. You don't stop and think, *Wait, what do I have to do again? What was that they taught me?* No, you *know* it instinctively. Without that repetition, you're dead.

The biggest morale lifter was mail call; we got letters and packages from home. We got mail about every two weeks. I wrote as often as I could to my parents, Frannie, and my brother Henry, who was also in the Army. I didn't write to Earnest in the Navy because he didn't know how to read or write.

We listened to all the great shows and music on the radio. If Glenn Miller was playing, *Shhhhh!* Nobody talk. Malarkey would kill you. He loved Glenn Miller. Malark got to see him in person on a pass to London during the war. Even without the radio, someone always started singing, and everyone chimed in.

We played a lot of sports, too. While we were in Aldbourne, Buck Compton came into Easy Company as 2nd lieutenant under Winters. He played baseball and football for UCLA. He had a hell of a throwing arm. The guys loved Compton; he would sit down and talk to us, play cards with us. Officers never mixed with enlisted men. Most of the time, he was segregated from the officers, didn't eat with them, didn't do anything but salute them. The officers didn't like it, but he never changed. Took care of the guys. He was a soldier's soldier. Very compassionate, a good man.

We got weekend passes to London here and there. In America, you read about what was going on in London, but you didn't realize, because you felt like it had nothing to do with you. When you got to London, then you saw. Hitler hadn't invaded England yet, but they were getting the shit bombed out of them for years, and it was still going on when we were there. Buildings were bombed out, fires smoldering all over. Thousands of people killed. The place was blacked out. They lived through hell and then some. They tried to get the children out, sent them to Scotland, America, anywhere. The air raid sirens were wailing all the time, scared the hell out of us. When the sirens went off, people ran down into the tube, the underground subway. The V-1 buzz bombs would fly over, and we'd chase them. You hoped one didn't land on you. You got used to it; you heard the sirens and all you worried about was the girls you were chasing.

When we were overseas, getting married was taboo. Lots of roadblocks to keep you from getting married in wartime. In the final analysis, most men didn't get married. We had no idea why they had that rule. The limey broads, they were no dummies, they got married thinking their husbands were going to get killed in the war and they would get insurance. It didn't become a racket but it became common among a group of people. We had no idea.

Leo Boyle—Fearless Phosgene—met a girl named Winn, a limey girl, a nice girl, and he wanted to get married in Aldbourne in May. He got through all the Army's roadblocks. They got the church and we were all ready to go to the ceremony. But I was always making trouble. I grabbed a Jeep and got a bunch of smoke grenades—yellow, green, red, purple. Leo was waiting inside the church for his girl, and I pulled up in the Jeep, and as soon as Winn got dropped off, I threw the smoke bombs in her direction, and the air was so smoky, nobody could see. Lots of confusion. I grabbed Winn, threw her in the Jeep—I had a mask on my face—and I drove her about ten miles away and dumped her off, then I went back. I acted completely innocent, went around blaming everybody else. "That dirty rat. Who done that?!" I blamed Smitty—Burr Smith—I always blamed Smitty. I blamed everybody, I acted like the innocent bystander. Winn eventually found her way back and they got married that day. I have no idea how she got back. Leo and Winn stayed married for a long time. I told Leo many years later, and we laughed like hell.

The reason I always blamed Smitty was when he came to Toccoa, we found out he was from around Hollywood, and his girlfriend was a movie starlet, and his parents owned stock at Kodak film. He came from good stock, went to military school. He was trained in garrison training, and he could do all kinds of things with the rifle. He was a nice boy, so you blamed him for the devilment, because nobody believed it.

Smitty wrote a letter to Dick Winters in 1979 and paid a nice compliment to me and Winters. Smitty was in the Army until 1980. He commanded a Special Forces reserve unit, assigned to the Delta Force. He told Winters, "I've been a soldier most of my adult life. In that time I've met only a handful of great soldiers, and of that handful, only half or less come from my WWII experience, and two of them came from ol' Easy—you and Bill Guarnere." Smitty was a good guy. We got along real well.

★ ★ ★

We never knew when D-day was coming, so we were always on edge. Training got more and more combat-oriented. Everything we did, we discussed what happened, how we reacted, what to do better. We kept making it better, getting into a rhythm with each other. The only problem was Sobel. As good a company as we were, as in tune to each other as we were, the minute we would get on the battlefield, we'd all be dead.

In December, the sergeants decided no way were we going into combat with Sobel. We didn't even have to think about it. We made the decision quick, fast, done. No one hesitated. We went right to Sobel and turned in our stripes. You can't run a company without sergeants. Had it been some of us, but not all, you got trouble. We stuck together. The news got to Strayer and regimental headquarters quickly. Here, Sink's got a company in his regiment that's disorganized. Sobel couldn't believe it. He couldn't do anything. He ranted and raved and screamed and hollered. But he couldn't do anything.

We knew all Sink could do was give us hell. He couldn't get rid of all the sergeants. The only way out was to get rid of Sobel. He put Sobel in training at Chilton Foliat. Training was what he was best at. They read us the riot act, but that was all they could do. We were all responsible, but there had to be a couple scapegoats. So they picked two—Mike Ranney and Terrence Harris. They couldn't get rid of all the noncoms; we were going right into combat. Harris got transferred, and ended up getting killed June 8 in Normandy. He was in 3rd Platoon, nice kid. Ranney stayed in 1st Platoon, but was demoted to private.

Lt. Thomas Meehan from B Company took over the company. Lt. Patrick Sweeney from A Company was our new executive officer. Winters took over 1st Platoon. Winters and Sobel had a falling out a few days or a week before, and Sink was transferring Winters out. But when Sobel got transferred, Sink brought Winters back. The mutiny turned out to be the best thing we could've done for Easy Company.

Right after that, Eisenhower and Churchill came to do inspections. Unbeknownst to us, Ike's team didn't want the Airborne drop to go forward; they thought we were all going to get killed. They figured on losing 70 percent. He came to see us off, and he felt bad, he figured most of us weren't going to make it.

They had all kinds of exercises for the brass; everybody was showing off. I had my mortar squad—the best mortar squad in the company, probably in the Army—fire at a couple targets, but they missed! We never missed. Thank Christ nobody was watching. Taylor came around, and the boys fired again—Malarkey and Muck hit all the targets. I told Taylor, "My boys never miss!" We still laugh about that.

We left Aldbourne for a few days to go to Slapton Sands, to do practice exercises as an entire division on the coast. Exercise Tiger, it was on my birthday, April 28th, how could I forget? They wanted to practice moving troops around at midnight on a beach similar to Utah, to prepare us for D-day. There were lots of simulations going on for all the Allied divisions. We heard shelling in the distance that sounded real. And it was real, we found out later. They covered it up until after the war. About nine hundred men from the 4th Infantry Division were killed; the Germans sank two of their assault ships. They got us out of there and back to Aldbourne, and I kept singing

"Happy Birthday" to myself and trying to get the guys calmed down. Everyone was hyped up. You knew something was coming.

We continued going out on problems, doing night problems, going out for three, four days, attacking roads and causeways, trying to survive outside, like we would do in combat. The kids took turns being an officer or a sergeant out in the field—they tried to prepare everyone to take over if you had to. I felt like I could take over the company if I had to.

They got the entire 101st together for a rehearsal for D-day, called Operation Eagle. They tried to get as close to the real thing as they could. We left from the same airfield, flew two and a half hours, jumped at midnight, did everything the same. There were lots of accidents, lots of men got hurt.

The end of May, we headed to the marshaling area at Upottery Field, where we'd be taking off. We knew it was time to go. There was a lot of military traffic in town, all of it moving south. The people of Aldbourne knew, too. As we left on trucks, the people all came out to say good-bye. There were tears in their eyes; they were sad to see us go. They got close to us. Nice people. We'd been there for almost nine months, in the middle of this village, so in a sense it was like our family.

Once we got inside the marshaling area, they sealed you from the outside world. You couldn't get in or out. That's when you knew the mission was set in stone and it was going to happen. We were set up in tents on the airfield, and they had GIs dressed in German uniforms walking all around to familiarize us with their uniforms, helmets, and guns. They were there all day and every night, and we wanted to kill them. We wanted to get started! Some people were sewing extra pockets on their uniforms to hide food and junk in, on their shoulders on the sides, front and back. I didn't do it. Guth and Liebgott were giving haircuts for cash. But I didn't have any money and there were no free haircuts. A lot of them shaved their heads, gave themselves Mohawks, and looked like Indians. I was a good-looking guy. I wasn't doing a Mohawk!

When we settled in, the officers were being briefed on the mission so they could brief us. Most of the men were cleaning their weapons and equipment. We took apart our guns, put them back together, cleaned them. We did it over and over again. The rifles were shining. We knew it was serious. At that point, we were ready. If you weren't ready, if you didn't want to jump into combat, you didn't want to be a paratrooper, and you should go join the supply house.

Nixon and Hester took all the sergeants into a tent; they had sand tables, ten to twenty feet long and wide. They built up the entire geography of Normandy with sand. A perfect miniature copy, it looked like a toy. It had the drop zones, the beach, the towns, the roads, the German artillery positions, their foxholes, hedgerows, everything. They showed us where we were landing, where our objectives were, where everyone else's objectives were. They had photographs, maps, diagrams. They went through the mission with us over and over. There were four causeways that ran up from the beaches, and the 101st needed to secure them so the seaborne troops could get supplies, equipment, artillery, tanks, and Jeeps up Utah Beach, and move inland. Everything was coming in by boat. When the troops got to shore, they had to take the causeway in—it was one way in, one way out, because the Germans were smart, they flooded the beach. We had to secure those roads, destroy German artillery positions trained on the beach, and keep the Germans from stopping those troops. If we failed, they'd be in trouble, and we'd be in trouble.

Second Platoon was dropping outside Ste. Marie-du-Mont, and securing the causeway that ran from the beach through the town of Pouppeville. Our orders were to kill any Germans we encountered and take no prisoners. They thought it was going to be quick and easy, they'd get us in and out, bing-bang-boom. I didn't think it was going to be that easy.

I spent most of the time at the marshaling area going over the mission with the other sergeants. We went over it forward and backward. We kept going over our platoon's mission, the other platoons' missions, the battalion and regimental missions.

Every day that passed, I couldn't wait to get the hell on the plane and jump already. You're there, you know it's gonna happen, but you don't know when the hell it's coming. The waiting part is hell. Most of us wanted to just get it over with. We figured we were going to knock the Germans off and come home anyway.

June 3, I was resting in the barracks, and Johnny's bunk was above mine, and I had to go to the latrine. I grabbed a jump jacket, thinking it was mine, but I picked up Johnny's by mistake. I sat down and while I'm there, I'm going through my pockets, and I felt a letter. It was from Johnny's wife, Pat. It said, "Don't tell Bill Guarnere, but his brother Henry was killed in Cassino."

It felt like the floor fell out from under me. I almost fainted. I read it again. I couldn't believe it. No one told me Henry was dead. I'd written him several times, but it took time for the letters to go back and forth. I didn't receive anything from him in months. Here, Frannie wrote to Pat, and Pat wrote to Johnny. Henry had been killed January 6, 1944, five months before, and nobody told me, that's why I hadn't heard from him. I sat there enraged, crying. I started thinking about my other brother Earnest, who was in the Navy, and Mom, and

Pop—how did they take it? My entire life with Henry went through my mind. I didn't have a chance to see him, say good-bye. A lot of brothers met up overseas, but I didn't have that opportunity. If I had been near Italy, and it was maybe forty miles away, I would have asked to get a truck to go see him, and they would have let me. The Army was lenient that way; they knew you were responsible.

I left that bathroom enraged, but I went out of there like a man. I never said a word to nobody. When I got back to the barracks and saw Johnny, I told him I read it, and he was sad, too, and felt bad that I read it. What a hell of a way to find out. I was mad because nobody informed me. I told Johnny they turned a killer loose. I was going to kill every goddamn German I came across. Just give me a gun and let me loose. Johnny may have told the rest of the guys what happened, because nobody came near me. D-day was coming, and as bad as I felt, I knew I had men to protect, knew what I had to do. But I felt like if anybody got in my way, they were dead. You didn't want to be a goddamn German when you met me.

The next night, June 4th, was D-day. We were all ready to go and they called off the jump because of bad weather. It was rainy and windy. We dropped our gear right by the plane, got off the runway, and went inside and had a beer and saw a movie. Guess what the name of the movie was? *Mr. Lucky*, with Cary Grant. I'll never forget it because I couldn't concentrate. I couldn't concentrate on anything. I wanted to get on the damn plane, get over there, and get it over with. Everyone was a nervous wreck. When they cancelled the jump, I realized the magnitude of what was going on, that we were just a tiny part of something huge.

No one slept that night, and the next day, the weather cleared, and we got ready to go. Everyone's faces shined like the moon at night, so we blackened our faces, and waited on the runway for the planes to be ready. Everybody had lots of nervous energy, the boys were wild as can be. We were exhausted, too, from all the tension and not sleeping. I was fuming thinking about Henry. We waited eight to ten hours for the planes, and the longer we waited, the madder I got.

When it was time to board the planes, that's when everyone got real serious. Everyone got quiet. We were packed up like elephants. Our uniforms were gas impregnated, and they were stiff as a board. Very uncomfortable. Then we had all our gear on top of that. It took three men to pick you up and put you on the damn plane. We had eighteen men to a stick, and two pilots. My mortar squad, and Joe Toye's rifle squad, was in my stick. At the last minute, they gave the first three men in the stick leg bags. The limeys came up with that idea, and we didn't know what to expect jumping with a leg bag. The thing weighed a hundred-fifty pounds by itself. It had everything but the kitchen sink in it, mortar shells, grenades, ammo, radio, machine-gun tripods, all kinds of supplies. Compton was first in the stick, he was jumpmaster, I was second, and Toye was third. Compton passed around airsickness pills. I have no idea why they gave us airsickness pills, but most of the men took them. I threw mine the hell away.

BABE

August 1942 to June 1944

Basic training at Fort Eustis, Virginia, prepared you for how to survive, how to kill. It was a lot to take in as a teenager. It was rough-and-tumble, the same as growing up on the streets. But it never affected me. You absorbed what they taught, and you got stronger and more prepared for what was to come, mentally and physically. Physically, I was already in very good shape from playing a lot of football at home. I always played sports.

Eustis had an obstacle course that was rigorous. You were timed, and you had to make the course in that time. We did calisthenics, learned soldiering, combat basics, how to use all kinds of weapons. The commanding officers were all stern, but nothing like Captain Sobel. You just had to do whatever you were told or you'd get kicked out. It was simple. If you did what you were told, you were okay. If you loused up, you lost your weekend pass and had to clean the barracks, latrine, or officers quarters. Whenever anyone got that duty, it made me think back to Sacred Heart school, and how the nuns used to find us on the street and make us come back and clean the convent. You'd be out playing on a nice spring day, when all of a sudden you heard, "Edward! John! William! I have something for you boys to do!" We knew our fun was over.

I was assigned to B Battery, 446, an antiaircraft unit, and I was on gun crew. I became a tech corporal, training officers-to-be for the officer candidate school. We trained them on the Bofors 40mm, a Swedish gun, and took them out on problems, taught them how to set up the guns. A funny story: One of the guys I was training was about twenty-five or so, a young colored fella, who lived near a reservation in Arizona. We were in a truck going out on a problem. He said, "I hope you give me good grades," and we got to talking about home. He said, "This may sound odd, but are you Catholic?" I told him I was. He said, "I was going to become a priest and try to teach the Indians in Arizona after I took my vows, but I went home one weekend and my sister had a girlfriend over and she talked me into going on a double date. Reluctantly I went, and that's why I'm not a priest today." I still think of that and laugh.

Every day at Eustis, my thoughts were on getting to the Airborne. I had put my papers in as soon as I got there, and they told me I had to finish basic first. I was just doing my time, and about six or seven months later, they put my papers through. It seemed like I waited forever. My commanding officer tried to talk me out of it. They were happy with my work in the battery, and they promised me everything, including promotions, to stay in the artillery. But I wanted to be a paratrooper. My buddies from South Philly were in the Airborne and I thought maybe I'd get in the same regiment. Just before my truck ride to Fort Benning, my commanding officer said again, "Heffron, anything I can do to change your mind?" I'd gotten really close to the guys and didn't want to leave them, but my only goal was to get to the Airborne.

It was February 1944 when I finally got to jump school at Fort Benning, Georgia. There were kids from all over the country, and everyone had their basic training in different places. When they got enough of us together they formed a company. They assigned me to the 1st Parachute Infantry Regiment, K Company. The jump training was three to four weeks and consisted of A, B, C, and D stages. The first two weeks was all physical training and learning to fold and pack parachutes, and then came the jump training.

The place was immaculate. It had the usual wooden barracks, but they were well manicured and very clean. They ran a very tight ship in the parachute infantry. The barracks were two floors, maybe twenty kids to a floor, with ten single beds on each side of the wall.

The first day I was so happy to meet a guy from my neighborhood. He was in the chow line. He saw me walking down the perimeter and he yelled, "Yo, Babe." A guy named Johnny Dougherty. We played football on the same team at home. He didn't end up qualifying for his wings, but I was grateful that he got me something to eat that first day, because I didn't know which end was up. The next day he came around and we took a walk through the woods. He told me to watch myself because there were dangerous snakes all over the woods between Fort Benning and Alabama, around the Chattahoochee River. I think he was trying to scare another city kid.

At night we read or talked about home. Someone had a radio at the end of the hall, and we listened to the big bands. Lights went out at ten p.m. and we had to be up at five. We didn't have much nightlife, and we looked forward to sleeping after long days of training.

Sometimes we went out in town to a little town nightclub called the Bama Club. It was just over a little footbridge from where we were. They had a band and the girls sang. One weekend I was there and a girl that was married to one of the officers got up to do a number. She said, "Any of you fellas want to get up and jitterbug with me? The winner gets a bottle of champagne." I was there with three other guys, one's name was Murray, he later got hurt on a night jump, and he said, "Come on Heffron, get up there and dance, you're always talking about jitterbugging in South Philly." Out of six or seven guys, I ended up winning the contest and the bottle of champagne. The girl was pretty good, too. She could dance.

A guy named Johnny Julian became my best buddy. You just looked at a guy and you liked him. John looked at me and thought I talked funny. I thought he talked funny. He was from Syspy, Alabama, and he had a strong Southern drawl. We got along great. He was just a nice kid. He was from a small town in the South, and I kidded him and said, "I'm from the South." He said, "You're from the South?" I said, "Yeah, South Philly!" He was clean-cut, believed in God, believed in everything I believed in, believed he was coming home. We could talk to one another really easily.

I also got close with J. D. Henderson, a really laid-back kid, a farmer from Oklahoma, and the three of us stuck together like glue all through jump school. We made a pact that if one of us bought the farm—if we got killed in combat—whoever was left would go to the parents.

After physical training and packing parachutes, we finally got to the jump training. The first stage was jumping out of towers. I hadn't done any practice jumping in basic, since I was training in the artillery. First you jumped from a thirty-two-foot tower with harnesses attached. Then you free-jumped with a parachute on—they pull you up two-hundred-fifty feet, and you jumped, and they told you what to do on your way down, how to maneuver your parachute. They told you left tumble, right tumble, and so on. Then D stage is five jumps from a C-47. The last one, your qualifying jump, was at night.

I wasn't nuts about the idea of jumping out of an aircraft at first, but once I did, I found it to be exhilarating. I loved my first jump. I wasn't scared at all. Once you left the door and you went under the tail of the plane, you saw the tail go over you, that's when your body would tumble under the plane in a somersault, and your chute would pop. And that was great. We were supposed to count to ten and then the chute would open, but I never counted, never met a guy that did. One guy said, "I say a Hail Mary, what the hell is counting gonna do?!" I knew when I went under the tail and it went over my head, and if I didn't hear it pop after I tumbled, I was in big trouble.

Once your chute opens, you look around and see the greenery of the earth against the blue sky. As I looked at the landscape, I always thought about the beauty of God's work. You saw colorful patterns of green and brown and blue. The air is soft and light. Nothing can hold a candle to the scenery. I always wished I was jumping in Pennsylvania, because the state is so full of natural beauty. As you start to come down, you think about not getting hurt and making a good landing. You stay away from water. You also want to come in front forward, because a lot of guys come in on their backs. I was lucky; I always landed right, in nice, open fields. But jumping out of planes wasn't for everyone. Some guys quit jump school after that first jump.

Night jumping I didn't like because you never knew where you were going. All you could see were dark patches of trees. The air was heavy and thick. But also, you relied too much on one man—the pilot. If he's on a bad decision day, you're going to be dropped in the wrong place. Sometimes a pilot got lost in his coordinates. You only had to go thirty to forty seconds off the drop zone to land somewhere dangerous. Maybe woods or water. If it's in combat, you're going to end up in German hands.

On the night of our last jump, the first plane up crashed, and all sixteen men on board were killed. An Italian fella from Conshohocken, Pennsylvania, got the soldier's medal because when they found the plane and the bodies, he had his hand on the guy jumping out of the plane, which meant he tried to get the guy out before he went out himself. The soldier's medal is the only Army decoration you can get stateside. The rest are combat awards.

They cancelled jumping for the night when the men were killed, and we were transferred to Camp Mackall for our final jump. Most of us had never been on a plane before we got to Benning, which was probably pretty obvious to the crew. As soon as we got airborne, one of the guys was looking out the window and hollered, "Hey, is the plane on fire?" We all got scared because it was just a two-engine job, a C-47. The crew chief told us it was just the exhaust from the motor—at night it looks like a flame.

I said a couple prayers. When it hit me that I was in a dark plane up in the sky at one a.m. getting ready to be dropped into the pitch black, I thought to myself, *What the hell am I doing up here? I could be back home on the corner in South Philly having a goddamn beer, or going to a dance.*

One of the kids, Murray, from Boston—he lost part of his family in the Coconut Grove fire, the worst fire in Boston's history—he broke a leg, an arm, and his back. He thought he was landing over water, but it was fresh cement and the minerals were shining in the moonlight.

We got our wings in March, and that was a great day. I was quite happy. I was proud. I was finally a paratrooper. I would rather have the wings than any other decoration. It was hard work. You had to have strength to maneuver the chute at times, and I still had that trouble with my hands, they would curl up and be in awful pain, but I did it. I got away with it. So I was happy.

We stayed in Camp Mackall, North Carolina, then went to Fort Bragg and back to Mackall. The training for combat intensified. We worked on night problems, we had fifteen-mile hikes in full combat gear. We had mock wars, and we'd send out a patrol and a point. Whatever had to be done in combat, we did it exactly the same way in training, and we did it over and over. We did a dry run and we found out what we did wrong, or who wasn't quick enough, and worked on resolving problems. We became a tight group.

At night when we weren't out on problems or maneuvers, we talked about home. Very seldom did we talk about the training. We cursed and hollered a bit about what we went through, but when we sat down to talk it was always about home. Everybody wanted to know where everyone was from, or the latest news from home, or about who was new to the outfit. The most popular state in the union was Pennsylvania, where most of the guys were from. If a guy said Philly, we'd ask where in Philly. He'd say Easton. We'd say, "There ain't no goddamn place named Easton!" Easton was on the outskirts of Philly, but you'd say "Philly" because everyone knew where it was. We antagonized each other a lot, but it was in fun.

In our downtime, we usually sat in the barracks and drank and played cards. Or we'd field strip our machine guns, or our M1s, or we'd do some cleaning. If we were inactive, that usually meant it was raining like hell out. Though if you had a bad officer, he'd have you marching out in the rain. But usually you got to stay inside, clean your weapons, listen to lectures, take tests. Like nomenclature of weapons; someone would call out a piece on your gun and you had to name it.

When it was time to head out overseas for combat duty, we were transferred to Camp Shanks, New York, on the Hudson River, and given one last weekend pass home. I came down my street and saw my mom on the pavement with the other women. I said, "Hi, Mrs. Gugan, Mrs. Daily, Mrs. Thompson." Just then turning the corner comes a Western Union guy on a bicycle. That usually meant a KIA. All the women watched him and seemed to be in unison: "Keep going, you son of a bitch, keep going." Nobody wanted him to stop at their house. I thought, *Oh, Jesus*. I had three brothers in the war. When he rode by, my mother went, "Whew." I said, "Boy, I got scared." She said, "Babe, this is all the time!"

We had mild spring weather, and I sat around with my family and a group of neighbors and had a few beers. Back then, even if you were underage, you drank beer. But also, nobody cared if you drank because nobody knew if you were coming home. People said to me, "Oh my, you're in the paratroopers? Oh my, that's bad." I heard it enough that I didn't have much confidence in coming home. People thought if you didn't get killed in combat, you'd surely get killed jumping out of an airplane! On one of my passes home, my mother said, "Edward"—she always called me Edward when she wanted something or she was mad at me—"why don't you go see Sister Mary Edna? She's been asking about you four boys and none of you have visited her." She was the nun we had in first grade, and we were all scared to death of her. I didn't want to go see her because even when you walked around in your own neighborhood, Army regulations said that you had to keep your uniform on; you couldn't dress in civilian clothes. When I walked around in uniform, I felt like I was flaunting it, like I thought I was some kind of hero, when I'd never even heard a shot fired. But to make my mom happy, I went and saw Sister Mary Edna in her classroom. "You know, children," she said to her students, "this fella and his three brothers were so scared of us nuns, they used to be shaking in their boots. Would you believe now he's dropping out of airplanes?" When I heard Sister Mary Edna thought jumping out of airplanes was such a big deal, I realized what I was doing was worse than I thought! She must have figured I was a little nuts. Really, we were all a little nuts.

I had a broad named Doris, and I didn't see her that last weekend. I had seen her the week before when I came home on a weekend pass, just after we arrived in New York. It was the most boring few hours I could've spent. I wasn't much for the broads anyway, never one for sitting and holding hands. I liked hanging out with the guys more than anything else. My brothers and friends were home on leave, and I didn't know if I'd see those guys again, so I wanted to hang out with them. Everyone asked me where I was headed, but we were told not to talk about any troop movements, and everyone understood. They only knew I was leaving the next day. I got a good night's sleep, and didn't make a big deal saying good-bye. You said good-bye at the door and you left. You didn't want a big deal.

It was the end of May 1944 when we left for England on the *Queen Elizabeth*. We were packed in like sardines. The boat was pretty well done in by the GIs. Everybody had carved their initials with their bayonets into the railings. We passed the Statue of Liberty, and that was the last lady I'd be seeing for a year. The ride was pretty smooth and all I recall about it is that when we went to eat, we had to go four decks down and stand in line. That was the big challenge of the day.

When we arrived in Liverpool, we learned that the 82nd and 101st Airborne Divisions had just jumped into Normandy. We loaded onto trucks and then took a train into Chester, England. They pulled all the curtains down on the train so nobody would know it was a troop movement. When we got there, they assigned us to our units. There were about five thousand of us, and it didn't matter who you trained with, they broke us up and sent us to different regiments, battalions, and companies. I got assigned to the 506th Parachute Infantry Regiment of the 101st Airborne, and was sent to regimental headquarters. Colonel Sink and his headquarters were at Littlecote House. It was an old castle. They let us flop there while they waited for the boys to come back from Normandy and they could see where replacements were needed. The little old lady who owned the castle owned Woodbine cigarettes. She would come out in the morning and I would be on sentry duty, and she'd say, "I'd say there, soldier, it's a lovely morning, isn't it?" She always had a cigarette hanging out the side of her mouth.

As soon as the guys were back from combat, I was transferred to 2nd Battalion, Easy Company. The good news was that my jump school buddies, J. D. Henderson and Johnny Julian, were assigned to Easy Company, too. You want to go in with a buddy or two if you're joining a unit that's been together in combat. We figured we better stick together.

3
★

D-DAY: WILD BILL'S REVENGE

Normandy, June 6 to Mid-July 1944

Everyone was quiet for the flight over the English Channel. The motors were loud and drowned everything out. The guys were praying, thinking, smoking, scared as hell. It was a two-and-a-half-hour ride, and our stomachs and bladders were working overtime. We trained and trained for this for two years and still didn't know what we were in for. I was praying. I said, "Dear God, help me get out of this goddamn plane alive and let me do what I have to do." I was thinking of my family and praying not to mess things up when I got there. Most of the guys were half asleep. I was wide awake thinking about Henry. I was obsessed. I was a madman. You never want to feel that kind of rage. I was burning to get at those goddamn Germans. I would kill every one of them. I didn't care if they killed me, I was taking them down with me. Everyone knew what I was thinking.

I didn't forget I was a sergeant, I had a squad to lead, and there was a larger mission at stake. I was still thinking clearly about the men. I looked around at their faces and thought, *I hope everything goes right for these guys.* They were like brothers to me, too. We had an unexplainable bond. We ate together, slept together, trained together every day for two years. But I couldn't guarantee what I was going to do when I got there. It became personal. I was ready to go in, kill a thousand krauts, and be dead by the end of the day. I didn't want to get anyone else killed, so I prayed to the man upstairs. A million thoughts go through your mind at a time like that.

There was fear on everyone's face. We all looked around, probably thinking the same thing, wondering who the hell's going to get out alive.

Around midnight, we were getting close to Normandy, and you could see thousands of ships below. The Allied invasion fleet was heading for Omaha and Utah Beaches. An amazing sight. You already knew how big this thing was, but that was a sight to behold. Made you more nervous, but proud, too. Just over the coast, we hit fog and clouds and couldn't see a damn thing, we lost sight of the planes in our formation. We were told to stand up and hook up. I stood up and fell right back down on my ass. My leg bag was loaded and weighed a ton, it sat on my legs for hours, and they fell asleep. We started getting a lot of flak, the antiaircraft fire was horrendous. Every third or fourth round was tracers. There was fire all over the sky, behind us, in front of us. The plane sped up and started going up and down and veering side to side. Your only thought was, *Get me the hell out of this plane!* The sky looked like ten thousand Fourth of Julys—bright orange and red lights and continuous bursts of gunfire. Planes were trying to dodge the fire and were flying haphazardly and I figured we'd crash even before we got there. We couldn't blame the pilots, they wanted to drop us and get the hell out. We had no time to think about our jump. We were too low. We weren't in the drop zone, but we didn't care. We just wanted out. We got the order to jump even though the plane was moving too fast. Compton went out the door, and my leg was still on pins and needles, so I dove out headfirst. Toye was right behind me. After I jumped, my leg bag fell off, and my leg woke up real fast.

Making it through the jump alive was a feat. Your heart's pounding. The sky's chaos. The planes are dumping men from Cherbourg all the way to Paris. All in the wrong places. Thousands of troopers coming down from the sky, it was like a duck shoot for the krauts. On top of that, planes are getting hit, shells are flying past your head, equipment and bundles are coming down all over the place. You prayed your parachute opened, you didn't get tangled with another trooper, you didn't land on the fires you saw burning on the ground, or get hung in a tree, or land on a German, or on something that would kill you. Put that all to chance!

I fell like a ton of bricks, thought I broke every bone in my body. Things were dropping from the sky, people, ammo, parachutes, you had to look up instead of looking down, because the big bundles could have killed you. They were attached to the bottom of the planes; they were filled with supplies, medical equipment—they had everything in them.

I had no idea where the hell I was, but it turned out to be Ste. Mere-Eglise, a few miles from the drop zone. We were lucky. Some of 3rd Battalion landed close to our drop zone and the Germans were waiting for them, killed them all. I landed in the 82nd Airborne's drop zone, just before they landed. If you saw the movie *The Longest Day*, I came down near the church where John Steele's parachute got caught on the steeple.

I twisted out of my chute in about three seconds—two and a half seconds!—damn right. My adrenaline was pumping. Dead troopers were hanging in the trees. Their chutes got caught, and the krauts shot them. My only thought was, *Get ready to fight*. All bets were off. I didn't feel any fear. The Germans had to be more scared than us because we were all over the place. Everywhere they went—*bing*—there was a paratrooper. All the chaos was beneficial to us. We learned that after.

I didn't have a gun, no cricket either. Everything went flying off me when my chute jerked open. I had a knife and a bent carbine. We all had a knife attached to our boots, and one in our jumpsuits. Dead soldiers were all over, Germans and Americans, you could scrounge up a gun. Keep your eyes and ears open, that's all. I grabbed my knife and went to look for a gun. It was chaos, and your senses were intensified. I don't remember running into a kid from Fox Company when I landed, but he remembers running into me. He was tied up in his chute, and he remembers me coming out of the shadows, holding him to the ground, pushing my knee into his chest and a dagger to his throat, and asking him over and over what side he was on. He said I was crazed. Damn right. I wasn't taking chances. I did that to a lot of soldiers. Hitler could have been there for all I knew. When I figured out he wasn't a kraut, I cut him out of his chute with my knife.

I went looking for a gun, and found a Thompson submachine gun. I also took a German MG-42 off a dead kraut and started shooting it, but the gun made a noise that was distinctly German. The

German gun went *brrrrrrrrt*. The American guns went *bap-bap-bap-bap-bap*. Every time I started shooting it, the Americans started shooting at me! I got shot at by a dozen or so of our own men. I threw it the hell away. You learn fast or you get killed. I grabbed an M1 instead.

The first thing I saw was a bucket brigade. German soldiers were watching French civilians passing buckets of water to put out the fires. We passed right by each other. They saw me. Hell, yes, they saw me, but they didn't do nothing. I felt like I didn't have to do anything, they were just putting out fires. I figured I better get out of there, find my men.

I had to backtrack on the stick. If you're the first one out of the plane, your stick is behind you, so you backtrack. If you're last out of the plane, your stick is in front of you, you go forward. No one was where they were supposed to be. Nothing was like what we prepared for. Everything we learned was out the window, it was one big mess, period. Nothing resembled what we studied in the marshaling area. But we were trained for surprises.

Right away I found Toye, Popeye Wynn, Malarkey, Compton, and Mike Ranney. We had blue metal crickets from the five-and-dime to identify each other. You pressed it, and it went click-clack, and the other guy clicked back. It was loud and high-pitched, you knew right away you were safe. If you lost it in the jump, a lot of men did, you used a password. The first person said, "Flash" and the reply was, "Thunder." You were so nervous, you'd forget the password, and then you just yelled, "Hey, you son of a bitch, I'm from Brooklyn, don't shoot!" As soon as you heard Indiana or California or something American, you stopped and checked the guy out.

We ran into Lieutenant Winters; he had about a dozen men with him, and we starting moving toward our objective to secure the causeways. Guys were joining up from the 82nd, 501st, 502nd, all different outfits. Some stayed, some left, some went and hid in a barn. Everyone was looking for their outfit. No one knew what was going on. There was lots of confusion. Lipton joined up, and Winters led the way to Pouppeville.

About four a.m., it was pitch dark, we heard something coming toward us getting louder and louder. A German supply train came into view—wagons, pull carts, donkeys, horses, dogs. They must have been pulling supplies up to the front. They made all kinds of noise, clip-clop-clip-clop. Sounded like they had bells ringing, too. They had to be stupid making all that damn noise. Thinking back, they were probably conscripted troops, not the elite soldiers. Jesus Christ, you got a million paratroopers all over the place and they're walking around singing a song. They didn't know we were there, and we hid behind hedgerows to ambush them. I was ready to kill them all. I had my Tommy gun ready, and I told Malarkey to get the hell out of my way. I was like possessed. They got past us, and we had them trapped. I let loose, started shooting from the rear to the front and back again, annihilated every last one. I took my vengeance out on those sons of bitches. I shot everything I saw that day. People ask if your first kill is hard. It was easy as squashing a bug. I released a lot of anger.

In the movie, Dick Winters orders us to hold fire, and I start shooting. If it happened that way, I don't remember, but it could have. I had so much anger I might have turned around and shot *him* if he tried to stop me. I wanted to shoot every German son of a bitch I laid eyes on. No one could have controlled me. To tell Malarkey, one of my best buddies, to get the hell out of my way, that tells you. It was kill or be killed, period. Another thing, I respected Winters as an officer, but no one proved themselves in combat yet. You don't know who's going to get you killed, make good decisions, bad decisions. He was a good leader in training, but combat could be a different story. I didn't know if Winters would kill. He was a Quaker. Quakers don't believe in violence. Winters didn't drink or smoke. He didn't curse. He was squeaky clean. He wasn't our company commander, nobody knew where the company commander Lieutenant Meehan was. We didn't know Meehan's plane was shot down until later. Your company commander can get you through, or get you all killed. I saw it this way: We got rid of Sobel before D-day—strike number one; then Lieutenant Meehan takes over the company just before D-day, and he's nowhere to be found—strike number two; now we've got Winters, a Quaker—strike number three. This was a quick change of command, bing-bang-boom. I thought, *We're all gonna die.*

In Ambrose's book, he says two wagons got away and we took prisoners. Nobody got away that I know of, and we didn't take prisoners. If you took prisoners, you had to guard them. Who was going to guard them? Our mission just started, and our orders were no prisoners. Meehan gave the order in England.

Right after we blew away the supply train, a French woman came out and screamed, "Why did you kill the horses?" I yelled back at her, "They're German horses!" You're not trying to kill the animals, but it's war.

We joined up with about forty kids from Dog Company, and Nixon and Hester from battalion headquarters, they had forty more men. We didn't know a few hundred yards away in St. Come-du-Mont the Germans had four 105mm cannons pointed toward Utah Beach. Our men were perfect targets. We weren't told this until we got there, but the sides of the roads were mined and flooded. They had Rommel's

Asparagus, like railroad spikes with points sticking up that went right through your body. That was for the gliders and seaborne troops. Unless you landed on it when you jumped, it would go right up your ass. It was one hell of a mess. So the troops had to stay on the road for the higher ground, and the Germans had them zeroed in.

Headquarters didn't know about that German battery. A lot of things they didn't know. We had to take everything as it came at us. When the tide rose, and the troops started coming in from the coast about seven or eight in the morning, the Germans started blowing away the troops on the beach and we learned where they were. They were firing continuously, we had no trouble finding them.

The battery was at Brecourt Manor; it had a huge field in front of it, lots of property, with hedgerows all around. The hedgerows in Normandy were bad news. They were like cement walls, branches all entwined, they were growing for seven hundred years. They were thick, ten feet high, six feet wide; the things were everywhere. This wasn't like you see at home. You couldn't see over them, you couldn't jump over them, tanks couldn't get through them. A tank had to have a special plow, like a big iron fork, to cut through. Good places for the Germans to dig in and hide, but it ain't easy fighting. Good for defense, not for offense. We were told about the hedgerows in the marshaling area, yes, but they said they were a few feet high, like you could jump over the damn things.

The krauts were dug into a long, winding, trench system along a line of trees, like an L-shape. The whole thing was well hidden. Could have been one gun, five, or fifteen in there. No one knew nothing. The only thing we knew was that Easy Company had orders to attack. With the nucleus of our company missing, they needed men to fill positions. We got promotions on the spot. We had no captain, no headquarters, I had no idea where my platoon sergeant Jimmy Diel was. They made Winters commander, he made me 2nd Platoon sergeant, Malarkey took over the mortar squad. A lot of promotions were made on the battlefield.

We had about eleven E Company men—Winters, Compton, Malarkey, Toye, Gerald Lorraine, Popeye Wynn, Lipton, Ranney, Plesha, Petty, and me. The frontal approaches to the guns were wide open, so we had to attack from the flank. Winters laid out a plan to attack the first gun closest to our position. We had to run about a couple hundred yards down an open field; we were an easy target for German machine guns covering the trench from across the field. They had them in the front and rear. The krauts wouldn't expect an attack over an open field. We had to lay down enough mortar and machine-gun fire to keep them from raising their heads. I had the mortar, but I couldn't find the base plate, so I put it between my legs and started shooting. We were doing like we did in training: Fire the mortar till we run out of ammo, then the machine guns open up on the flanks to keep the krauts' heads down, then we advance under cover of machine-gun fire. Plesha and Petty were on the machine guns, and Lipton and Ranney were covering us from the flanks. Lipton went up in a tree in the middle of the field, a skinny tree, you couldn't miss him. Nobody told him to, he did it himself. The Germans were so busy with us, they didn't have time to see him. You do stupid things, you're so full of vim and vigor, you don't care. Afterward you say, *Holy Christ.*

Winters picked me, Compton, and Malarkey to hit the first gun. We had to crouch down and run across the field. Winters, Toye, and Lorraine were coming up from the rear. We spread out, but stayed close enough we could see each other. Luckily, the Germans stayed down. You would hide, too! There was fire coming at them from three sides. A hedgerow and trees were blocking the trench, so we didn't know what we were going to find, how many Germans we were going to come face-to-face with. My heart was pounding. It was scary. We didn't know what the hell we were doing yet, either. Nobody did. But we didn't really give a damn.

Compton reached the trench, burst through the hedgerow, and tried to shoot a Thompson he picked up after the jump, but it didn't work, so he threw it. The barrel was bent. The British made a bunch of guns—they called them grease guns, they were cheap Tommy guns. They got so hot, they wouldn't fire, so you unscrewed the barrel and pissed on it or put it in water to cool it down. That's what Compton had. I jumped in the trench right behind him, and we started lobbing grenades. The Germans ran like hell down the trench in the other direction. Winters and the other guys were right behind us, and all of us started lobbing grenades and shooting everything we had. Tossing grenades and attacking, it was stupid, but we did it so quick, so fast, they thought an entire company was attacking. We caught them with their pants down. When they ran down the trench, we saw there were a lot more of them than we thought. About forty of them manning the 105s, plus the machine gunners on the flanks. They were all firing at us. Next thing we knew, Popeye Wynn got shot in the ass and fell—two years of working and the first day in combat, *bang,* you blink your eyes and you're done. We didn't let up, we kept chasing the krauts, shooting and shouting. They were firing at us, too. It was chaos. I was raring to take out those Germans. You get the strength of an ox on the battlefield; your adrenaline's going, you're hyperalert, you see, hear, and smell everything. Your movements are quick, your body is in survival mode. You don't think, you react.

A kraut threw a grenade at us, and we all took a forward dive, and it landed between Joe Toye's legs. Winters hollered at him, and Toye jumped, and the grenade exploded on Toye's rifle. He was lucky, the rifle took the brunt of it. Otherwise he'd be singing soprano. He got sprayed with some wooden splinters, but he was okay. We chased the Germans, throwing grenades and shooting, and they started jumping out of the trench and running down the field. Me, Winters, and Lorraine started shooting. They got two of them, I missed my target. I never missed! Never missed! But I made up for it. That kraut was full of bullets when I got done with him. No one got away.

We got down low and ran to the second gun. The krauts kept firing those machine guns so we had to stay low. That's when Malarkey ran out in the field because he thought he saw a Luger on a dead kraut. He was a Luger nut. I guess he wanted to give it to someone at home, but he almost got himself killed. How he lived through it, I'll never know. It wasn't a Luger either, the dummy! I'll tell you something about Malarkey, he was the best of the best, an expert marksman, a great soldier. But he ran out in a field with ten machine guns firing at us, that's how bad he wanted a Luger. I think he wound up with about seventy German guns by the time the war was over.

Winters had to call headquarters for ammo, guns, and backup. We didn't even think about what we had, we were so gung-ho, we threw everything at them, and it was almost too late when we realized it. We charged the third gun, firing at them, them firing at us. We had to make sure every shot or grenade counted, because if we ran out, we were done. We were under constant fire. I don't know how more of us didn't get hit. We had a kid named Hall with us; he was one of the kids who couldn't find his company. His head must have gone above the ditch, and *bang*, a sniper got him, killed him instantly. But we kept going and captured the third gun. Nothing we could do. Wrong place, wrong time. You thank God it's not you, and you wonder if you're next, but you don't have time to think about it. You learn real fast about war. Men drop dead right in front of you, and you better keep moving. You don't get used to it, believe me. But it's war, kid. You can't be affected, or you're dead. Later, when you're alone with your thoughts, you can think back to all the men you lost, and then it hits you.

Winters had to make sure the Germans didn't come back and use the guns, so Captain Hester and Nixon came from headquarters with TNT and blew the barrels and breeches apart. I think we tried grenades first, but they didn't even scratch it.

Lt. Ronald Speirs and some men from Dog Company came down to reinforce us. Speirs went right in to take the fourth gun, and I was so hyped up, I followed right behind him, covered him from the rear. Speirs was as nutty as I was. He sent the Germans fleeing, and took the gun, but he lost two men.

I picked up some field binoculars and was looking over a hedge at the German machine-gun positions on the flanks, and I fell sound asleep in the ditch. After all the chaos, if you stop moving, the adrenaline leaves you, and you poop out. Joe Toye smacked me in the back of the head, he thought I was dead, and I jumped ten feet in the air. He scared the hell out of me, and I scared the hell out of him! Jesus Christ, I felt like I slept for ten days. We were awake for two days at that point, and had nine or ten hours of straight combat. When you thought you had nothing left, I have no idea how, but you kept moving.

We killed a lot of Germans, wounded a lot, and got a lot of information on the Germans' positions, where their supplies were coming from, what outfit we were fighting. Winters grabbed hold of maps that showed where they were, where the machine guns were, everything. Probably helped us in future battles. For what we accomplished, we were lucky, and they had to be stupid. We didn't know there were forty, fifty of them, and they didn't know there was just a few of us. They thought it was a bigger force coming at them. They weren't ready; we hit them at the right time and place. It was a normal maneuver we done in training over and over. No guesswork involved.

We saved the lives of the kids coming in on the beachheads. We saved quite a few. We got a letter from a guy who came in on the beach and thanked us for knocking out the guns. I think the 4th Division wrote in their history they came in and knocked out the guns, and that was squashed real fast.

We had one hell of a baptism of fire. I got a lot of kills. When it was all over, I got the shakes pretty bad. I thought, *What the hell did I just do?* You don't realize what you're doing. It felt like it didn't happen. During the action, my brain was blank. I didn't feel a damn thing. You act and react, that's all. Even if I had got hit, I don't think I would have felt a thing. Would have kept on running.

We left that field and sat around for a while talking about what we did, thinking back about who did what, how, who got hurt, who got killed. We couldn't believe what we just done. We couldn't believe we came out of it alive. We proved Easy Company was damn good. What we knew about each other in training held over in combat. We knew each other's next move, we trusted each other, it went right back to that bond. You'd give up your life for the man beside you. That's when boys became men.

Winters turned out to be a great leader in combat. He called all the shots, and we followed his orders. He was smart, quick, efficient, resourceful, intuitive, fearless. Very good officer. I had a lot of respect for him. He wasn't a Quaker in combat. He proved himself. A hundred-eighty degrees different than Sobel. We'd have all been dead if it were Sobel. I think one of us would have killed Sobel if the krauts didn't get him first. That's no joke. It happened in combat. Not all the time, but it happened. Someone was a bad leader, made bad choices, his own men killed him so they can stay alive. But I knew after the first bullets came in that day, and what we did at Brecourt, we had a good commander leading us. You knew you could follow Winters anywhere.

Machine-gun fire was still coming from around the house. Malarkey got on the mortar and Toye got on the machine gun and blasted the hedgerows across the street. I jumped on a gun, too. With me, Malarkey, and Toye they didn't have a chance. We blew those krauts out of there. Nixon came in with the heavy stuff; he brought a couple Sherman tanks and took care of the rest of them. We got every last kraut.

More men were showing up, and we were getting bigger and bigger. We talked about who was missing, who was dead. I never saw Punchy Diel, never saw Johnny Martin. Leo Boyle joined up. It was a relief to see each man's face. The men who missed the Brecourt action, we filled them in. Each one told their stories. We all had crazy stories about the jump, who encountered what, how we found each other. We slept in the ground near Culoville for the night, and I don't remember anything about it, except that I was thankful to come out alive. It took my body a long time to stop shaking. I don't know how I made it. Never thought I'd last one day. If I could make it through D-day being as stupid as I was, then maybe I could make it one more day. I was a little nuttier than the next guy. I took a lot of chances, kid. But we did what we had to. When the events of the day started to sink in, I thought I done a good job, accomplished the mission, got out alive. If you get most of your men in and out alive, you done a good job.

★ ★ ★

It took a week to get the company together. Everything was slow. It wasn't well organized. We were supposed to leave Normandy and go back to England for another jump, but they wanted us to take Carentan. Carentan connected Utah and Omaha beaches and they needed it to link up the seaborne troops and bring them inland. It had to be taken, period. But it was defended by the *Fallschirmjäger*, the German paratroopers—the best Germany had. That's why they kept us there. You put the best against the best. We figured we'd get the job done in a couple days and go back to England.

When we marched toward Carentan, we marched into a couple companies of *Fallshirmjäger*; they were trying to keep us out. Most of the 506th was there. We killed a lot of Germans, took a lot of prisoners, and pushed them back. But these guys were like scallywags. Unorganized. They weren't the best of the troops. These were put outside Carentan, let them get killed first. The better soldiers were in Carentan. We found all this out later.

We got Angoville secure, and we went over the Douve River—there were more rivers and springs than I can name—in the pitch dark, in the rain, we got terrible storms, thunder and lightning, and everything was mud. It was hot, wet, miserable. Your feet got stuck in the mud. We were tripping over logs, dead GIs, dead animals, shells, we couldn't see a damn thing, but it was nothing new to us. We trained and trained and trained for it. Times like that you thanked Sobel in your mind for the hell he put you through.

On the way, we were following Fox Company—they were on our flank—and we kept losing contact with them, so we kept stopping. Someone was always carrying a phone or a radio to keep up contact. I carried a phone. Rod Bain, George Luz, and a couple other guys had radios. Company headquarters had the big radios, they were huge, and had long range. The rest of us had a small, portable radio, about four times the size of a regular phone. You had to be within range to hear someone talking. Usually company headquarters was on the other end, we could also talk company to company, or relay a call, if someone came on from Able Company, he could transfer you to Easy. We had a good system, but if you were out of range, you lost contact with everyone. That's what happened going into Carentan, we lost the company we were following, and we could have all gotten killed—the Germans were waiting for us. The officers were at fault for that, but you don't think about that until later. Somebody said the regimental officers made themselves scarce during night training exercises, and that's probably true. At the time, you have no idea what the hell is going on, you're just following orders.

We were attacking at dawn at a Y-intersection, you had to go left or right. Houses and buildings were on both sides. The Germans were no dummies, they had the high ground. Once you control the high ground, anyone who attacks has got big trouble. They called the Y-intersection Dead Man's Corner. A lot of men from the 101st Airborne got killed there, and they piled them all on top of each other, right at the crossroads. It was kind of a warning to you—if you got down to the intersection alive you were lucky. We knew we were on low ground and were going to attack on high ground. We waited in ditches on the side of the road for orders. Second Platoon was attacking on the right. We had to run down the road in the open to get to the buildings, then do house-to-house fighting to flush the Germans out. Winters gave the order to go. Lieutenant Welsh ran out with a few men from 1st Platoon behind him, and all hell broke loose. The Germans opened up on us with an MG-42 straight up the road. Everybody froze in the ditch. We were pinned down by the machine-gun fire. If you lifted your head it would get blown off. Winters didn't care, he wanted everyone to move out, he wanted us right behind Welsh. He was yelling "Go! Go! Go!" but no one budged. He ran into the middle of the road, bullets flying by his head, hitting at his feet, he's hollering, and waving his hands, running from one side of the road to the other and back, screaming and yelling like a lunatic, trying to get us to move out. Everybody was looking at each other saying "Is he friggin' nuts? He thinks we're going to get up?!" I never saw Winters that mad in my life. I think we figured Winters was going to get himself killed, so we better get the hell up. We ran right through the machine-gun fire, and I think Welsh took out the main gun with a grenade.

At some point, Shifty Powers picked off a couple snipers. When there was a sniper, you sent Shifty in to take him out. Shifty was a damn good soldier in 3rd Platoon. He was from the mountains in Virginia, born and raised with a gun in his hand, not like us city slickers. He was like an Indian, lived off the ground, was very observant, was in tune to nature. He could pick out movement a mile away.

Rifle and machine-gun fire was coming from the windows and doors, and we paired off and ran house to house. You threw a grenade through a window or open door, kicked down the door, and ran inside to kill anyone left alive. At one point, I was paired off with Lipton—he took the upstairs and I took the downstairs. You don't shoot unless you see somebody. You don't want to give away your position.

Then we got split up and Lipton got hit by sniper fire in the groin and was evacuated. I got my kills, but I was also running around giving orders, telling my men where to fire. It was a bad battle, but we got the Germans flushed out pretty quick. They got the hell out of there. Problem was, they had us zeroed in from another location, and started pounding us with mortars and 88s. They shoot those 88s and the ground explodes and blows out everything above it. Best weapon ever made. Everyone was running, you had no idea where they were going to land. There was smoke everywhere. It was chaos. Everyone's screaming for medics. Father Maloney ran around giving last rites. He was the chaplain for the 506th. He was awarded the Distinguished Service Cross for his action in Normandy. He had no weapons on him, just carried a cross. He was all over like a ghost, running in and out. If you were fighting and not hurt, you didn't pay attention to what he was doing at the time, but if you got wounded, and you didn't know if you were going to survive, his presence was important. Thinking back, he inspired the men, it was like having the Lord himself come down to visit you. You know you're not alone, someone cared for you. Even the rabbi came, he would bless you, too. Religion made no difference. When Father Maloney died twenty years ago, I went up to New York with George Vanderswick, who was also from E Company, and we helped bury him. I had flowers made up into a Screaming Eagle, three feet high and two feet wide, and put it by his side. We painted a helmet gold, and put the Distinguished Service Cross on it with his name. The chaplains and the medics were the real heroes.

The shelling stopped, and we had about a dozen men hurt. Winters got hit in the leg, and got treated. We got orders to clear the Germans out of Carentan. We tried moving out and there was so much chaos—the Germans were firing at us, we were firing at them, and our battalions were firing at each other. We dug in for the night to hit the krauts at dawn.

The sergeants are in motion before the battle starts. You go back and forth with the company commander and headquarters. They map things out, coordinate the mortars and machine guns of every company. You look at a big booklet with a grid, and the grid gives you distance, you can see where every company is, where their mortars and machine guns are, where the Germans are, what the ranges are, and where you want the men to fire. It changes minute by minute so you gotta think fast. I coordinated a lot with headquarters on the fire. Not every sergeant did it, some did. I ran back and forth. Headquarters had the heavy artillery and mortars, so in a battle you called them for support. I knew them, they were former E Company guys.

As soon as it got light, both sides were waiting, right away all hell broke loose. We were firing back and forth, machine guns, lobbing mortars and grenades, and then all of a sudden, their tanks rolled in. Once the tanks roll in you're in trouble; we didn't have any armored with us. They were shooting 88s. The earth was shaking. We were getting the hell beat out of us. Everyone was screaming for medics. The NCOs were running back and forth hollering at the men to fire at everything they could—"keep shooting, keep shooting, keep shooting!" The forward observer calls the range, and you run around making sure the guns are trained right, the men keep firing, and the Germans stay pinned down. I ran back and forth not just watching my platoon, but also 1st and 3rd. You have to make snap decisions, change positions, get new ranges; it's continuous action. Meanwhile mortars and 88s are hitting around us, and you can't even see through the smoke. We were losing men left and right—and getting our kills in, too—but we couldn't let the Germans take Carentan. Too much at stake.

This was hedgerow-to-hedgerow fighting and we were at a constant disadvantage. They were ten feet high, for crying out loud. They would gouge you, too. We had to climb under the damn things. We climbed over them, but you risked getting your head blown off. The Germans were no dummies. They waited for you to come out of the hedgerows, come over them, come around them—every corner was a tanker with a machine gun waiting. They hid right in the hedgerows. They'd come busting through and surprise you. The Germans were good on the defensive, bad on the offensive.

John McGrath and Lieutenant Welsh set up their bazooka and knocked out a tank that was headed right for us. The bazooka was the only thing we had that could take out a tank. Twice the size of a mortar, but lighter. Then we heard the Sherman tanks. Our own 2nd Armored Division coming in with dozens of tanks. Those tanks made a racket, clanking away, but when it's your own, it's like music. Since I worked at Baldwin Locomotive before the war making Sherman tanks, I could identify them real fast. You still don't want to stick your nose up if it's your own tanks. You don't know if the gunner will mistake you for a kraut.

Our tanks started blowing away the Tigers and everything else. We were shooting, our tanks were shooting. We boxed those Jerries in and shelled the shillelagh out of them.

Thank God 2nd Armored was with us. Not only did they have tanks, but tank destroyers, too, heavy stuff. They massacred the krauts. We were able to hold our ground long enough for them to get there, and they finished the job. You see, they put us against the panzer (tank) division, and the German paratroopers—we loved fighting against them, that's the elite of the German army—and we whooped their goddamn asses!

We got extreme confidence right away in Normandy. When you meet the Germans face-to-face, you see they're not superhuman. A German soldier puts his pants on just like you, he's a man just like you. Once you lick them, you figure you can lick the world. You had that feeling, like you could lick them all. They were good, but we were better. We could thank Sobel for that.

We took Carentan, and got relieved, and were billeted in stables, and the men went on a looting spree. We were raiding houses and taking liquor. They had a lot of cognac and Calvados, those Frenchman. That stuff will straighten you right out. Heavy duty. When someone found some, they took a swig and passed it around. We passed bottles around all the time. Good thing it wasn't poison!

The civilians were hiding, sometimes in the cellar; they were never out in the open. The entire time in France, I never saw a French civilian. Some guys said they had contact with civilians, I never saw a one. They didn't want any part of us. Years later when I went back to France, and they asked me for a passport, I said, "You didn't ask me for a passport on D-day. I never saw one of you then."

We were in Carentan for about two weeks, and there were dead horses and cows and dead bodies everywhere, and they were rotting and starting to stink. They were mounting up and weren't being buried fast enough. The smell was unbearable. Made us all sick. You can't close your nose and not breathe! The Graves Registration Team, they were part of the army, their job was to come after the battle and bury the dead, even if they got relocated later. They had the worst job of all. I don't know how the hell they done it. I tried to find them after the war. I wanted to thank them for the work they done; they didn't get any recognition. But I never found them.

We went back to the line after a few days and dug in. Winters asked for volunteers for a patrol to check out some farmhouses nearby. They knew the Germans were in the area, but they wanted more info. So he asked for volunteers and like I said, my policy is *never* volunteer. You don't know what the hell they're going to throw at you. No one volunteered, so Winters picked me to lead the patrol. They briefed me, gave me a map, and I took the patrol out with Albert Blithe, Maxwell Clark, Joe Lesniewski, and Eddie Joint. I made Blithe point man, put Lesniewski behind him on the right, Clark in the rear. We crouched down and advanced toward the farmhouse, along a line of hedgerows. Now like I said about those hedgerows, those Germans were waiting around every corner. Just when we got past the hedgerows, when we could see the farmhouses, *bam!* A sniper fired at us and hit Blithe in the back of the neck, and he dropped to the ground. I yelled for covering fire so we could get to him, and someone yelled for a medic. His wound had what looked like red wooden splinters in it, like they hit him with wooden bullets. We seen clips of wooden bullets around Brecourt. Who knows what the Germans were doing with wooden bullets? Maybe they thought it was better to wound a soldier rather than kill him; his buddies will try to retrieve him and they could get a few more kills. Normally, if the guy is shot bad, and Blithe was, you leave the man there and get the hell out. But we never left a man. We went and got him and tried to patch him up. Lesniewski tried to stop the bleeding with a handkerchief. Then we grabbed Blithe and got the hell out of there. The krauts fired at us all the way back, so Malarkey got on the mortar and blasted them. Blithe was evacuated back to England and never saw combat with us again.

We called Blithe Alby for short. He was in 1st Platoon. The movie portrays him as scared, everybody was scared. But he was a good soldier, that's why I put him on the point. I think he ended up back in combat in the Korean War.

At the end of June, we went in reserve, somewhere around Utah Beach. We got our first showers and sleep, and our first real food. The K rations that were supposed to be breakfast, lunch, and dinner were enough to gag a maggot, and just enough to survive on. You got a little box with four cigarettes, chocolate bars, stale crackers, a can of eggs and cheese, or Spam and cheese, or just cheese, some coffee and a fruit bar. Same thing every day for a month. Luckily, you never worried about eating in Normandy. It was all farms, there was always something—a potato, a head of cabbage. You survived. We shot a cow over there and ate it, too. I don't know who shot it, but Brad Freeman, who was in the mortar squad, was born and raised on a farm and he told us he would dress the cow, which meant cut it up. I'm a city kid, I don't know, I thought he was going to put a dress on the cow. I thought, *This guy is nuts*. We cooked it and ate it, ate around the shrapnel. Another thing we could always find in Normandy was liquor. The French enjoy their liquor.

After it's all over, when you're back in garrison, or you get time to rest, which is almost never, *then* you start to think. When I first got to Normandy, every day for a week I got up and wanted to kill as many Germans as I could. I took chances you had to be stupid to take. I didn't care. You don't know what tonight brings, what tomorrow brings. It was terrifying. There's so much uncertainty. Every day I thought I might die tomorrow. When I lasted one day, I thought okay, maybe I'll last two. And every day you make it, your drive to live gets stronger. I got a taste of making it through six or seven, then I thought, *Jesus Christ, how lucky I am.* Then I planned to get out alive. But combat happens so damn quick it makes your eyes spin. You can't think. You must be callous to death. It's all around you. It's war. It ain't no damn picnic. The enemy is waiting for you around every corner.

There were times after a day or week of combat when I thought about the guys killed and said to myself, *You crazy bastard, look what you done.* I called the shots for my men, I felt responsible. But you can't second-guess. You don't know if you done it some other way, or ten other ways, if it would have been worse. So why question? It was sad when one of our guys got hurt or killed, but you didn't have time to cry. Some guys did. You couldn't let yourself get soft. I kept telling the men, "You can't think. If you do, you're dead. Just keep moving forward." When you lose your buddies, it makes you go forward with more vengeance. The guys talked to each other about the men we lost, and what we'd done, the close calls we had. After three weeks of fighting together, we were bonded in a different way than before. We saw and experienced the worst things humans can see or experience. We saved each other's lives. It was give and take. The bond really came out. These are the same guys you entered training with, the same guys you survived Sobel with, the same guys you spent every day with, and slept with every night. Then in combat, it's life or death, it bonds you even more.

You learned over and over your body could take more than you thought. At night, you sat down and thought, *What the hell did I do? Jesus Christ.* You reflected on what you done, and you said, *That can't be me, I gotta be nuts, I can't believe that was my day.* In combat, your body just responds automatically, and then your brain catches up later and goes, *How in the hell did I do that?*

We found out that Captain Meehan and eighteen Easy Company men were killed on D-day when their plane went down. Most of them were from company headquarters. That was very sad.

We left Normandy on the LSTs, about mid-July, and we saw the armada of ships, like we saw coming in on D-day. Thousands of ships with Allied troops and artillery. I thought, *I hope they get out of here alive.* We were leaving, but those guys were just going in! But then I wondered, *What the hell's going to happen to us next?*

Johnny Martin said, "Jesus Christ, we just jumped here a month ago and half the men are gone. We just started. None of us are going to get out of here alive." We figured we better go back and have the most fun we can have because tomorrow we might all be dead.

4

★

ENGLAND: GARRISON DUTY AND PICCADILLY LILIES

Mid-July to Mid-September 1944

BILL

Aldbourne was like a homecoming. The civilians were happy to see us, and we were happy as hell to be alive. As soon as we got back, we got seven-day passes, new uniforms, all our back pay. I got about two hundred dollars, a lot of money for a kid from South Philly. I always sent most of my money to Mom and kept the rest. The Army took out allotments, sent them wherever you wanted. It wasn't much, but it helped.

The men were all fired up. Most took off for London. We were the first GIs back from combat, and we went all decorated with our ribbons and medals. In London, everyone knew you were just in combat. Nobody wanted to mess with you. They were afraid. They knew you killed people.

The Americans made three or four times what the English soldiers made, and paratroopers got that extra fifty bucks jump pay every month, so we went to the pubs and threw our money away. We'd slap a ten on the bar, we looked like big spenders and it impressed the girls. The English soldiers made much less, and we'd take their girls, so we got into a lot of brawls. A lot of their soldiers hadn't come back yet, so we benefited there, too. We drank, danced, binga-da, banga-da, bonga-da. A lot of sex. We raised Cain in London. Oh boy, did we have a ball.

First thing me and Johnny Martin did, we went to Edinburgh, Scotland, and got tattoos. We were drunk as sixteen skunks. Woke up the next morning and looked at our arms and said, "What the hell is that?" We had matching tattoos of a paratrooper coming down from the sky. If I was sober, I'd never get a tattoo. But I figured if I had one, I may as well have three. So I got two more in London—an eagle, and a skull and crossbones.

We were on pass for a week, and one night, it was late and we couldn't find a place to sleep, so Johnny said, "I'll get us a place to sleep." We went to a USO club, but there were no beds left. So Johnny said, "Watch this." He went to the door and yelled, "Fire!" Everybody ran out. We ran in, got under the sheets, and went to sleep. No one said a word. We would have killed them. We were crazy kids.

When everyone got back to Aldbourne, we got stars put on our jump wings. When you made a combat jump, you got a star. We never knew about it until after the fact. So we wanted to do more combat jumps. It sounds crazy now, that we'd risk our lives to get a star on our wings, but it was true. I got a real nice honor, too. Captain Winters recommended me for a Distinguished Service Cross for my actions at Brecourt. He told me about it after the battle. I was awarded the Silver Star instead because the Army didn't give too many DSC awards. Only two of us in the company received the Silver Star, me and Buck Compton.

I was officially promoted to staff sergeant when we got back to Aldbourne. Jimmy Diel was made officer and sent to Able Company. Once I was promoted, I had three more squads to lead. A big responsibility, but it came naturally to me to look out for the men. I would do it without a promotion. I reported to Buck Compton. He was 2nd lieutenant, oversaw all three of Easy Company's platoons. We had two lieutenants that oversaw the company, Compton and Winters, then Winters was promoted to company commander in Normandy, and Compton became 1st lieutenant.

A lot of promotions after Normandy. Burr Smith became a staff sergeant. Muck and Malarkey were made sergeants. Leo Boyle was promoted to staff sergeant and put in headquarters company. He was a good sergeant, but could not handle men and lead them in combat. In combat, the leaders stand right out. Someone may be a leader in training, and then they can't handle leading in combat. It happened sometimes. When it came to responsibility, most men turned it down. Your actions can kill people. That was on your mind at all times. Leo was a very nice kid, quiet, just didn't have leadership quality, but he was a good sergeant. He was in charge of our gas training back in the States. When we jumped on D-day, all our clothing was gas-impregnated. The Germans found out that if they use gas on us, we have much more of it, and there would be one big mess. Thank God they never used it.

Lipton became 1st sergeant of the company. He wanted to be an officer. He had the moxie, he could use his brain. He was my mentor; I looked up to him. He was calm, and he would discuss any situation you got into. We had brains between us. No quick reactions—he thought things out. Like Winters, but you didn't have too much time with officers, so Lipton was the guy you went to. I trusted him with my life. We were both senior sergeants, and a lot of the men looked up to us.

We were training six days a week in Aldbourne. We went over the problems we had in Normandy, and figured out the who, what, why. We got smarter and trained harder. Replacements came in, and we had to train them, too. You learned in Normandy, replacements come in, you don't learn their names. Before you know it, *bang*—this one's gone, that one's gone. Someone would say, "Oh yeah, he come in about a week ago." Nobody ever knew them. As quick as they came in, they were gone. We tried not to get to know them. You're not out there to socialize anyway.

Winters sent me a new replacement from Philly. It was Babe. He came into the barracks, and he walked like a penguin, side to side, like a duck. He did the South Philly shuffle. You couldn't miss it. We started asking each other who we knew back home. I thought he was as goofy as I was. He liked to have fun; I liked him right away, the dirty rat. I told him he was on the machine gun, sent him to Joe Toye, 1st squad sergeant. I knew Toye would take good care of him. Now I think back, *How did I make a machine gunner out of him?* He was a midget, five-foot-four! The gun was bigger than he was. These guns are not like machine guns you carry. These are 30-caliber jobs, about twenty-nine pounds. Like a small cannon.

BABE

The Easy Company barracks were converted wooden horse stables in Aldbourne, a little English village just like you'd imagine an English village to be. Cobblestone streets, little stone houses with gardens, a corner bakery. Easy was stationed right in the middle of it. We walked in and met Captain Winters, and he assigned us to our platoons. Julian was sent to 1st Platoon, J. D. to 3rd Platoon, and I was sent to see Bill Guarnere, 2nd Platoon sergeant. Winters told me he was from Philly. I walked into the barracks and threw my bags down, and Bill Guarnere said, "You from Philly?" I said, "Yeah." He said, "What part?" I said, "South." I found out he lived at 17th and McKean; I lived at 2nd and Wilbur. We lived so close we could walk to each other's houses. Our birthdays were eighteen days apart—he was born April 28, 1923, I was born May 16. It was good to meet someone from the neighborhood.

Bill made me a machine gunner. Back in Fort Eustis, I taught machine guns, 30s and 50s, to officers in officer candidate school. He sent me to Joe Toye's squad, and I met some of the guys—Eddie Barnett and Eddie Joint, both from Erie, Pennsylvania, Jim McMahon, Al Vittore, and Stephen Grodski. All good guys. Our squad was in horse stables. They were pretty private because they only had six bunks.

I learned pretty quickly you couldn't just come in and expect to be one of the guys. You'd hear someone say, "Oh, he's one of those replacements." The Toccoa men were together for a long time, and they were combat veterans. They had five weeks of fighting in Normandy behind them and they were tight. They didn't want to be sent into combat with any damn replacements. Some people say it was easy to get in with them, but I can tell you it wasn't easy. The Toccoa vets were not overly friendly, and they made you feel like you weren't worth getting to know. I heard Earl "One Lung" McClung say they didn't want to get to know replacements because they'd be the first to be killed. I don't believe that for a minute.

For three weeks, I thought, *Boy, I wish I made that Normandy jump.* I wanted to be where the veterans were. It really burned me up that I didn't get to jump into Normandy. I hated being on the outside, feeling like I had to prove myself. Some guys like Joe Toye and Chuck Grant didn't care nothing about who was a replacement and who was a vet. They took care of everyone. Chuck Grant even gave me a nickname—Jigger—because I called everything a jigger.

Right away you knew who took care of the guys and who the respected veterans were. Buck Compton, he was a quiet and compassionate guy, an enlisted man's officer, took things to heart, and worried about us guys. You didn't find many like him. Then there was Guarnere, they called him Wild Bill because he went nuts in Normandy killing Germans. He was tough on everybody, strict, didn't take no guff. You did what he said or else. He'd say, "You want to make it home? Then do it right. If you want to die, don't listen." He was just trying to get us all home. As gruff as he was, you could tell he loved the men, took good care of everyone. The same with Chuck Grant, Joe Toye, and Ken Mercier.

I was raised on the streets, so I didn't care how they treated me, I just did my own thing. If I didn't like a sergeant, I stayed away from him, or just didn't go out of my way. For guys like Toye, Grant, Guarnere, Mercier you did extra.

Outside of Bill, I didn't get close to sergeants. They were on their own planets. If you hung out with one, it looked like you were brown-nosing. You could think the world of someone, but you didn't try to be friends with them if they were in a different rank. I was accepted a little faster than the others because Bill was looking out for me. But I knew my place. The replacements stuck together and just tried to fit in. I stuck with my buddies, J. D., John Julian, and Jim Campbell. We were all in the same boat, we came in after the Normandy jump, and didn't yet rate. We knew we had to prove ourselves.

I found the most well-liked guy in the platoon was George Luz, one of the Toccoa guys. He was the company comedian. He could imitate people, and he was always telling jokes. Good jokes, not like Bill Guarnere's jokes! Luz was actually funny. He always told me I reminded him of his parish priest. He was a great soldier, all-around 100 percent great American. Serious when he had to be, but he kidded with everyone he liked. He knew who could take a joke and who couldn't.

I thought training would intensify when we got to Aldbourne, but it wasn't any tougher than it was in the States. Winters had us train with real ammo, but we were used to that; we did it at Camp Mackall and Fort Bragg. They used live rounds. We kept our backsides down and crawled as low to the ground as we could. They fired high enough above your head to give you the leeway. If you stood up, you were a dead man. The machine guns were fixed in place, locked in, we found out later. The replacements didn't know it, the rookies didn't know it. You wanted to survive, so you listened closely. If you're not listening, you're in trouble. You did what they told you.

My machine gun was a light 30 shoulder type, and it weighed twenty-eight pounds. Your assistant carried a bipod for it, and the ammo weighed seven pounds. I used to be six-foot-two. Now I'm five-foot-four-and-a-half. That's what being machine gunner can do to you!

I got to talk casually whenever I could to Bill—in the woods, in training. We'd say, "I wonder what's going on in South Philly?" We had a couple guys from Philly. If a new guy came into the outfit, we'd always ask where he was from. Everybody always wanted to talk about home.

Speaking of home, a few weeks after I got to Aldbourne, I got a letter from my girl Doris. A "Dear John" letter. She was breaking up with me because she met another guy. She was a nice girl, but I didn't care all that much. I didn't even visit her before we were leaving for England.

BILL

We ran through the training over and over, again and again. There were mistakes made in Normandy, the ones that made them got killed. The officers saw those mistakes and set out plans to correct them. We went over them in Aldbourne and drilled them into the replacements, too. We started training with live ammo, it was good for the kids who were never in combat. When you see bullets flying, you learn to crawl as low as possible, to move on the ground like a snake. We trained on different types of terrain, trained at night, during the day, in all kinds of conditions. All kinds of exercises, over and over.

You're always on edge, even when you're not on the battlefield. You can get called any minute. Weekend passes to London became the highlight of our time there. You had a change of scenery and felt like the war was behind you for a little while. The guys got to enjoy each other more, too.

We all loved London. You saw so many different people, Englishmen, Scotsmen, Australians, New Zealanders, Canadians. So many different uniforms—air force, sailors, marines. Lot of women in uniform, too. The English women in the military never left England, they did all the work on their home turf.

Babe was into jitterbugging with the girls. We went to a lot of dances together, well-known dance places with the limey broads, like Charing Cross and the Cove and the Gardens, right near where we stayed. Babe was an expert jitterbugger, danced all night with the broads; they lined up to jitterbug with him. He won contests, too. We went to a joint that was a bomb cellar. You couldn't even stand up. It's called the Windsor Dive. You go down all these steps, and when you get to the bottom, it's a big, round, stone cave. One way in, one way out.

We used to take double-decker buses to Trafalgar Square and Piccadilly Circus. Piccadilly Circus is a big attraction in London. Like Times Square in New York. That's where all the girls of the night used to hang out. We'd go there at night, and it was always blacked out, so when you go walking around, you can't see people unless you light a light in their face. We had some money on us, we had our Zippo lighters, and when we ran into a broad, we flipped the lighter on, put it in her face, and she says, "Ten pounds, Yank." So I said "Ten pounds! I come to save your ass, not buy it!" We called them Piccadilly Lilies. Oh boy. Don't even ask about *those* broads. They were all over us, aggressive. It was a den of iniquity, is all I'll say. That was a favorite spot for the GIs. If you got half crocked, it rocked. Johnny Martin would say, "Let's go visit Gonorrhea's clap house." Johnny gave me the nickname Gonorrhea as soon as we got overseas. Guarnere, Gonorrhea, they sounds alike. I have no comment at present!

One time I had a girl in the barracks, and we had morning inspections, so I hid her in the storage area. Lieutenant Peacock, our 1st lieutenant, came around snooping. I was holding my breath. I never liked Peacock either. He went by the book. Didn't smoke. Didn't drink. Wasn't a soldier's soldier. He looked around, everything looked good, clean, proper. All of a sudden a leg came crashing through the ceiling. He said, "What's that?" I said, "It looks like a broad's leg to me. I have no idea what it is." He looks at me, "Do you know what's going on?" I said, "Nooooo, I have no idea what's going on." Then the girl came down, and said, "Oh, Billie . . ." and my goose was cooked. I had two broads up there. Peacock said, "Who's got the other broad?" It was Gordy Carson's broad, but I didn't tell him. Then he'd go raise holy hell with Carson. I said it was only me, I had two broads. He threw them out and gave me holy hell and I got KP, kitchen police. We all hated it. I had to peel potatoes. While I was on KP, the men were given a night march. There they were, all lined up, equipment on their backs, and I'm sitting there peeling potatoes. They were cursing me out, and I was laughing. I said, "Where you goin' fellas?"

I had fun, but I never forgot I was a sergeant. I spent a lot of time anticipating what we had to do next. I was always looking ahead, looking forward, wanted to be one step ahead of the game. I studied a lot of manuals, and just like before Normandy, I kept up training myself on the guns, artillery, ammo, tanks. I was nosy. I tried to find out where we were going, what we were doing. Snooping all the time.

We didn't get much downtime, but I played baseball, football, basketball, craps. We played for money. I played Jew Pinochle with Babe.

I knew the game well because at home we played Pinochle or rummy under the streetlights until four, five in the morning. We put the table in the middle of the street. Growing up we watched the adults. You stood behind the players and you watched and learned. You knew to keep your eyes and ears open, but you didn't speak, or you'd get whacked. By the time I got into the Army, I knew how to play real well, but I didn't win much. Malarkey was the one who won all the time. Malarkey liked money. He was as tight as Kelsey's nuts.

We listened to the propaganda on the radio for fun, too. There was Axis Sally, Tokyo Rose, Lord Heehaw—he was a limey that was a British spy. It was so goofy. Everybody had propaganda, the Americans, British, French. All kinds of pamphlets were thrown around, it was all a bunch of baloney. You didn't know what was true and what wasn't. We just knew we had to kill the Germans. We didn't care about Axis Sally and Tokyo Rose. I think Tokyo Rose was from Chicago.

In August, we were getting ready for a jump outside Paris. Eisenhower came to inspect us. It got cancelled because General Patton's Third Army overran the drop zone, they liberated the towns before we could jump in. Patton was one of the most feared military commanders the Americans had, the Germans were afraid of him. His army moved fast, like a whirlwind, captured entire divisions, probably killed more Germans than any other unit. He was nuts.

We didn't think about it at the time, but after the war's over, you start to look at the context of things. All the politics. Like, who was going to liberate Paris? You've got ten to twelve Allied nations—America, Britain, Canada, New Zealand, Australia, even Spanish troops, all different nationalities, and all the generals up there deciding who is going to do what. There's de Gaulle, there's Montgomery, there's Eisenhower. If anyone is going to liberate Paris, be the first ones there, it has to be the French. The rest of us were right behind them but they had to be first. And Patton overran it. Those are the politics you find out after the war. When we were in it, we didn't care if we jumped on Paris or Hitler's head.

BABE

You learned pretty quickly what the British had to deal with from the krauts. One night I was in a pub in Bristol with my buddy J. D. and all of a sudden we heard an explosion, it cracked a mirror on the wall, and me and J. D. hit the floor. A German V-1 hit nearby. The Brits looked at us and laughed. They figured we were scaredy-cats. We were taught to take cover, but in the pub, it seemed a little ridiculous.

That place went through a lot of hell. The destruction in a place that was once beautiful, it was a bad scene. They didn't like us to go on leave in London, because you never knew when the Germans were coming over. The British and American air forces had control of the skies, but the Germans would send over the V-1s, the buzz bombs. They were guided missiles that looked like rockets, they had a flame shooting out the back, and if the flame went out, they crashed and exploded, and they were fully ammoed, so they caused a lot of destruction. It happened every day and the Brits just got used to it.

The GIs still had a good time there. Not long after we got to Aldbourne, I went on a weekend pass in London with two of my buddies, Jim Campbell and John Julian. Jimmy was a rugged-looking guy and John was a handsome, quiet kid from Alabama. We went to Piccadilly Circus, and ended up on Archer Street at an after-hours club called the

Bow and Arrow. As we sat upstairs where the piano player was, and all the action was, a buxom lady who weighed about four-hundred pounds said, "Hey, Yank, give us a fag, will ya?" Fag is slang for cigarettes in England. As she lit up, she said, "How 'bout I sing a song for you Yanks." She sang "A Nightingale Sang in Berkeley Square," and believe me, toots, this broad could sing! Everybody in the club had a tear in their eye. My mother always said that fat ladies could sing, and she was right. I went back there as often as possible when we were on pass. London became my favorite place in the world.

One of my favorite spots was a dance club in back of the Strand Plaza called the Cove and the Gardens. They had two big dance halls, one on the left and one on the right, and live bands. We would jitterbug all night there. But I'll tell you, nobody could jitterbug like the girls from South Philly. That's a fact!

When the night was over, when you were on weekend pass, you hoped you had a girl to go home with. Sometimes one or two of you had a girl, and whoever didn't was on his own. You looked for a place to sleep. You had very little money left because you blew it at the clubs.

I went with Bill to Piccadilly Circus a couple times. We called those girls Piccadilly commandos, that's what they call the girls of the night. I tell people today, that's the only group we never got decorated from. Every country decorated us, but the Piccadilly commandos never gave us nothing. We spent enough time with them they should have gave us something!

Bill didn't have to look for girls, he found them wherever he went, and he brought them back to the barracks. Like the broad whose leg came through the ceiling. And instead of KP being a punishment, Bill made out. That was typical Bill. There we were at four a.m. the next morning, loaded down with full field packs and rifles on our backs, and Bill's sitting there peeling potatoes and laughing. Everybody was yelling, "You dago bastard, you son of a bitch!" KP isn't a punishment if you miss out on a twenty-five-mile forced march. I thought, *Boy, that lucky son-of-a-gun.*

When we got weekend furloughs, we went to London. But if you couldn't get to London, we went to Windsor, just to get out of Aldbourne. It was the biggest village around and a fifteen-minute ride by bus. We met some of the local girls and danced. The toughest part was the blackouts. The bars and cafes closed at ten p.m., so the bus came at ten thirty to get you back to camp, and you better be there. The walk took three hours. I never had to walk, I wasn't that stupid, but some guys walked.

One of the pubs we would go to in London was called the Windsor Dive. There was always a fight in there. Everybody was fighting. The Airborne, the tankers, Canadians, Americans, British. Good old-fashioned brawls. Somebody would say something like, "What comes out of the sky?" And one of his buddies would say, "Birdshit and paratroopers," and then it would start. We'd all go after them.

We made more money than the British so the women were hanging out more with us. We made more money in a lot of ways. If you were a private, you got a base pay of fifty dollars a month, plus hazardous duty pay, combat pay, jump pay, and if you were in for more than three years you got longevity pay. Then higher rank got you more money. It went private, private first class, corporal, sergeant, staff sergeant, 2nd lieutenant, 1st lieutenant, and so on. We did pretty well for GIs. When I joined the Army, I was a corporal, then a technician. When you got broken down for combat and joined another area like I did—I was in the artillery and then went into the

Airborne—they took your former rank off you. I didn't care. It was all the same to me.

We worked hard and trained hard. But overall, Aldbourne was a fun time. We went into pubs, and we were only nineteen, twenty years old. Some of the kids were seventeen, eighteen and they're the ones who couldn't handle the beer. You had to help get them back to the sleeping quarters. There was a horse racing track nearby called Membury, that's where we took off for the invasion. They had horse racing there, but during the war, they closed the track and made the stables into barracks, and sent the horses out to pastures. It's back in operation now; the British love their horse racing.

We had a few D-days called off. At the end of August, we took trucks to the marshaling area at Membury and then that jump was called off. We were supposed to go to Belgium. Boy, did we have a good time after that was called off! Everybody was happy. Bill put Chuck Grant on detail and guard duty at the sheds where our chutes were stored, and he told Chuck to take me with him. I thought, *Boy, this is all right.* We never made it to the packing shed. Chuck took me right to a pub, and I wasn't going to disobey his orders! Chuck was one of those guys, besides being a great soldier and great guy, he loved life, loved women, loved a beer. He always wore his hat sideways, so it was hanging over one ear. He looked like a movie star—tall, slim, blond, curly hair. That night, he hit on one of the prettiest girls I've ever seen in England. And then her husband walked in. He was an English officer, and he was looking at Chuck like he could shoot him. We never did guard the shed. Every night, we'd sneak away and go to the pub in Membury. Bill would've raised hell with us if he knew.

(Bill chides Babe: "The reason you had to guard the packing shed was because when we left for D-day, we packed all our clothes up.

When we came back, someone cut all our stuff open, cut the patches off everything, it was turmoil. If I knew you were at the pub, I'd have shot you both, and missed. Lucky you didn't get us all killed, you dummy!")

At the end of our stay in Aldbourne, a couple days before we were sent to the marshaling area for the last time, we were in our billets, waiting for our last replacements. One of our sergeants walked in with a runt of a guy and introduced him as Miller. Miller tossed his duffel bag on the floor, and grabbed a lower bunk near the door, like he was already one of the guys. I thought he was a little cocky at first, but he turned out to be a pretty likeable guy. His first night in the barracks, a drunk soldier in our platoon who had a habit of pissing anywhere—I won't name names, he took Miller's bunk for a latrine and pissed on his head. Miller screamed and woke us up and a couple of us jumped up and grabbed the soldier. I told Miller that where I grew up in South Philly, if a bird shit on your head or a dog pissed on your leg, it was good luck. Somebody on the street corner would say, "You're gonna hit the number today!" So I told Miller he would definitely get through the war without a scratch.

It was around September 10 or 11, we went back to the marshaling area at Membury Airfield for a jump in Holland on the 17th, which was code-named Operation Market Garden. They put us behind barbed wire. Once you're in, you're in. They make sure you can't go out and discuss it in bars and say, "Oh yeah, we're leaving tomorrow to jump in Holland." They put up sand tables and diagrams, explained the objectives of every division going in, and showed us the exact locations and situations we'd be running into, up to every detail.

At night, you had your own thoughts. We sat on our beds and thought. And we'd bullshit. Some guys played cards. I never got into playing cards. But I played Pinochle—me, Eddie Stein, and Dick Davenport. We called it Jew Pinochle. Eddie Stein was a Jewish kid from St. Louis. This was his version—it's three-handed and cutthroat. Guy makes the bid and then you got to put 'em up, the other two work against you to put you up so you don't make your bid, and it costs you the game. We enjoyed it.

Some guys played darts. I'd rather sit at the bar and have a beer. Pinochle was my way of gambling. Some guys played poker. I thought it ruined friendships and I stayed away from it. We got a lot of laughs playing Pinochle. A lot of kidding. Whoever lost, we antagonized him all night. They did it to me, I did it to them.

We tried to keep things light. Every man had his own feelings about going into combat. We had no idea what we were going to face. But we were raring to go. After all, why did we enlist? Some guys were nervous, but we trained for this, we were ready to do what we were trained for.

I couldn't wait to jump. Just like with my first jump in training. How am I gonna get a taste of it if I didn't do it? I wasn't afraid. I wanted that star on my wings. You got one for every combat jump. The guys who were in Normandy had one. Your jump wings mean more than anything. You can have your Purple Heart and your Bronze Star, but don't ever take the jump wings. You worked hard for them and knew what they stood for and what that entailed, and you were ready to face whatever was coming. If you didn't feel that way, you wouldn't make it through training. So damn right, I was ready.

We had to wait, it seemed like forever to board the planes. Our gear was so heavy and uncomfortable. It felt like a hundred pounds of extra weight strapped to you. We had two boxes of machine-gun ammo, rifle with bayonet, musette bag, six grenades, two bandoleers of rifle ammo, reserve parachute, Mae West, two knives—one was a trench knife with brass knuckles and a long knife, smoke grenade, main parachute, and gas mask.

At one point, I was lying on the ground on the airfield, with my chute under my head, taking the weight off my back from my backpack. Jim McMahon, my assistant machine gunner said, "Yo, Jigger, I hope that ain't our plane." I looked up and there's the name Doris in big red letters on the fuselage. He said, "Christ, we're going to get blown right out of the sky." I said, "Jim, you always got such kind thoughts?" Sure enough, that was the plane we got in.

BILL

In the marshaling area, we were briefed on Market Garden. There were three Airborne divisions going in, the 101st, 82nd, and British 1st Airborne. We had to keep one road open that ran from Son in the south straight up to Arnhem in the north. The 101st was jumping in at the south end, in Son, the 82nd was jumping in the middle at Nijmegen, and the British troopers were jumping at Arnhem. If we secured the road, and kept all the bridges open, the British tanks could advance up to Arnhem, and cross the Lower Rhine into Berlin with the British Second Army. We studied maps and sand tables, mock-ups of the geography, like for Normandy, but in Normandy, there was so much chaos, all the preparation was for nothing. They told us this jump would be quick and easy. The war would be over by Christmas. We all thought, *Thank Christ for that.* But who the hell knew?

The road we were securing was what they called Hell's Highway. Believe me, the name was correct! If the Germans took the bridges on that road, we were in trouble. It was one road in, one road out, and Allied troops would be trapped.

Our first objective was the Wilhelmina Canal bridge in Son, then the city of Eindhoven, meet the British Armored there, and get the road secured all the way up. Lots of risks being taken, but we didn't know. Only the generals knew. Everything the Army had—money, resources, everything—was put into Market Garden. Everything was at a standstill until it was over. Huge risk.

What worried me was the entire mission was under British command. It was strictly a limey deal, under Montgomery. The Brits were different fighters than us. We figured that out real fast in Normandy. They were fighting the war for years and were tired of war. The soldiers were lions—they fought like the Americans—but they were led by a bunch of damned donkeys. Ever hear that said? The ranks were handed down, like with British royalty. They weren't earned. So *who knows* what was leading their army. See, now I'm educating ya! Their leaders were very leisurely in their way of fighting. They liked to stop for tea and crumpets and set up housekeeping in the middle of a battle. True. Tea and crumpets. I saw it for myself.

Mentally, the Holland jump was different from Normandy. When you been on the front lines in combat, one day is enough, one week is plenty. We were on the front lines in Normandy over a month. When you think back you have no idea how you done it. When you're in it, your only thought is, *I've got to get the hell out alive.* Your body is performing superhuman feats. When you get out you think, *How in the hell did I survive that?* You look around, you see this guy's wounded, this guy's gone, that guy's gone. You can't believe it. The replacements didn't have that, they were looking at combat from an entirely different perspective. They were going in not knowing what's coming. We were going in knowing what was coming, and that was another kind of fear. What we saw in Normandy was still fresh in our minds.

Some were more willing to go through it again, some weren't. I was ready to go through it all of the time. Hell, yes. If you weren't, you shouldn't be there. But you looked at it differently. Before you see combat, you're eager to get in; once you get in, you want to get the hell out. We went into Holland more cautious, more careful than the replacements. We knew from experience what the alternative was—death, *see ya later*. Ain't no recourse from that, kid. It's final. *Bing, bang, see ya later.*

Popeye Wynn, he was hit in the backside on D-day, he met us at the airfield. He went AWOL from the hospital, just made it. He still wasn't recovered, I think he could barely walk, but he wanted to jump with the company.

When we boarded the planes at the airfield, I thought, *Here we go again.*

5

---⭐---

HOLLAND: PARADES, GRENADES, AND HELL'S HIGHWAY

Mid-September to End of November 1944

BABE

Going to Holland we flew in C-47s, with P-38 fighters trailing us for safety. The P-38s fired at anything they had to. Once we got close to the drop zone, we heard occasional bursts of antiaircraft fire, but not much. Things were pretty quiet. Looking out the door of the plane, I saw a windmill, might have been on the Belgium side of the border, and shots were firing out of it at the planes in the sky. We had been told the Germans used windmills to hide their antiaircraft batteries, and sure as hell they did. Right away a couple P-38s that were escorting us flew straight under the tail of our plane right for that windmill. They blasted it, and all we could see were plumes of black smoke. The windmill was destroyed.

The plane's crew chief, who was an old guy to us kids—he was in his late twenties—went up and down the aisle telling us all what a credit to our country we were. "You guys should be proud of your-selves," he said. "I wish I could do what you do." He made us feel really good about what we were doing. He told us he'd mail letters for us, so some of the guys scribbled off letters and handed them to him. I said, "By the way, who's Doris?" He told me it was the pilot's wife. I told him about the broad back in South Philly and the Dear John letter. He must have related the story to the pilot, because the pilot, a really nice guy from New Jersey, came out to shake my hand. He looked at us all and said, "Don't worry, boys, I'll be dropping you right where you belong."

The mood in the plane was tense. Guys were praying, sitting in contemplation. We felt some flak on the tail of our plane, and the order came to stand up and hook up. Sometimes you felt that order in the pit of your stomach. When you stepped out that door, you knew full well you might not be alive when you hit the ground. We were told to check equipment and stand in the door. Joe Toye was push-master. They make sure you get a good fast stick out of the plane. The green light came on, even though we weren't by the drop zone yet. We jumped from about twelve hundred feet, which is pretty high for a combat jump, but the area was supposed to be quiet. We were glad to go out that high because that meant there was no major threat in the area.

I heard a story later that in Bill's plane, a few of the guys were cut-ting up and laughing, I guess to relieve the anxiety. Bill was watching all the guys, like he always did. He was standing up, and he turned to the rest of the guys and asked, "You guys doing all right?" Then he said, "I just want to remind you, the krauts are down there waiting for us." All of a sudden, it got quiet. He was saying, *If you don't want to think about what's coming, I'm going to* make *you think about it.* He wanted the guys to be in fighting mode before they hit the ground.

The jump couldn't have gone better. It was noon on Sunday, September 17. A bright, beautiful, sunny day. We landed in a giant field. I could hear rifle and machine-gun fire in the distance. The Germans must have been shooting blindly from somewhere far, because shells would go past our ears and just drop to the ground. Projectiles that had no spin on them and just ran out of steam. A crashed glider and C-47 were burning on the field, and chaplains and troopers were trying to drag the dead and wounded off the drop zone. When you landed, you were supposed to move fast—cut your chute off, gather your gear and get off the drop zone to your platoon, and get into formation. One reason you had to move fast was so you didn't get hit with anything. Gear was raining down on us, guns and ammo, and equipment. Landing troopers were running and grabbing whatever they could stash on them. As I was running to get to my platoon, a trooper lying on the ground cried, "Help me, Heffron, please! My leg is broken. Don't leave me for the krauts!" I recognized him from jump school, so I stopped to help him. He was in Dog Company. I tried using a rifle to splinter his leg, but we figured out he could use it better as a crutch, and then I carried him off the field. Lieutenant Peacock, who I never liked—he's the one who turned Bill in for having a girl in the barracks—wasn't far away and he barked, "Heffron, join your platoon!" I carried the trooper to the road where he could get transportation and took off. I told him to be happy for his broken leg.

He had a million-dollar wound there. He was hurt just bad enough to be forced out of combat, but not critically wounded. Being hurt and in pain meant nothing. A good soldier still fought like that, most Easy Company men did. No one wanted to let their buddies down. You *wanted* to do your part. And you wanted to do it well. On the other hand, you were happy for fate to intervene and take you off the battlefield. That broken leg was a ticket home.

As machine gunner for 2nd Platoon, I had to be ready to set up my machine gun at any moment, wherever they told me to. The gun was heavy, about twenty-six pounds, you threw it over your shoulder; it had a shoulder sack that it fit right into. It was an air-cooled 30-caliber automatic machine gun. The regular outfits had water-cooled. We had no way of using them. We had to carry a light 30 shoulder type. Jim McMahon was my assistant then. I always had different assistants but everyone knew what they had to do. You set up the bipod in the dirt, the bipod strapped right on the gun itself. You threw it down and you stayed there. Your assistant fed the belt of ammo into the gun so it didn't jam. Our job was to provide cover fire for the rest of the platoon's advancement whenever we were under attack or on the offensive. Then you picked up the gun and advanced with them, and set it up again. Mostly, it was used in defensive position. You set the gun up, wait for the krauts to come over, and you nail them. My job was to repulse any attack or patrols. If everyone was digging in for the night, you became a defensive machine gunner. Once you opened fire, you gave your position away, so you had to move from that spot quickly. We moved around a lot with those heavy guns.

The Dutch were out to greet us. They were so happy. They called us angels from the sky. They hated the Germans. The Germans came around to their farms every three to six months with wagons and trucks and took all the newborn animals and first fruits, took whatever livestock and produce they wanted, and brought it back for the German farmers.

When we entered the village of Son on the way to the Wilhelmina Canal, the Germans hit us with an 88; they hit a big vacant department store window, and the glass blew out, and the pressure blew me into the center of the street and knocked me unconscious. When I came to, I was dizzy and I hoisted my gun over my shoulder, and a kid from Dog Company said, "You all right?" I felt something warm running down my arm, and I looked and I was bleeding. It wasn't nothing. I was okay. A couple days later, my hand got swollen, it had dirt in it, and I went back to the aid station to get it lanced and bandaged, and I was fine after that. But when it first happened, I caught up to my squad, and my squad leader, Joe Toye, said, "Where the hell you been, Heffron?" I told him I got tied up for a while.

BILL

It was a beautiful day when we jumped into Holland. Absolutely gorgeous. Nothing like Normandy. This jump was so beautiful you might have thought the war was over. The people from the town of Son saw us before we saw them. They waved orange flags from their windows and doors and came running out of their houses to greet us. They knew they were liberated; it was a celebration in the streets. They hugged us and kissed us, gave us food and drinks—beer, milk, apples, honey. They didn't have much themselves, but they shared what they had. They were so grateful. Some of the men got caught up in the fun. Broads were grabbing them, kissing them, it was a den of iniquity! I was ready for the krauts to surprise us any minute. The drop was quiet, but you knew the krauts were around. The Dutch called them *Boshe*. Might have been code for "German." As we advanced, they were trying to keep us informed. They kept hollering, *"Boshe, Boshe!"* Let me tell you about the Dutch: I thought they were the most beautiful people alive. They were so friendly. Couldn't do enough for us. They spoke English. They were so appreciative that we'd come to help them. Not like the French. I didn't see a Frenchman anywhere. Somebody told me before we jumped in Normandy, "Don't turn your back on a Frenchman." That was good advice. A lot of them liked the Germans a little *too* much.

As we went through the crowds, I piled a bunch of green apples in my pockets, and hoped I didn't accidentally throw one at a kraut instead of a grenade. You're not going to stop a Nazi with a piece of fruit.

Things were fairly quiet moving toward the bridge at Wilhelmina. Just as we were about a half mile in front of the bridge, the krauts woke up from their little nap. A machine gun and German 88 fired at us. One of the shells hit a big department store window, and the impact threw Babe across the street, knocked him out. He was shook the hell up, that's all. Then just before we got to the bridge—*bam!*—it blew up right in our puss. Big chunks of debris flew everywhere. We hit the dirt and fired back at them. Nobody got badly hurt. Damn krauts were waiting for us. The problem was, the planes dropped us eight miles away. Too much time passed by the time we jumped, got together, got through the crowds, and got to the first bridge. If they dropped us right on it, we would have beat the Germans there. But that's hindsight, kid.

Babe and the other machine gunners laid down cover fire and pushed back the Germans. Some of the men tried to get a makeshift bridge up so we could cross the canal. We got resourceful, tore down barn doors, whatever we could find heavy enough to get everyone across. Later, the engineers came, they built something stronger to get the tanks over.

BABE

We spent the night in Son, sleeping on the ground. You made a hole for yourself and stayed there. In the morning we had orders to move out and take Eindhoven. As we marched, everyone was spread out. You always spread out. If you bunched up, and an 88 came in, it would take everyone out at once. Lt. Bob Brewer walked ahead of us as lead scout, when suddenly sniper fire came from a church and hit him right in the throat. We had to keep advancing. Outside Eindhoven, we had to regroup, because we lost some men and we lost Brewer (he ended up surviving), a lieutenant. So we sat on the steps at St. Katrina's Church for an hour before moving out again.

Before we jumped our orders upon landing were to find anything with wheels to help carry our supplies. A Dutch woman gave me an old baby carriage. So there I am pushing a baby carriage with ammo, weapons, and supplies. As I'm pushing it through the streets, crowded with people partying and singing, my mind went to South Philly. Four blocks from where we lived was the Delaware River. Ships would bring coal and the coal would be transferred to trains that ran along Delaware Avenue. My family was poor, and my mother would send my three brothers and I down to Delaware Avenue with my sister's baby carriage to pick up any stray pieces of coal we could find. It meant we'd have heat from the coal stove. We'd fill the carriage with the coal and push it home. If there was snow on the ground, we used a sled. This wasn't easy. There was a mean railroad dick we called Duckfeet. Everyone in South Philly has a nickname and this man walked like a duck. He wouldn't hesitate to shoot anyone he caught stealing coal. I don't know if he'd have shot us four little kids, but we were scared of him. Pushing the stroller down the streets of Eindhoven, I wondered what mean old Duckfeet would have done to the krauts if he was so quick to shoot someone pocketing coal. Believe me, I would have given anything at that moment to be back in Philly with Duckfeet.

Popeye Wynn threw his weapons in my baby carriage. I said, "You do the pushing then." I picked up my machine gun and hoisted it over my shoulder and gave him the carriage.

BILL

The next morning, we marched through pastures and fields into Eindhoven. Now we thought Son was a celebration, but Eindhoven was a sight to behold. The streets were so crowded we could barely push our way through. It was one giant party. Civilians grabbing and kissing us, giving us food and beer. One woman was shoving an autograph book in our faces, saying "Sign, sign!" We had a war to fight and she's looking for autographs! We scribbled in her book "John Wayne," "Cary Grant," "Kilroy," "The Andrews Sisters." We just wanted to get the hell away from her.

You know why the Dutch were so aggressively friendly toward us? I mean *aggressive*. It's because they never knew what it was to be occupied. They weren't in World War I. They were a peaceful people, always neutral. After five years of oppression, we came and liberated them. They were so grateful. One Dutchman said to us, "Can you define freedom? You can't," he said. "Because you don't know what freedom is until you lose it." I'll never forget that. Babe was there, too, when he said it.

There were women who collaborated with the Germans, they were kissing us, too. But the Dutch didn't waste time taking care of the traitors. Right away, they rounded them up, grabbed the men right off the streets and killed them. The women got what was due them, too. The Dutch threw them into the middle of the street, ripped off their clothes, shaved their heads, beat them, publicly shamed them. They deserved it. What should you do, kiss them? They were sent off like homeless lepers. We saw them wandering in the countryside and we didn't say a word to them. We knew what they were, what they done. Someone probably killed them eventually.

BABE

We were the first platoon in the city, and we secured the bridges over the Dommel River and set up outposts. I had orders from Bill to set up my machine gun by a footbridge going over a small canal next to a set of row homes. I'll never forget that spot, and actually when I went back to the spot ten years later, and asked someone about the footbridge, the man said, "You have a good memory. The people have moved now, but yes, there was a footbridge there."

We set the gun up and had it facing a secondary road on our right coming into the town. We had the larger roads coming out of the woods already secured. All our guys were in place and we were waiting for a counterattack, and one of the heads of the underground—they wore an orange band on their arms so we knew who they were—came over and said to Compton, Toye, and Bill, "We have a horse and wagon coming up the road with about eight German soldiers, and a large artillery piece on the back of the wagon. Would you give us the pleasure of taking them out, instead of you?" We looked at each other and Compton said, "If anyone deserves to take them out, it's the Dutch." They suffered through five, six years of occupation. So we said, "Go ahead." They hid on the side of the road in a doorway, and when the horse and wagon made a move with the artillery piece, the Dutch opened up and killed all of them. All except one, a tall blond-haired, blue-eyed kid who was badly wounded in the left shoulder. He was holding his shoulder, moaning in pain, and they marched him over toward us so headquarters could get some information out of him. We were all hollering, "Suffer, you son of a bitch!" when an old Dutch woman in her eighties came out, and asked him in Dutch, "Where does it hurt?" It looked like she was going to help him. He pointed to his shoulder, and she started hitting him over and over with her pocketbook right on that shoulder, screaming something like *"Moffe! Moffe! Moffe!"* She's screaming at him, and he's screaming in pain. Turned out the woman had put a brick in her pocketbook. She made my day, she made everyone's day. We asked around what the woman was yelling and found out there was no translation for it in English, but it was something like "evil."

BILL

The Dutch underground found us right after we landed. Told us where the Germans were, what their plans were. They hated the Germans, wanted to get in on the killing, too. They gave us accurate info, became part of our combat team. One of them was John van Kooijk. A good Dutchman. A good source for us. He pointed out who the collaborators and the rat finks were. Told us everything. He stayed with us, and fought the entire war with 2nd Battalion. I think they put an Airborne uniform on him, too. The Dutch women sabotaged the German telephone lines and communications, we found out later.

The days after we secured the bridges, word came from the Dutch underground to get the hell out of town. The Germans were planning to bomb Eindhoven that night. We didn't have the fire or air support to do anything about it. As we were marching out, we felt like hell. The people in Eindhoven must have felt like we abandoned them. But what could we do? There was no way we could have spread the news fast enough. Put it this way: *Eind* means land, *hoven* means farms— land of farms. There were green pastures as far as the eye could see. Everything was too spread out. If we stayed and tried to inform the people, we would all be dead. We sat in our foxholes and felt terrible.

The next day, the nineteenth of September, I went out looking for Able Company to find my buddy James Diel. I found a couple kids from Able, and asked where he was. They said "You just missed him. He was on the road and a shell hit him, cut him right in half." It was a shock. He was my sergeant back in training, and he was a good buddy of mine, but I couldn't stop to think about it or I'd be buried there, too. When someone got killed, you just got more fired up for the next battle. Somehow I ended up getting his dog tags, I have no idea how, but after the war, I gave them to his family.

BABE

One of the men in 2nd Platoon, Stephen Grodski, who we called the Brow because he looked like the character from the *Dick Tracy* comics—he had one big eyebrow across his forehead that looked like it was drawn on with some grease paint—he would make us the last hot meal I remember having for seventy-some days. We were in the middle of an apple orchard, and he made a stew out of everything we could find. He put it all in a helmet and cooked it with a Bunsen burner.

In the morning, we had a forced march to Neunen. Some of the guys piled onto the British Cromwell tanks moving with us into the village. We heard there was nothing there, and it was pretty quiet as we came up to it, except for some Dutch civilians cheering us on from their windows or the streets. There were beautiful buildings, old country inns, and farmhouses. We took a secondary road in, but all the land was flat, it was all farmland, so we were in plain view. The roads were raised a few feet off the ground, too, which made you more conspicuous, and along both sides of the roads were drainage ditches. Those ditches ended up being an advantage and a disadvantage, depending on whether it was us or them hiding in them.

We led a frontal assault, and luckily we were on the flank, in a wooded area, because suddenly, we heard the rumbling and clanking of metal, and it wasn't our tanks. German tanks came rolling out from behind the trees about four hundred yards away and let loose with a barrage of 88s. There were dozens more tanks behind them. We only had about four or five. We dove into the ditches just as our rear tank got blasted.

Johnny Martin saw a German tank hiding in a hedgerow with its gun pointed right at one of the British tanks just waiting for it to advance a few feet. I covered him, and we ran over to warn the tank driver. Martin jumped up on the tank and pointed to where the German tank was hidden and said to the driver, "Shoot him! Shoot him!" But the Brit wouldn't listen, he couldn't see the tank. Boy, they were laid back, those Brits, even with 88's exploding all around them. He was more concerned about his orders not to destroy property. We hightailed it away from him, not a minute before the German tank let loose and blasted him, and then blasted another one of our tanks behind him. The crew from the first tank escaped, but the gunner, he got both his legs blown off, all that was left of him was a torso. Our regimental chaplain, Father Maloney, ran over and pulled him from the tank, laid him down in the ditch, and gave him his last rites before he died.

Let me tell you about Father Maloney. Now *he* was a hero. As spiritual guide for the 506th, he had twelve rifle companies to worry about, not counting regimental headquarters. He went from company to company holding Mass, giving last rites and spiritual aid, wherever he was needed. He risked his life going onto the battlefield to save someone's soul. His job was saving souls, not lives. He didn't carry a gun, only his chalice, crucifix, and sacramental stuff. I imagine he enjoyed meeting his maker, because that's the way he treated people and that's the way he served. He went out of his way to make someone feel better. He got the DSC in Normandy for courage.

One day when I came to a confession, he said, "I don't see many of you guys when there's no fighting." He said, "The Catholic faith is the hardest to live by but the easiest to die by. When you meet your maker it's all forgiven." That thought helped me through every day.

★ ★ ★

Neunen was overrun with German soldiers and tanks, firing at us with everything they had. Mortars, pistol fire, MG-42 fire, and 88s. You couldn't see through the clouds of dust and smoke, and there was debris flying everywhere. A machine gunner from Dog Company got hit. He yelled, "Son of a bitch, I'm dead!" and he dropped dead. It was the strangest thing to see.

We were pinned down in a ditch, trying to advance and staying low, when clouds of heavy smoke came wafting down the ditch toward us. The Brow yelled, "Gas! Gas!" We went to grab our ankles for our gas masks, but most of us left them in the plane. Usually they were right above our knives, which we had on our right ankles, unless you were left handed, then it was on your left ankle. We'd taken them off, along with our reserve parachutes, to lighten the load before jumping. Those things were big and bulky, not like gas masks today. We never figured the Germans would actually use gas, even though the generals and higher-ups expected them to; we even had gas-impregnated jump jackets. At that moment, we were scared as hell, cursing ourselves for being so stupid. We were sure we were going to die. Then Joe Toye yelled, "They're smoke pots!" When the air finally cleared, we could see it was smoke from a burning English tank that the wind carried down the ditch. What a relief! We'd have all been dead if it had been gas. Bill was pissed. He shouted, "Who the hell hollered gas?!" but nobody would rat. Under our breath we were calling the Brow a dumb son of a bitch; he scared the hell out of us. Bill would have given him holy hell.

Tanks were burning all around us, and the kids inside were dead, so the tanks kept rolling on their own, and would stop only when they rolled into ditches. While I was in the ditch manning the machine gun, one of the tanks rolled into the ditch on fire. I couldn't go running out, or even raise my head, the place was like a hornet's nest. I would have got my head blown off. I was pinned down. Getting a shot off was out of the question. I don't know how I escaped that burning tank, but somehow I did.

We never succeeded in pushing the Germans back, and we were ordered to withdraw. It's hard to take when you get that order to pull back. You feel defeated. But you do what you're told, and we had full confidence in any order Dick Winters gave.

I was providing cover fire for the rest of the platoon, when I felt something hit my leg hard. I thought I was hit. But it was Buck Compton's head. He fell across a wheelbarrow right at my feet. A sniper got him right in the backside. He looked up at me and said, "She always said my big ass would get in the way." He had four holes in his rear end. He was a strapping guy, too heavy for anyone to drag, and we were being bombarded with heavy machine-gun fire. I tried to help Buck, but he told me to leave him there for the Germans. (Bill adds: "When Compton got shot, he wanted us to leave him there to die. He didn't want anyone else to get hit trying to save him. He was no midget. Six-foot-two, two hundred forty pounds. I told him he was going to get shot in the ass because he was too big to run fast. Our company medic, Gene Roe, tried to patch him up, and we had to get him out of there. Malarkey, Babe, Joe Toye, and I and some others tried to lift him, but it was like picking up a damn elephant. We had to rip a door off a barn, make a stretcher out of it, and get him up onto a British tank. He was mad as hell that we were trying to help him. Mad as hell. Cursing us all. He wanted to kill us. But Compton was lucky. He got four holes in his rear end from one bullet, and I'm saying he was lucky. It was a fleshy spot, they could fix it bing-bang-boom, so he was lucky.")

That was a pretty amazing feat that Bill, Malarkey, and Toye pulled off. They did it in that open field with machine fire coming from every direction. Especially considering we were the only platoon there, the others were off to the flanks.

To get beyond the German fire, I had to climb over a six-foot hedgerow. These damn things were four feet wide. You ran at them, trying to get over, and bounced off. And I was bogged down by my machine gun. John Sheehy yelled from the other side, "Come on, Heffron! Give it a running start!" I threw my machine gun over the hedgerow to Sheehy, but to get a running start, I had to move back into German fire. My heart was pounding. It was like you see in a movie. Bullets were kicking the dirt up next to my ankles and whizzing by my head. As I ran, my rosary beads flew off my neck, but I jumped the hedgerow and Sheehy grabbed my jump jacket and yanked me over. I didn't want to leave without my rosaries. I thought I wouldn't come out of this war alive without them. "To hell with the rosary beads," Sheehy yelled. "Let's go!" I stooped down to pick up my helmet, which had fallen on the ground, and the rosaries were right inside the helmet. Lying right in there. By some stroke of luck, the rosaries had come over the hedgerow with it. If Sheehy hadn't waited for me and helped me that day, I never would have made it. I never forgot what he did.

On the other side of the hedgerow, one of our guys was wounded and lying in a ditch, and we were withdrawing, so I ran over to throw him over my shoulder and put him on a tank. Then I heard Sergeant Ranney's voice come from the tank: "Leave him, Heffron, he's dead." When I laid him back down, I saw he had a hole through his left temple. Then I saw his face. It was Miller, the guy I told a few days before that he would get through the war without a scratch. I didn't want to leave him, and we always brought our dead back, but Ranney had given the order. Maybe there was no room on the tank, or maybe someone got him later. I know they had to take his dog tags and personal things, they had to report him dead. But boy, seeing Miller hit me like a ton of bricks. I had to sit there for a minute. I didn't even know his first name. When a replacement got killed and no one knew his name, you described him: "The little skinny guy that came into the outfit as we were leaving." I always tried not to get close to anyone because it hurt like hell when they died. I think about Miller a lot. He was just a kid.

BILL

During the fight, one of our sergeants, Denver "Bull" Randleman, got caught between a burning tank and the Germans and was missing in action. We didn't know where he was, so after we pulled back, I said to the men in Bull's squad, "Let's go find Bull." Bull was in 1st Platoon with Johnny Martin, a great soldier. A great squad leader. You didn't mess with the Bull. He was a big man. Tough on the outside, but a softie on the inside. His men loved him. In Easy Company we had the best NCOs in the Army. The best.

Everyone went out looking for the Bull, not just Easy but a couple of other companies, too. You'd never see that happen in any other regiment but the 506th, everyone out searching for one man. By the next day, we had Bull back. The krauts had him in a barn. I don't know who did what or how we got him back, but we were lucky, and boy, were we relieved. We looked out for each other, and the impossible became possible. We're able to say that no man in Easy Company was ever taken prisoner.

We took cover in Dutch houses, set up our machine guns and mortars from there, to try and push those krauts back. They had us zeroed in the whole time, and were shelling us. We went house to house looking for Germans, and throwing grenades. We blew apart a lot of Dutch houses. We didn't know which houses had Germans in them, and we couldn't take any chances. I noticed at the doors of the houses they had those little miniature silver spoons, the kind you find in souvenir shops. There was a spoon on the wall for every family member, each one had a name and birth date on it. Like a history of the family on the wall. It was sad. All those Dutch houses, destroyed. You felt bad because you liked the Dutch people. At the time we couldn't think, we had a job to do. Later, I thought, *What the hell did I do?* And then I realized, *I'm alive. And we're here to liberate these towns.* Wouldn't you rather be liberated and have no house than the other way around?

BABE

The Germans ended up pushing us back. We had to fall back and regroup. There were more of them than there were of us. Before we left, Winters wanted someone to penetrate German lines and get a prisoner. Toye volunteered and he needed two more to go with him.

I wanted to go but Toye wanted me on the machine gun, so he picked Siles Harrellson and James Campbell. Brother, talk about being in with the enemy. We were surrounded and they were hitting us from everywhere. It was so bad, we had to withdraw, and there's Joe and his patrol going right in. They got fired at, but Joe pressed on, and sure enough, came back with a prisoner. No one could believe it. Later I asked him, "How in the hell did you pull that one off?" He said the kraut was on guard, dozing off, so he got behind him, put his hand over the kraut's mouth, and put a knife to his throat. The kraut dropped his weapon and walked back with Joe. Why Joe didn't get a commendation for that one, I'll never know. The prisoner was a fresh one, too. Kept telling us in broken English we were going to lose the war.

BILL

We were no match for German artillery. They had those Tiger 88 tanks. Our Sherman tanks and the Brits' Cromwells were pussycats, didn't hold a candle to kraut tanks. Everything the Germans had was superior. When the war started, the Germans knocked out the French in less than a month with the Tigers. We weren't prepared for them either. Those Germans were technologically advanced. They were fighting and perfecting their arsenal for decades. Think about it. Fighting since World War I. Their tanks were superior, and the MG-42 blew away any guns we had. They had a lot of firepower. The bullets go *brrrrrrrrrt!* Four hundred bullets come out at once. American machine guns went *bap-bap-bap-bap-bap!* The best weapon the Germans had was the 88. They had them on the tanks, they could blow a house to pieces. We had the 75mm on our tanks, and headquarters had the 81mm mortar—the biggest piece of artillery we had. The Germans had the 105mm howitzers, they were at Brecourt, and the 270mm railroad gun that was like forty freight trains and nineteen semis all at once. It was so big, it needed two tracks to support it. They fired them in Holland and Belgium. Nobody ever knew where they were; they were a son of a bitch. You thought there was an earthquake when they fired it.

That night, we could see from where we were the krauts were bombing Eindhoven. They kept their word. Damn krauts bombed the shillelagh out of it. The railroad station, everything. All you saw was fire and smoke in the sky. The krauts were infuriated at the welcome the Dutch gave us. They wanted the Dutch to stay in their houses and keep the German flag flying. They also figured we'd still be there. We would have if the Dutch underground didn't warn us. We marched back into Eindhoven the next day, the town was in shambles. Over two-hundred Dutch people dead, and eight-hundred wounded.

The civilians kept getting caught in the middle. They'd see us coming and put up Dutch flags. Then the Germans would knock us back and put up German flags. All along Hell's Highway, same thing every day. The Germans would cut the road, we'd open it, they'd cut it, we'd open it, that's how it kept going. We couldn't let them take the road, somebody would get trapped—the 82nd, the British troops, the Guards Armored Division, the 501st, 502nd. Too many to take a chance.

BABE

The Dutch underground warned of an attack in Uden, so we moved with our trucks and tanks through Veghel to Uden. On the way, the

Germans cut the road between Uden and Veghel, and about nine of us got cut off in Uden from the rest of the platoon. The rest of them were in Veghel. I was with J. B. Stokes, another trooper named Mauser, and one of our officers, who I won't name because he was an idiot. Bill yelled at him in Neunen, gave him holy hell, because he wasn't doing his job. The same officer gave Mauser a few rounds of armor-piercing ammo and told him to put them in his rifle and stay put in a nearby building. He told Mauser, "If you see any tanks, get off some good shots." We looked at each other. *Was he crazy? A rifle against a tank?* The only thing that will take out a tank is a bazooka. And only if it's aimed perfectly. The officer didn't know what the hell he was talking about. You always worried someone incompetent could end up giving orders and getting men killed needlessly. Soon after that, the same officer shot off his own hand, I'm pretty sure on purpose, and we were glad to get rid of him. Made me appreciate that I was fighting alongside the best soldiers in the Army, and the likes of that officer were few and far between.

Luckily for us, the Germans never attacked Uden. But we could hear a lot of heavy shelling nearby. J. B. and I found a church with a good, high belfry, and churches were always suspect, because the belfry was a nice high spot for a German sniper to hide out. So after checking it for krauts, I left my machine gun at the bottom of the ladder, and we climbed a ladder to the belfry to try and scout out the rest of our platoon. We saw Germans coming toward us, and next thing we knew, the Germans must have seen the glint of the gunmetal from J. B.'s rifle, and they started shelling us. The shells told us they had us zeroed in, and we flew down the ladder as fast as we could, and into the backyard. There was a huge cemetery back there, full of graves of early World War II fighters. We stood by a wooden gate for a minute in awe of this graveyard and more rounds started hitting the church. J. B. shouted, "Let's get the hell out of here!" We didn't get twenty yards away before a shell landed on the wooden gate and blew it to pieces. One of many close calls.

The men trapped in Veghel finally got relieved, and we got our troops back. We didn't know what happened to them. I looked at Bill and the guys and I couldn't believe what I saw. They had a look on their faces like I'd never seen before, a dead stare. Distant. Like they'd seen a ghost. I don't know. I still can't explain it to this day. It was scary. I asked Bill, "What the hell happened?" He said, "Babe, you ain't never ever seen such artillery fire in all your life. You couldn't come out of your hole, you couldn't do anything. They were hitting us from planes, with 88s, everything. It was bad." I tell Bill once in a while, "In sixty-some years, I still have never seen a look on you like that day." The Germans had all their artillery there, and they used it.

A couple days later, I found out my buddy J. D. Henderson was hit in Veghel. He was in 3rd Platoon. He was one of the guys I made a pact with, he and Johnny Julian, that if one of us buys the farm the others have to go see the parents. But J. D. was going to be okay. He was evacuated back to England, spent forty-five days in the hospital, and came back to Easy Company.

BILL

The krauts attacked Veghel instead of Uden, and when they cut the road, they had the entire 506th surrounded. It was raining like hell out, and we got caught in bad artillery fire. The Luftwaffe bombed us from the air, the SS shelled us from the ground, the tanks hit us with 88s. It came from all sides. We couldn't get a shot off, we couldn't do a goddamn thing. All day, all night they shelled the shillelagh out of us. They weren't sparing those 88s either. You never exposed yourself. They'd fire an 88 at one man running across the field. Those damn 88s blew craters into the ground. There was no cover to move out. Most of the time we were hiding in an orchard in foxholes that we dug so fast your eyes would spin. If we could have dug thirty feet down, we would have. When there were breaks in the shelling, we returned the fire, otherwise we sat there with four feet of water under our ass.

After a few days, we heard the Typhoons above our heads, the English air force. They could see the German positions from overhead. They started strafing the hell out of the Germans and gave us air cover so we could get out. The British Armored also came in and pushed the Germans back, and opened the road, so we were able to get back to Uden. That was a bad one. We lost a lot of men.

To be in an artillery bombardment is hell. Beside the fear—fear is something you feel every second in combat, I don't care who you are—when artillery starts flying, it's worse than anything else you can imagine. Machine-gun fire is bad, but when artillery starts coming in, you're going to see some gruesome things. It's those things only a combat veteran knows, that's what bonds you for life, because no civilian could ever understand. In ordinary life, a man will never see his buddy's limbs blown off into the trees, or a person explode into thin air, nothing left of him. This is not something you ever forget, or you can put into words. When you think about it, it makes you sick. All of us out there saw the same damn thing. It's one of the worst things a soldier sees in war. But if you couldn't handle it, you couldn't be a soldier. You had no choice but to ignore it. You hoped you had the next day to look forward to, and every day after that. It made you appreciate every day that you were still alive.

We met the rest of the platoon in Uden, and they sent us right back somewhere near Veghel with the entire 506th, in the pouring rain. The 502nd was there, and the 501st was in a hell of a battle nearby, maybe worse than where we were. I noticed every windmill we passed was blown apart. The Germans used them for sniper points and artillery, and the British planes destroyed them.

BABE

In the morning, we were outside of Veghel preparing for an offensive, waiting to get the word to attack, when we noticed a Dutchman kept riding past with a kid on the back of his bike. Five minutes after they'd ride by, we'd get shelled with heavy artillery. We had quite a few casualties, and by the third time, we started to think it was a little too coincidental that every time they rode through, we get shelled. Someone said, "Grab that son of a bitch," and an Easy officer, a replacement no one liked, stopped the guy. Sure enough, under the seat was a two-way radio. The officer took the kid, the man, and the radio to headquarters, and we never saw them again.

We started our advance, and we had to go through an open field. Winters was in front, I was in back with first squad. Second Platoon was leading the attack. All of a sudden, automatic-weapon fire came at us from the right flank. It was going over our heads and it looked like they were trying to get a bead on us and were lowering the trajectory of their machine guns. Winters hollered, "Bring your guns up! Fire into those woods!" I said, "Lieutenant, they sound like our thirties."

He said, "I think you're right." Here, Fox or Dog Company got trigger happy and opened up on us. Winters ordered someone to send up a smoke pot, and as soon as it went up, the firing stopped. If Winters hadn't made the call to send the smoke pot, a few of the boys would've bought the farm. In a tight spot, Winters always thought quick. He always used his head. Shows you how nervous and confused everyone was. And tired.

BILL

The Germans started firing at us, and Malarkey got on the mortar and I gave him range and direction and we blasted a machine-gun nest. We were good on the mortar in practice, but when we got to combat, we were at our peak. We could hit any target. We had tanks with us, and the krauts took a couple of them out, we had to pull back. That's where Babe came in. The machine gunners covered us when we needed to pull back or advance under fire. You can't do it without the machine gunners.

BABE

At one point, we were caught in a ditch, the krauts were firing at us, and Joe Toye wanted me to return the fire. He told me to throw my gun up on the ridge. As I went to put my head up out of the ditch, Bill kicked me in the left shoulder and knocked me back down into the ditch. He saved me from taking a shot, while he stayed right out there in the middle of it. I learned pretty quickly what kind of soldier Bill

Guarnere was. He made good snap decisions, and he was watching our every move. He expected the same dedication out of us that he put forth. He was wild, yes, but in the paratroopers you needed the fearless ones who were willing to do whatever it takes. They didn't call him Wild Bill for nothing. He'd stand up when everyone was crouched down and run straight into enemy fire, yelling, "Let's go, let's go, they couldn't hit the side of a barn!" It's true, the krauts were pretty piss-poor shooters. He was always straight up, never hugging the ground. Joe Toye, too. They were stand-up guys in more ways than one. Nothing scared either of them. If you couldn't find Bill, you asked, "What the hell platoon is under fire now?" That's where you'd find Guarnere. He'd run back and forth, and we'd get irrigated, because we had our trouble, too. But never as bad as 1st Platoon, they were always in a bad firefight.

BILL

Nighttime, we sat in foxholes in the rain. Malarkey and the mortar squad fired back and forth with the krauts. Usually at night, things quiet down till daybreak, then all hell breaks loose. The 502 was attacking the krauts, too, from a different area, so you heard shelling all night. When they saw we had them from all sides, the krauts retreated.

We did our job on Hell's Highway, so they took us off the line. We needed it. It was ten days we were on the front lines.

We got good news. Mail got through. When you heard "Mail call!" oh boy, you ran. Perconte did the mail. He called out names and kept throwing letters. When you got one, the whole war stopped for you. You crawled into a hole someplace and you read it. Everyone perked up. Frannie and I wrote a lot of letters. Everyone knew I wanted to marry the old gal. We V-mailed each other. Victory mail. We didn't have e-mail, we didn't have fax! With V-mail, they turned the letter into a tiny film the size of your thumbnail, and blew it up to normal size when it got to its destination. Some people sent regular letters, but V-mail saved space, helped the war effort.

Mail call had its sad points, too. Like when we're standing around getting our letters and suddenly there's only seven or eight letters left and twenty of us standing there. You looked at each other, and you hoped it was for you, but you hoped it was for the other guys, too. A lot of them never got letters. So after you read your letter, you sat down and gave the other guy the letter to read, too. Even if it wasn't for them, they liked hearing what was going on back home. It made us feel better that normal life was happening somewhere. Gave us hope. The letters back then were simple and clean, no hanky-panky like today. Somebody got a little package sometimes, they'd share whatever was inside with the guys—cookies, a candy bar. Nobody was selfish. In Easy Company, we all shared everything we got even before we got to combat, even in the States. Little things like that were even more of a big deal when you didn't know if you'd live to see tomorrow.

In Holland, guys got more sentimental because we didn't expect what the Germans were throwing at us, and who knew if you'd be going home. That's when I thought of Frannie a lot. I carried her picture with me all through the war. The picture of her in a grass skirt. I'd keep it in my pocket, in my helmet, in my musette bag; I kept moving it to keep it safe. I knew she was there with me, that's all. And I hoped she was waiting for me. Who the hell knew? But I didn't talk about her much. As soon as the kids got real sentimental, I told them,

"Knock it off! You can't afford to be sentimental. You'll get killed, you hear? You got to concentrate on what you're doing now. If you get sentimental and soft, before you know it, *bang*, you're hit, you're dead. Stay on your toes."

★   ★   ★

In the first week of the Holland campaign, we knew Market Garden failed. We didn't get into Arnhem, and we took too many casualties, but we weren't defeated. We captured the bridges in Eindhoven, the 82nd Airborne took the bridge in Nijmegen, but we couldn't keep the road open for the advancement down Hell's Highway, and the British and Polish in Arnhem, who were supposed to be the first into Germany, got slaughtered.

Too many loose ends. Take the larger context of that operation. Three divisions. Together we're supposed to form a corridor right into Germany, hit the Germans from the flank. The first problem was there were just too many damn Germans. But even if we had more men, it wouldn't have mattered. As soon as we jumped, the British were supposed to come up with all their arms and their tanks. They got held up. We needed the British to come up the road faster than they did. For Operation Market Garden to work, everything had to be timed to perfection, and everyone needed to move fast. There was too much stopping, too much inefficiency, not enough of a push.

Now, we never fought with the British in the war. They are supposed to come up and meet us in Eindhoven. The British were good soldiers. They had a lot of time in combat. But their leaders had them stopping for friggin' tea in every town. Maybe if they met their own troops in Eindhoven, not us, they would have fought better, instead of throwing two different armies together. That was a risk.

Strategy-wise, it should have been the opposite—the British should have jumped where we jumped and met their own armored division, and we should have been in Arnhem. If you watch the movie *A Bridge Too Far*, that tells you what happened when the British were dropped in Arnhem. They jumped on top of a German armored division. And the Dutch warned them the German armored was there! They told Montgomery; he knew all about it. And still they jumped right on top of them. The Germans were waiting.

If we were in Arnhem, we'd have gotten the shit beat out of us, too, but we fought differently, and we may have succeeded. If Patton was there, he'd have blown right through to Arnhem. He would have hit them like a brick. Instead, Montgomery wanted all the glory. He was an egotistical son of a bitch. No one liked him. Montgomery led this operation, so who was going to be the first one into Germany? Montgomery gets first pick, of course he wanted to be the first one in Germany, to be the hero. So that, to me, was failure because of a political move. First into Germany, the British?!

So yes, with Market Garden they left too many loose ends. That's my own concept of the war. You read about this stuff after the war is over, and sixty years later you still analyze it. A lot of mistakes were made.

BABE

After the Neunen fight where we had to fall back, I thought we did a good job. We regrouped, got our tanks rolling, moved down Hell's Highway, and took every town we needed to. Hell's Highway was two weeks of the same thing every day. We'd be sleeping in apple orchards, the Germans would break the highway, we'd go out and get into a firefight or tank battle, go back to foxholes, and get called out again. We'd advance, dig foxholes in another orchard, or in the woods, and do the same exact thing the next day. Half the time we didn't know where the hell we were. We moved from Son all the way up to Nijmegen that way.

★　★　★

We were heading up to Nijmegen, where the 82nd Airborne captured the bridge that would allow the English tanks to cross over toward Arnhem. The entire 506th was taking up new positions on the Island. It was a stretch of land sandwiched between two rivers—the Waal River and the Lower Rhine. But our immediate plan was to get showers. By the bridge, there were portable showers maintained by black troops attached to the Canadian army. The water from the showers came from the river. I thought of my mother always telling me, "Wash behind your ears, Edward." Well, that was the least of my worries now. But we'd gone a few weeks without a shower, and our uniforms were drenched with rain and sweat and covered with mud and soot. We all stunk to holy hell. We couldn't even stand the smell of ourselves.

When we got there, the soldier standing guard at the bridge, said, "You fellas here for a shower?" He told us the Germans blew the showers to hell when they tried to bomb the bridge. Boy, oh boy, were we mad. We were so desperate for those showers, we almost jumped in the damn river. We thought two weeks was bad. We didn't know we'd end up going seventy-two days without showers.

We took up positions along a dike by the river. There were huge dikes maybe two stories high to keep the area from flooding. They had roads on top of them and then they sloped down on the sides.

They were steep enough you couldn't see what was on the other side of them if you were on flat ground. So we dug in behind the dikes, and our front line was all along the dike, to prevent the Germans from coming over it.

We couldn't move around by day, you were too conspicuous. We only moved under cover of darkness. At night, it was eerie in the foxholes. You heard the rumbling of German motorcycles going up and down the dike all night long, and you couldn't tell whether they were coming over it or not.

It was cold and dreary, always raining, and the lower ground was muddy and flooded. Rats were all over the place trying to scrounge food, and there were also pigs running around unattended, eating everything they could find, even dead corpses. You saw them in ditches wherever there were dead bodies.

Sitting in our foxholes, we'd see our own B-24s flying overhead to Germany. First, you'd hear a noise, and you'd wait and wait to see the plane, and they would drop silver foil all over to louse up German radar. It all fell on top of us. The sky would be full of American B-24s, I mean full, and we would yell, "Go get 'em!" What a great thing to look at and think, *I'm glad they're on our side.* We put the silver foil in our pockets for souvenirs.

BILL

Easy Company was all set up at the perimeter, and all of a sudden I hear Babe screaming and hollering, so loud the Germans could hear him screaming, too. I ran over, tried to find out what the hell was going on and shut him the hell up. Here, he was on outpost and dozed off next to his machine gun, when he felt something like rain. He woke up, and Bill Morganti was taking a piss on his machine gun. It was pitch black, Morganti couldn't see what he was pissing on. Babe's ranting and hollering, ready to go fist city with Morganti. I said, "So he peed on your machine gun, what's the difference? Shut the hell up. You're gonna get us all killed." He still didn't shut up. Babe's still pissed off, or pissed on! He's still looking for Morganti.

When our platoon was in a static position, I would go out and help 1st Platoon fight. They were usually the first to encounter the enemy. We were second, 3rd Platoon was in the rear. It ended up 1st Platoon took the most casualties and 3rd took the least. It just happened that way. I was always worried about what was happening in all three platoons, not just my platoon. I couldn't help myself. I was a snoop, always asked questions, had my nose in everything. Always wanted to know where 1st and 3rd Platoon were, where headquarters was.

It was around Opheusden, 2nd Platoon was doing patrols, relieving other companies on the lines. Dick Winters took out a patrol to make sure our lines were secure. We were spread so far apart on the island, you never saw anybody on your flanks. His patrol found a bunch of SS nearby. Now SS troopers, these are no-good sons of bitches. This wasn't the ordinary German or Polish kid who was ordered to fight in the German army. These were Nazis. Gestapos. They started training as young boys to be loyal to Hitler. They lived and died by Hitler, did all his dirty work. They wore long black coats; you could spot them anywhere.

Back in Normandy, I caught two of them off guard, two SS. I came up behind them and grabbed them. Pointed my M1 at their heads, they handed me their weapons and surrendered to me, and I blew their brains out. I had no sympathy. We killed a lot of Germans that surrendered. The same ones would kill you if they got the chance, so it was easy as killing a bug. Today, you'd get arrested. I took their guns, gave one to George Luz and one to Johnny Martin. Martin kept his, and Luz's we hocked in London. We had no money, so George says, "How about that gun you gave me?" I think it was a Luger. We sold it and had a ball.

First Platoon beat the shillelagh out of those Nazis. It was like a duck shoot. When our platoon joined them, they were already at the end of the action. I would have liked to have blown them all away myself. They killed Dukeman. William Dukeman. He was a Toccoa man. No matter what platoon you were in, these men were like family. It affects you, but you can't stop to think about it.

At night, when the battle is over for a short time, that's when things like that hit you. You think of who got hit, who got killed. Sometimes I got the shakes. When you did get a minute to yourself, and you weren't on the line, you felt the effects from the day, but you didn't want nobody to see you. I imagine lots of guys sat in their foxholes crying like a baby. But no matter how bad it got, I couldn't let my guard down. I couldn't stop to cry. I had men to lead.

You have so many mixed emotions in combat. You don't know what's going to happen today, tomorrow. No idea. Some days you want to get hurt and get out. On the other hand the war's got to be won, too, so you don't want to let your buddies down, you don't want to be what they call a goldbricker, trying to get out while you can still fight. Half of you wants to get the hell out and half of you doesn't want to leave your buddies to do this on their own. You'd give your life up for them. That's how I felt. Each man felt differently.

I remember thinking, *Lord, get me the hell out of this place*, and my next thought would be, *But If I leave, then what's going to happen to my men?* You go through so many conflicting emotions. You jump from one conclusion to another real quick. And on top of that, somebody's trying to kill you every goddamn minute.

I went to help Johnny's platoon at the front; they chased the SS over a dike to a river crossing. The SS started shelling the hell out of us with artillery to keep us away. We were trying to withdraw back over a dike, and they had it zeroed in. They bombed the hell out of us. The ground was exploding, men were getting hit left and right, limbs flying, and everyone was yelling for medics. It was a bad, bad scene. I got to the dike just as Leo Boyle got hit and fell flat on his face. Shrapnel hit him in the back of the leg, and ripped open his thigh, he was bleeding something terrible, there was almost nothing left of it. There were a few of us who were able to stomach seeing blood and guts and patch up a wound when no medics were around. Not everyone could, but it didn't bother me a bit. Me and Pat Christenson ripped off Boyle's pant leg and put sulfa powder on his wound, and tried to help him best we could until the medics came and patched him up. He went out like a light, but we knew he'd be okay. Poor Boyle was shot in the leg in Normandy and wasn't recovered from that yet.

BABE

My buddy Jim Campbell and I were sitting in an apple orchard, and he seemed upset. He had a letter from his wife, and he wanted me to read it. He said, "Well, she got another guy. I don't know what's going to happen to our baby." I didn't even know what to say.

October 6th, our platoon was relieving B Company in a defensive position on the dike. The stupidity of it was they brought us up by truck in broad daylight, on a main road. The Germans had the high ground, so you had to figure they could see us. When we got out of the truck, a kid from headquarters company went over to a wooded area to go to the bathroom, and a shell exploded on him, and a piece of him flew over the truck. I know that's hard to hear, but that's how it happens in war.

Bill was taking some of the men to set up a mortar, and he gave the rest of us our orders. We were walking up beside a house to go occupy it, and as B Company was leaving, they told us things had been pretty quiet. "The only action was a round of mortar shells on a nearby house," one of the troopers said. He kind of shrugged it off. We knew the Germans had a bead on the area. Joe Toye was ahead of me and hollered, "Hey, Heffron, bring your machine gun up." I started up in back of him when Jim Campbell—he was Toye's assistant—says "Heffron, you stay here with the gun. *I'll* go with Toye." As soon as they turned the corner of the house, a German 88 exploded right on top of them. The side of the house came crashing down on us, and we were buried in white chalk and debris. You could smell the spent shell. I ran over to check on Toye and Campbell. There was a large cloud of shell powder, like a mushroom cloud, and Toye stepped out of it. He said, "Don't touch me, I'm hit all over." He was hit bad in the back and legs. His neck was all chewed up with shrapnel, it looked like rats got to it. It was his third time hit in four months of combat. I looked at Campbell. Before I could check his pulse, Toye said: "He's dead, Heffron, I checked." The shell had hit Campbell in the back, killing him instantly. He had a pair of Dutch wooden shoes, a gift from a farmer, in his musette bag, and the shell sliced those shoes right in half. But what I couldn't believe was that Joe Toye, bleeding and in pain himself, reached over to check on Campbell. That was the kind of soldier Toye was. I threw my topcoat over Campbell—I had nothing else to cover him with—and said a prayer for him. Then I threw Toye over my shoulder and carried him back to the aid area. We were being shot at and mortars were falling all around us. I stumbled a couple of times and fell, but we made it. For days, I was in a stupor over Campbell's death. It was supposed to be me that went up with Toye. I can't figure out why at the last minute Campbell said, "I'll go." Why was I allowed to live? He took that shell for me. He saved my life. I never, never forget it. I eat it, sleep it, breathe it. Still, not a day goes by I don't wonder why *I* got to go home, get married, and have a family, and he never got that chance. When I talk about it, Bill says, "You were just lucky, forget about it." When someone takes a shell for you, it's hard to forget about it.

BILL

About a week after we got onto the Island, Winters was promoted. Finally we got rid of the Quaker! Nah, Winters was the best CO we ever had. Probably the best CO in the Army. The men were pretty upset when we found out we were losing Winters. The CO can make or break the company. He can get the men killed or keep them alive. Luckily, we had the NCOs, all Toccoa men, to hold the company up if leadership was poor. Because who knew what we'd get?

The first replacement for Winters, you never saw the guy. They got rid of him quick, and sent in Lt. Fred "Moose" Heyliger from headquarters. Moose was an E Company man, who was promoted to HQ before D-day. We all liked Moose. He was a good man, a good officer, always out there in the field with us, made good decisions.

We stayed in static position for a while, on outpost duty, sending out constant patrols, trying to keep the Germans from breaking through our lines. We could only move around at night; we got very little sleep. We slept when we could, shivering and wet most of the time. Couldn't do a damned thing to get dry. But you couldn't complain. What were you gonna do? Where were you going? It's not like home, kid. If you didn't feel good, tough shit. You have a stomachache? Well, unless you prefer getting killed to a stomachache, you're going to take the stomachache and fight.

We lived on K rations and apples. Lots of orchards around, and we'd hit the trees with our guns and get the apples to drop, and that was most of our diet.

Joe Toye would try and lighten things up at night by singing "I'll Be Seeing You." Or he'd be humming it wherever he was. It would be quiet at night, and when it's been quiet for so damn long and you're out there all by yourself, you think of a million things. He'd sing a line of that song and before you know it, the guy next to him starts singing, and the guys next to him, and soon everybody's singing. Even I'm singing, and thinking, *What the hell, we're all nuts.* The Germans could follow the whole front line! Sometimes I was trying to sleep, and all of a sudden I heard the singing start and I'd think, *Shut up, you sons-of-beetles! You're in a foxhole!* But I didn't say it out loud. Nah. Every time I hear that song, I think of old Joe Toye. Yeah, there were some good times. Little things like that never leave your mind.

Babe sang all the time, too. He sang all the old Irish songs, like "Bridget O'Flynn," or he'd get us all singing "Mares eat oats and does eat oats and little lambs eat ivy." He sang pretty good, too. I tell him he chirps, so he don't get full of himself. Music was very important to us back then. It was a big part of our lives. The music during the World War II era was very soothing. Took you away from where you were.

My days were spent running around all over the place trying to figure out what's going on, in the front, in the back. My right-hand man was Rod Bain. Very quiet, very nice kid, you never knew he was there. He was our platoon's radioman, and every time I wanted information whether it was from one of the other companies, platoons, or headquarters, I hollered "Bain!" and he found out what was going on. I always called him because he was a good soldier, very dependable. I don't know how he put up with it, but he did everything I asked, and then some. Probably cursed me under his breath! Anytime I needed help, I called on him, Babe, or Toye first. Whatever you called on them to do, they got it done, no questions asked.

Bain did a lot of running around as the radioman, too. He had a tough job, he was a technician, a T-5. We needed to communicate, especially on patrols, but if you did it by radio, the Germans could tap in. So he laid wire from outpost to company CP a couple hundred yards away. They had a phone and outpost had a phone. The krauts would break the wire when they shelled us. Bain had to crawl out there by himself, find the break in the wire, and connect it. He done that over and over. I give him a lot of credit.

When we were attacking, or on the defensive, I ran back and forth making sure guns were trained right, and directing 2nd Platoon's fire. When I gave an order and a man didn't like it, I told them I don't give a goddamn whether you like me or not, I'm going to get you out of the battle alive. I told them I don't give a rat's ass if you like what I'm telling you; they looked in my eyes and knew I was serious, and they got it done.

Everyone was spread out on the island. We didn't know it at the time, but the front line was like a mile long. I checked on the men constantly. Your job as a leader, beside doing your own reconnaissance and giving orders, is to let the men know you're there with them. You didn't have to give pep talks; as soon as they saw you that was enough. Sometimes you sat there by yourself in a foxhole so long you felt like you were fighting the whole goddamn German army yourself. You're not of course, but that's how you felt. *Where the hell's everybody at*, you're thinking. You have no information. So if your sergeant comes around, you see his face, you know you're doing okay.

The middle of October, we were doing the same as we did every day—patrolling and doing outpost duty. I was trying to get somewhere fast and stole a motorcycle from a Dutchman. The entire island was flat, and you were conspicuous wherever you were. I was stupid, drove the motorcycle across an open field. Didn't even think about it. If I had, I wouldn't have done it. If I thought about half the things I done, I probably wouldn't have done them. All of a sudden—*bam!*—a sniper shot me in the right leg. Blew me right off the motorcycle. I couldn't walk. It hurt like holy hell. I had some shrapnel in my rear end, too. I was evacuated back to England. Fractured my right tibia, and they put a big walking cast on me that started at my foot and went up to my thigh.

The hospital was a nightmare. GIs were being carried in on stretchers, they had no heads, no arms, bodies bleeding like holy Christ almighty! Some were burned beyond recognition, moaning, crying. In bad, bad shape. A thousand times worse than me, and there's me with a goddamn scratch. I wanted to get the hell out. I was going nuts. I asked them to send me back to Easy Company. They said, "We can't do that." Well, there ain't no such thing as "you can't." I started plotting how I was going to get the hell out.

When you were better, they sent you to the rehabilitation ward and then to a replacement depot—repo depot, we called it. You could be half dead, but if you could *walk* to the front lines, you were considered walking wounded, and returned to combat. Repo depot sent you to any unit that needed bodies, whether it was artillery, infantry, tankers, truck drivers, anything. Everyone in Easy Company knew about repo depot. Quite a few already went AWOL and hitchhiked back to the unit. Whoever was going your way, you jumped on a truck. Most of the time the 101st was at the front lines, and everybody knew it.

I sure as hell wasn't going to no repo depot and getting assigned to another unit. I found some black shoe polish, and rubbed it all over my cast to make it look like a black boot, put my pant-leg down over it, and walked out. I couldn't even walk, but I walked anyway. I was weak, limping. I tried to get to an airfield and catch a plane, but that plan failed. I made it to the beach and was sneaking around trying to catch a boat across the English Channel, when an officer caught me. They threw me back in the hospital and court-martialed me. I said, "I'll just go AWOL again tomorrow, and you'll have to court-martial me again. I want to go back to my outfit." So they said, "This guy is a nut." They cut my cast off and said, "Now walk." I couldn't even stand on that leg, it got so skinny from being in the hospital, but I opened my big mouth so I had to walk, and they made me run, too. It was killing me, but I did it, and they shipped me back to duty a week later.

BABE

One night at the end of October we moved to an area closer to Arnhem where they told us we'd be out of the elements. My squad was positioned in a barn with no roof, so it wasn't exactly out of the elements. We were relieving B Company, we always relieved B Company, and when we got to the barn, there was this big dead kraut lying there. He was about six-foot-four, black uniform—he was SS. He was lying next to a dead cow. A kid from B Company said, "You should've been here last night, we had a party." The story was, the SS officer followed the rope down to CP, where Welsh was. They were all sitting on boxes, so you floated in the water. The kraut walked in by himself and said in perfect English, "Put your hands up, you are now prisoners of the German Reich, the barn is surrounded." One of B Company's forward observers was sitting in the corner, and drew his pistol, and shot the kraut in the head. They all started fighting over his Luger, and the forward observer got it. Meanwhile, the kraut's squad heard the gunshot and took off back to their lines, so the B Company guys threw the dead kraut next to a dead cow. Someone said, "He was an animal, that's where he belongs." We all concurred.

The German lines weren't far away, and our barn was in a spot where, if the krauts attacked from their position on the dike, we could put up enough resistance for the rest of the platoon to get a counterattack ready. The morning after we got there, a German soldier stood up out of his foxhole, and faced our lines and put his thumb to his nose, grabbed his middle, like he was laughing, and waved. I thought, *Well, there's a fresh son of a bitch!* The next morning, same thing. The morning after that, we had two British snipers sent to our line to take him out. They set up positions twelve hundred yards away, he did his nose-thumbing thing, and they shot, and missed! He was too far away and too well dug in. A sergeant with the 377 Para Artillery that was attached to us devised a plan to get rid of him. He said "I'll have a surprise for him tomorrow morning." Next morning, the kraut stood up and did his thing. The sergeant picked up a phone, called in the coordinates, and said, "Fire," and shells flew over our heads. They gave him what they call "air burst." The shell blew before it hit the ground and took the German soldier with it. We were all hooting and hollering. Let's just say you could find that kraut up in Scranton "spreading the news." We have a law in combat: If you're a wise guy, you're on your own.

At night, in the barn, we crawled into bins full of hay to get some sleep. You went in feetfirst, with your head out, so you could see. At two a.m., the lookout ran in and hollered, "The Germans are coming over the dike!" We all fell out, and one of my socks came off in the straw. I put my boots on and went out the door. My assistant was with me, and as we ran up the road, I yelled, "My sock's back there!" I had my bare foot in a wet boot. We repelled the Germans and went back to the barn, and I went searching for my sock in eight to ten feet of hay. I gave up. One night, C. T. Smith, our supply sergeant came up, he had colonels Sink and Strayer—they were going around with a microphone trying to get the Germans to surrender. I told C.T. "I ain't got no socks, and we need clothes, we need underwear." I figured I'd put my order in for the guys. He said, "I'll be up in the morning," but he never came. I tried putting a GI handkerchief around my feet, but they stayed soaked. Holland was always underwater. You couldn't even walk along the dikes, your feet got stuck in the mud. For the next two weeks, I had one sock between two feet. I took the sock off every three days and put it on the other foot.

(Bill adds: "I don't have that trouble!" Babe replies: "Yeah, ain't that odd?")

One day in the barn, I heard a noise outside, so I borrowed a rifle, headed outside, and a big shadowy figure started coming toward me. He had to be over six-foot-five. He put his hands in the air, and shouted, *"Comraden, Comraden! Nicht Deutsche, Nicht Deutsche! Polsky!"* I threw him against the barn and held my rifle on him. He was about thirty years old and explained in his broken English that the Germans made the Polish boys fight or they'd kill him. It was true. The Germans put a lot of the Poles in slave labor camps and conscripted the good men for the army. Who knows how many Americans he killed up to that point, but he found a chance to escape and took it. At least that was his story. I searched his pockets for weapons and found nothing. I hoped he had something to eat on him, and he did. A crust of hard bread. I said, "This is hard as a rock!" and I handed it back to him. He had torn newspapers for relieving himself and some German money, which I took, and still have. I was leading him back to the barn to turn him into our platoon CO, Harry Welsh, when a fellow Easy soldier ran over and said, "Let's kill the son of a bitch right now!" I explained the situation, but the other soldier was adamant. He kept yelling, "Kill him!" We argued for a few minutes, and finally I got the POW sent to headquarters. Turned out the prisoner was able to tell headquarters who was where, and what outfits. Welsh told me, "It's a good thing you got that prisoner. He really helped us out." It just so happened that the night before when colonels Strayer and Sink came up, they were trying to get these guys to surrender, but they didn't succeed. I guess this guy changed his mind.

A lot of the time we did kill prisoners. You can't have them tagging along with you. The only time you could take them was when regimental headquarters had a place for them. We captured a bunch of POWs and put them in a schoolyard, and they all escaped. After that we learned not to take POWs. Plus, it's a risk. They're just waiting for you to turn your back so they can kill you.

I think sometimes about the power I had over that Polish man's life. I let him live when another soldier would have killed him instantly. It's frightening to think any human being has that kind of power over another. I hope he lived a long, full life after being released from prison. I'd like to think that with whatever years I gave that Polish soldier, he said a few prayers for me and maybe said a few kind words about me to his family.

At the end of October, a British colonel swam across the river to tell us he had a bunch of troops trapped across the river that the Dutch were hiding, and he wanted our help getting them across the river to safety. They had British soldiers and American flyers that got shot down. We formed a party of men, got some boats, and I was on my machine gun covering the withdraw, them going over and bringing the troops back. They did it in the pitch dark, of course, you didn't do anything in the daylight, but they got them all back safe. When they got back, there was a little Irish paratrooper, he was carrying a club, and he said, "Once I get back to Ireland, I'll never go back in this man's army again." He wasn't at all happy about how the British fought.

Here's another thing about the British: Their cigarettes were terrible! They were like straw. They'd try to con us, "Hey, I'll trade you Players or Woodbines for Luckys or Chesterfields, mate." First we'd look at them like they were crazy. Then we figured, *What the hell, they're our fighting buddies.* We'd give them a few packs and they thought they got the better of us. Then we'd take their horrible cigarettes and give them to the Dutch civilians who were dying for any cigarettes, and we'd tell them, "These are English cigarettes, they're not American." We didn't want to make *our country* look bad!

★ ★ ★

We spent most of November on outpost duty and doing patrols. Unfortunately, we lost our CO Moose Heyliger when he got shot by one of our own men who was on outpost, and he was evacuated to England. The first week of November, we had a new CO, Norman Dike. He was from division HQ, a real stiff military-career type, completely inexperienced in combat. We learned right away Dike wasn't a good soldier, let alone a good leader. We called him Foxhole Norman because whenever there was action, he wasn't around.

When I didn't like an officer, I just stayed away from him. It didn't matter who the officers were, because we had great NCOs in the company.

Right after Dike came in, Gen. Maxwell Taylor, the commander of the 101st Airborne was wounded inspecting the 501st and I was sent over in a Jeep to be the guard at his command post, which was a trailer in the woods. They would only give that duty to a soldier they trusted. It made me feel good to know my superiors thought that highly of me.

At the end of the month, Canadian units relieved us and we took trucks to France to recoup. We figured the war was just about over. The bad news was that six Easy Company men were dead, and fifty were wounded. We took a beating in Holland. It was awful. Montgomery did an awful job.

Many military people regard the drop in Holland as a failure, but the two American Airborne Divisions, the 101st and 82nd, did their jobs, secured their objectives, won their parts of the battle, killed and captured a lot of Germans, succeeded in pushing them back and liberated Holland. I've always thought the British high command could have done a better job of helping their men trapped at Arnhem, but the British army never seemed to be in a hurry. Patton should have been there; he would have kept that road open all the time. One thing I can tell you, it was quite a privilege to have the 82nd Airborne fighting alongside of us. They were great soldiers.

6

★

MOURMELON-LE-GRAND: R & R INTERRUPTED

End of November to Mid-December 1944

BABE

We were so happy we could finally rest and get a bath. We went eighty days counting the marshaling area with no bath. Seventy-three days on the front lines. We stunk to holy hell. Then when we got to Mourmelon, we all got dysentery. We had a hot meal of chicken and vegetables when it happened, and who knows if it was because it was our first hot food in months—maybe it was too heavy for our digestive systems after eating only apples and stale bread—or if the chicken was bad. But it seemed to affect the guys who'd been in Holland. My God, we were a mess—cramps, throwing up, running to the latrine every minute, it was coming out both ends—I remember being in so much pain I had to hold on to the bedpost. It was awful, and the officers wouldn't let you stay in the barracks. We had to go out on the road with the new replacements and teach them how to survive. As sick as we were, we took them out and brought them back every day. Every morning Roe came around and gave us some medicine on a spoon to counteract all the symptoms. It was hell! Bill got lucky it didn't happen to him, because he wasn't with us when we came back to Holland. It wasn't lucky of course that he was hit, but at least he missed being sick.

BILL

After I went AWOL, I took a boat back to France and hitchhiked to Mourmelon-le-Grand, where the 506th was resting and refitting. I got there around the 10th of December. It was like coming home. Boy, was I glad to see those guys again, and see them alive. Buck Compton went AWOL and came back around the same time.

Winters wasn't surprised to see me. When I reported in, I told him I was court-martialed and demoted to private. But records weren't kept, there was a war going on. I was put right back in charge of the men. I can't say what I would have done if I wasn't. Malarkey was acting 2nd platoon sergeant after I got hurt in Holland, and I knew he done a good job.

Word was that the war in Europe would be over in a few weeks. The generals told us it was going to be over by Christmas. We heard we were getting passes anywhere we wanted to go—Paris, Reims, all over.

We had training exercises almost every day and were waiting for more supplies and replacements, but we mostly practiced for a football game. We had a big game planned, the 506 against the 502—the Five-0-Deuce, we called them, or the Five-0-Ducs. They were a pretty good football team, and we were getting ready to kick their asses.

You kind of felt like combat was behind you for a while. Our next jump was supposed to be in the spring. So me and Johnny Martin, Burt Christenson, Joe Toye, Chuck Grant, and a couple other sergeants went out and robbed about twenty cases of champagne. We threw a party in our barracks, got drunk as skunks, and trashed the joint. We ripped the bunks out of the floor, threw them out the windows, broke everything we could get our hands on. Lit things on fire. Just destroyed the place. Lipton was the first sergeant then, he came in and gave us all hell, made us clean it up. He was a lot more conscientious than I was. Lip was a good guy. Even though I was a sergeant, had responsibilities, I was a wild man. I was like Jekyll and Hyde, a troublemaker outside of combat, but in combat I was focused. Everything else became secondary.

The next morning, we had football practice for the big game, and then I had a pass to Reims for the day after that. I still have that pass. I never made it to Reims.

BABE

Everyone was excited because we had weekend passes to go to all these great places. We'd been talking about it for days, who was going where, what we were going to do when we got there. Early in the morning, I think it was the 17th, Bill came running in hollering, "Get off your asses! Let's go! We gotta go! Krauts broke through the

Ardennes!" We all looked at each other and said, "Where the hell's the Ardennes?" Bill said, "Just get your ass out of bed!" So instead of getting weekend passes, we had to run around and get ourselves ready to move out again.

Everybody was looking for ammo and clothes. The first thing I did was look for some extra pairs of socks. I couldn't forget after Holland—I lost a sock, and for the last couple weeks had to keep switching the sock from one foot to the other. That was bad. I wanted to make sure I had enough gear this time. We knew it was going to be cold. It was the middle of December, and it was Belgium we were going to. We had no winter underwear, we had only our regular gear, but when they said grab everything you can, my only thought was socks. I took a few extra pair.

BILL

We had less than twenty-four hours to get ready to move out. Everyone scrambled to dig up whatever they could find—mostly ammo and warm clothes. The sergeants ran around trying to find out who had what. We didn't have nothing. We were waiting for supplies to arrive before this happened. There was hardly any ammo around, we had no waterproof boots, no winter coats, no long underwear. For the other jumps, we knew they were coming, just didn't know when. This time, we weren't expecting to be in combat again. It was like being blindsided. But you have to get focused real fast, and that's what we did.

It made you nervous to have so many replacements going in. A lot of the original company was gone, and you have no idea what these new kids are going to do. But the noncoms are the backbone of the company; good NCOs means a good, strong company. Thank God the original sergeants were still there.

The men that went away on passes, the MPs went around and picked them up and brought them back to barracks. Chuck Grant was taken off the street in London and had to jump in. One of the few men who made a jump into Belgium. The ones that got picked up by the MPs while on pass, all they had was their dress uniforms. It was one big mess. They just wanted to get the troops in.

We weren't briefed. Nobody knew what the hell was going on. Even the generals didn't know. All we knew was the Germans launched a surprise offensive in the Ardennes forest in Belgium, on the border of Germany. We got little bits of information, took us a week to figure out what was going on. The Germans were trying to secure Antwerp before Allied troops got there. Everyone wanted Antwerp. The Germans wanted it, the Allies wanted it. It had a big seaport into Germany, and the Germans were advancing with tanks through the Ardennes to get there. They needed the roads. The 101st was going to defend the town of Bastogne—it had seven crossroads the Germans needed. We had to put a perimeter defense around it and block the Germans from getting through at all costs.

My leg was still kind of weak, but I never gave it a thought. I didn't feel my leg. Some people can't stand pain. Pain doesn't bother me one damn bit. If there was pain, I didn't feel it. That's my nature. If I get a headache, I bang my head against the wall, curse somebody, and it goes away *bing-bang-boom!* I just ignore it. Once you're thrown out on the front lines, you don't pay attention to your body. You get stronger and stronger.

BABE

They had a church service before the trucks came in to get us. The priest from the 501 was saying mass, his name was Father Sampson. He was a jolly Roman Catholic priest; we admired him like we did Father Maloney. We felt the chaplains were, like the medics, the real heroes. Father Sampson was captured in Normandy and released. We didn't know it then, but he would be captured and held prisoner for months in Bastogne, too. He wrote about it in his book *Look Out Below!*

He looked us all over, and seeing more of us than usual at Mass, and not just the usual suspects, he said, "Look how many men we got here, what's going on? We going up again? It's the only time I see all you guys." He said Mass, and as I was kneeling, I looked over and right next to me was Gen. Anthony McAuliffe, the division artillery commander. I thought, *I'll never be this close to an Army general again.* I was pretty excited about it. I didn't know then he would later be famous all over the world for saying "Nuts!" at Bastogne.

At about two or three in the morning, we boarded the trucks. All we had were regular fatigue clothes on, we had no combat gear, no winter gear, no winter underwear; they sent us up as we were. No supplies, no ammo. In my squad we dug up two boxes of 30 caliber, I had one and Jim McMahon had one. I don't know who else had one. Everybody was hollering for rifle ammo, carbine ammo. It was a sad affair.

We went up on trailers, and as we drove up, it rained, it snowed, and these trailers were like boxcars, open on the top, no shelter, and it's December, and it's Belgium's coldest winter in thirty years. We didn't know that at the time, we just knew it was cold. So we were wet and cold to start with. But we didn't worry about it. We were tough. We were kids. My only thought was about what the hell we were getting ready to do. Nobody knew.

7

---★---

BASTOGNE:
CODE WORD FOR HELL

Winter 1944

(Bill's Stories in Italics)

The Red Ball Express drivers drove us to an area just outside Bastogne, Belgium. Joe Toye and I were up front with the machine gun. The driver was a black man from Philly, so we chatted with him a little bit. You could see and hear the shelling in the background, it started out faint and got louder and louder as we got closer. Our driver was getting pretty shaken up. We moved along at about forty miles per hour in the pitch dark, and every blast we heard, he would say nervously, "That's theirs!" He knew what we were heading into, and wanted to drop us off and get the hell out. A couple of shells hit a hundred yards to the right of our trucks, and the recoil of German artillery was lighting up the sky. Light travels faster than sound, so the sky lights up, then you hear them coming over your head. By the time you hear them it's too late to do anything about it. We had to keep moving in a straight line, even if shells fell around us. When we got as close as we could, the trucks stopped, dropped us off, and took off. I give the drivers a lot of credit, because they got us where we needed to go.

The Army was segregated, the time dictated that, and blacks were usually put in transportation jobs. Everything we got was through them—equipment, ammo, supplies, food. It was a team effort, that's a fact. Without everyone doing their part, we wouldn't have won the war. There were some black soldiers at the Bulge, but they weren't paratroopers. They were tankers or infantry. I never saw them.

The broads had important jobs in the war, too. Lots of women took part. The British had the Wrens (Women's Royal Naval Service). We had the WACS (Women's Army Corps) and the WASPs (Women's Airforce Service Pilots). Whenever a plane was finished for the war, the girls delivered them to the military bases in a hurry. They were fly girls. They flew bombers, those broads.

We got off the trucks and fell into our columns. We didn't try and bunch up, and we didn't walk slow, we walked double-time. The quickstep. You follow whoever is up front telling you where to go. If he's doing eight steps a minute, you do eight steps a minute. We had to get to wherever we were setting up a main line of resistance (MLR). No one seemed to know what we were supposed to be doing.

There was a major battle going on nearby. Lot of shelling. As we advanced, infantry troops were running toward us, scared as can be. We're going forward, they're running back. A lieutenant named Rice, I don't know where he was from, he was stopping these kids, making them pile their weapons, clothes, ammo in one big pile. They threw their stuff down and ran. The pile was getting bigger and bigger, so as we walked past, we fished through it and grabbed whatever we could carry. First thing I grabbed was ammo. You tried to load up on guns, ammo, and grenades. Food and clothes were secondary. When your hands were full, you threw what ammo you found in someone else's hands.

Bill said, "Look at the patch, 28th Division." I'm telling you I never seen men with a look like that in my life, running, scared to death. No helmets, no weapons. They threw their guns down, they threw their bandoleers down, they threw everything down. The kids were all out of breath, yelling, "Don't go up there, there are so many Germans, they're gonna kill everybody!" We said, "That's our job!" They said, "But there's a million of them!"

I stopped one of the fellas—he was an artillery man—I said, "What the hell outfit you in?" He mentioned some artillery. I said, "Jesus, I hope you at least lowered your gun and blew them." He said, "No, we didn't have time." I said, "Oh my God." Bill would have said—any of our leaders would have said—"Stand your ground!" That's what would have prevailed in our company. We were more ashamed than anything else. These were American soldiers.

We walked through the town of Bastogne; it was a sad sight, a beautiful town in shambles, just destroyed. We went about a mile and a half outside Bastogne and set up our MLR. The town had a railroad running through and was a crossroads, seven roads ran through the middle of town. They would have made the German advance much faster, trying to get to the seaport in Antwerp. The Germans and the Americans wanted that seaport. We had to set up a perimeter defense, surround Bastogne in a circle, and hold it. This was nothing like France or Holland. In France we were on the move. In Holland, we were all spread out. In Bastogne, the company was all together in one place. Our job was to hold the line and try to stay alive.

When we got to our position in the Bois Jacques woods, that was kind of a safe haven for a little while. You could see they had a hell of a fight there. The ground had craters from the 88s, shell cases and tree branches all over, dead GIs, and limbs—an arm here, a leg there, blood and guts. That was Bastogne, kid. Ain't no damn picnic. We knew trouble was coming. Luckily, it was quiet while we set up a permanent defense. We dug our foxholes about thirty to forty feet into the woods, put out outposts just behind the front of the woods, Winters set up headquarters behind us. The 501st was on our right flank. We had an artillery battalion and an armored division with us. The 10th Armored's Team Cherry and Team Desiree were in Bastogne before we got there and got surrounded with us. Thank God they did because we needed them. Otherwise, we didn't have much contact with the other regiments and divisions that were out there. We were all spread out, a lot of ground to cover. No one knew what was going on that first day; we were sent to see what's cooking, and patrols were sent out all over the place. You could have been on a patrol and not even known it. Everything was just chaos.

Our medics, Gene Roe and Ralph Spina were low on medical supplies, and Ralph—he was also from South Philly—and I went back to the town of Bastogne to see what we could find. Ralph got some supplies at the aid station, but everyone was low; the Germans had captured the 101st Division's medical company on their way into Bastogne. We lost most of our doctors, aids, and supplies. That was certainly a blow to the division.

Ralph and I took advantage of being off the line for a few minutes and stopped to eat the only hot meal we would have in over a month. It was getting dark, and we were freezing, so I suggested we try a shortcut through the woods. We were trying to figure out where the hell we were when suddenly I fell into a hole. A voice yelled out from under me, "Hinkle, Hinkle, *ist das du*?" I scrambled out of that foxhole and yelled, "Hinkle your ass, Kraut!" and ran. Thank God it was dark or he probably would have got a shot off. I found Ralph and we found our way back to the line. Ralph liked to remind me of that incident often. He'd say, "Hey Babe, how's Hinkle?" Or "Have you seen Hinkle lately?" I wonder if Hinkle ever did make it back to his foxhole.

For a few days, we kept up constant patrols. Everybody in every company and every outfit had patrols out. The 501st, 502nd, everyone. You know what I say—just don't volunteer! The Germans were patrolling, too. Whenever the Germans fired on us, we fired back. Whatever they gave us, we gave back. Machine-gun fire, artillery fire, mortars. Don't forget, we were low on ammo. We were low on everything. We had to conserve, so we couldn't go crazy, or we'd be like sitting ducks. Dead. The Germans didn't know what we had, so that saved us.

I was in a foxhole with Buck Compton. Our foxhole was like the Platoon CP. I was the sergeant, and he was the boss, he was my lieutenant, so anything that had to do with the action up front started from our foxhole. He was in command—if something happened to him, I was the boss. We had phones to the guys on outpost, and they'd report to us what was going on. They'd tell us if it was quiet, or they saw something, and we'd dispatch orders. One of us watched the phones while the other slept. Whatever was going on, we were in contact with Captain Dike, Foxhole Norman. He wasn't worth the room he took up.

It would be quiet, and then a quick firefight, and you'd hear the men in the woods screaming and hollering for medics, and that's how it went for a few days. When it got quiet, we'd wait for the Germans to shell us again. They had Screaming Mimis, too, six rockets together, they'd shoot it and it screamed so loud it pierced your ears. Nothing you could do but sit there and take it. They kept probing and pushing. They'd fire at us, shell us, and try to break us down. Like a boxer, they'd jab, jab, jab, and hope to find a weak spot so they can hit you with a haymaker. You hope every line is secure, that's all. You have no idea where they're going to hit next. We had to be sparing, so a lot of the time, we sat there and took it. We still killed more krauts than they got of us.

We couldn't appreciate the lulls in the fire, because we were freezing our skidonies off. It was snowing, it was minus five degrees, we were sitting in an icy foxhole, like being in a freezer, with no winter clothes—no long underwear, no warm socks, no overcoats, no blankets, nothing. We looked like shivering, homeless ragamuffins. The Germans had long wool coats on, and winter boots; they were ready for the cold. But even if we piled on winter clothes, we still would have froze. A few of the guys got hold of winter coats before we left, I think Bain and Malarkey had wool coats and hats, and they still froze. Never been that goddamn cold in my life. Belgium's coldest winter in thirty years. How's that for luck? The only way to describe it is tell you to go outside in your pajamas, in a snowstorm, in wind and subzero temperatures, and once you get nice and wet, stay there for a week. There was nothing you could do to get warm. Nothing. At home you go inside to get warm, and you go out again. We didn't have anyplace to go into. When it got quiet for a little while, you got out of your foxhole and moved around. That's how you got warm, by going outside.

The sergeants were in charge of waking the guys up and getting them to outpost. We switched up every two hours. Getting to outpost was a little eerie. You're out there all by yourself. You never knew if you'd get there alive, or if the men on outpost were alive. Germans would sneak up on the guys and capture them. There was heavy fog at night and in the morning. Add that to the rain and snow, and you couldn't see two feet in front of you. You had your gun ready, and you listened first, and tried to see the outline of the helmets and clothes, see if it's your own guys, before going in.

The Germans had the high ground. There were hills all around Bastogne. We were on a hill, but they were higher than us because a lot of them were positioned in homes and a church. They were in the town of Foy, no farther than three hundred to four hundred yards away from the wooded area that we occupied, about four football fields away. That's another reason when you had outpost, you were so glad to see the guys there and alive. We had to send outposts to lie outside Foy all night. Chuck Grant had his squad out there every night watching everything. Then we had our outposts about forty feet in back of them, then you had another outpost behind that one, then the woods where the men tried to get some sleep. If outpost heard something, they opened fire, and you heard it and got the hell up. All you had to do was hear fire. The guys that were in the woods had to come out and hold them off.

You took the heaviest weapon in the platoon on outpost, a light 30. We also had the 60mm mortar, but you used the 30 to repulse any German attack, even though it couldn't do much against tanks. Sometimes Chuck's squad came running back and we'd say, "What the hell's the matter with them guys, they're coming back?" and we found out they encountered a German patrol with more firepower. Then we had to stand our ground with our guns, and wait for an attack, and usually, luckily there was no attack coming.

We didn't get much sleep. The Germans liked to shell the woods with mortars at night. The more men we lost, the less we slept. We started with two men on, four men off; then went to two on, two off; then one on, one off; then you're never getting any rest, you're at it all the time. We were so tired, guys would fall asleep walking. The guy in front of you would drop his rifle, and you'd see he was asleep.

You got so tired you didn't know what the hell was going on. No sleep and constant stress. Joe Toye tried to lighten it up, singing all the time like he did in Holland. Same song, too—"I'll Be Seeing You." We had no entertainment, so he sounded good to me.

If Joe was singing or anyone else was singing, it meant we were okay, so you felt good about that. But some men couldn't carry a tune. That includes Bill. The worst singer up in the Bulge was Ralph Spina. He couldn't sing a note. He sang like South Philly Willy. He thought he was Mario Lanza. He said, "Well, I come from his neighborhood." I said, "Well, you ain't got his voice!" When he started to sing we all yelled, "Will you shut the hell up!"

It didn't take the Germans long to figure out what was going on— that we surrounded the town—and they started hitting our defensive perimeter from all sides. They pushed so far into Allied lines, they created a bulge in the line, that's why they call it the Battle of the Bulge. A couple days in, we had a foot of snow, the wind kicked up, we were freezing our cods off, we were running out of food, and the krauts had the entire 101st Division surrounded. It happened so quick, no one knew what was going on. The generals didn't even know. We knew we were surrounded because we saw the antiaircraft gun the Germans use, we saw it on all four sides of us. They fired at any Allied planes or pursuit planes they saw. You could tell we were in trouble, getting fire from every direction. You couldn't miss it.

We were dug in a circle and that's where we were staying, hell or high water. Just don't let them break through, was all that was on our minds. Paratroopers are used to having front lines facing every direction—east, west, north, south, so it was nothing new. We said, "They got us surrounded, the poor bastards!" Those krauts didn't know who they were dealing with.

One day Ralph Spina and I were sitting in a tree trunk that had been blown down by artillery fire. We were talking about home when we heard Bill arguing with a second lieutenant who had just joined the platoon from West Point. The lieutenant was looking for volunteers for a patrol on the other side of a hill, and Bill, who was much more experienced in combat, was arguing that no patrol was needed because they already knew the German position. The lieutenant kept on it and found seven volunteers to go with him. Of course, they were replacements. When the patrol returned later that night, two of the men were dead and one had his hand torn apart. The lieutenant apologized to Bill for not listening to the more experienced soldier, but it was too late for those kids who trusted him. We saw most of the West Pointers as cocky and not into combat. They were military-career types more than they were soldiers, and the actions they took seemed to be about earning promotions, not for the sake of winning the war or keeping their men safe. There were the exceptions of course. Some great soldiers came from West Point, but we always mistrusted them until they proved otherwise. This West Pointer wasn't well liked in the platoon after that incident.

Father Maloney came up in his Jeep to do Mass for the men. The driver of the Jeep, a Catholic kid, acted as the altar boy and if he needed help, one of us would pitch in. When we saw the Jeep come up, we had to separate to walk toward it, you couldn't bunch up. One shell comes in, it could kill up to eight men. So we had to stagger, we all knew to do that, any soldier in any infantry organization knows to do that.

It was snowing, and Father Maloney gave us a pep talk, "You guys are doing a good job for your country, you're heroes, it's a pleasure to be your spiritual guide, and I'm proud to be part of the 506th."

He used the hood of the Jeep as an altar, and we knelt in the snow to get communion. Skip Muck was kneeling by me. He was a likeable, funny guy, and Irish and short like me. I got my wafer and he got his, and Father Maloney ended the Mass saying, "God bless you, good luck." In the Catholic faith, when you receive communion and you die, you automatically ascend into heaven. So as we walked away, I said to Muck, "At least if we die, were going to die in a state of grace." Muck said, "You're right, Heffron."

We knew where the Germans were, they knew where we were. The snow was deep, and moving through it made a lot of noise, and we were slipping and sliding through it. They could see and hear us, and they were always sending shells over trying to break through, but they couldn't do it. The weather was a problem for them, too. They had a lack of ammo and fuel and the same problems we had. But they were in houses, we were in the ground. They also had winter clothing. We had GI gloves; they were no good. They were wet, if you lit a fire to dry them, the krauts would start throwing artillery. So you threw your gloves away. We were given two burlap bags apiece for our feet. Our boots were already waterlogged, and after you walked around with the burlap for a while, the burlap got wet and froze, and got heavy with snow and ice; it was like walking with cinderblocks on your feet. But we knew never to take our boots off. You couldn't get them back on because your feet swelled up. It's not like you could ever dry your socks and boots anyhow, everything was full of snow. When you moved an inch, wet dirt and snow dropped down your back, down your front, down your pants, everywhere. It was awful.

We spent a lot of time on outpost, and if you were on outpost during the day, you had the open field in front of you, and you could see the German V-1s flying over, probably headed to London or Coventry.

They sounded like a motorcycle or freight train, and moved parallel to the ground about two thousand feet up, and you thought, "Keep that flame lit, keep that flame lit." When it went out, the motor stopped and it crashed and exploded. We also saw the V-2s, they were supersonic stratosphere jobs, they went straight up into the heavens, like a streak of light. We didn't worry about them, they weren't landing on us, but those V-1s made us sweat a little.

I was usually on outpost at night, and one night I was with Al Vittore from Pennsylvania; he was my assistant machine gunner. He was a few years older than us, a good guy. I shared a foxhole with him. We were out there every night. One night Sal Bellino from Brooklyn came running out into the forest to our outpost in his bare feet, in the ice and snow. What happened was, 3rd Squad was sent out on forward outpost every night, and since we had two-man foxholes to take up less space for artillery bombardments—but also for body heat—Sal figured he'd spread out a little in one of 3rd Squad's empty holes. He took his boots off and settled in when a Tiger Sixer tank pulled up and fired an 88 at his foxhole. Somehow the shell overflew the ditch and missed him, and he bolted into the forest. That was the end of Sal for a while. He ended up in the hospital with a very bad case of trench foot. That was December, he came back in August, that shows you how bad it was. Trench foot was a big problem for a lot of the guys. The doctors told us, "Take your boots off and rub each other's feet." We said, "Let them try it, with the krauts out here. They're crazy!"

That same night, we came back from outpost and Al said, "I'm gonna hit the sack." We were tired and cold and hungry, and we got back to the foxhole and tried to sleep. It wasn't easy to face the night. Living in the ground night after night, in five below zero, the wind whipping through at thirty to forty miles per hour, no bark on the trees, no leaves to protect us. It was very eerie. The snow would drop down your back, it was itchy, and you shivered all night. Finally I dozed off and was lying on my side, and I felt this heavy object come over my leg. I thought the lumber we had over the foxhole to protect us had fallen in on me. But it was Al's leg. I punched him in the side with my elbow. I said, "Yo Al, what are you doing?!" He said, "Oh, Babe," and he looked at me and said, "Oh, I'm all right," and he fell asleep again. So I fall asleep again, and a few seconds later, he's got his hand inside of my shirt! I gave him a shot in the belly and said, "You son of a bitch, what the hell are you doing?!" He said, "Oh, Babe, Babe, I was dreaming of my wife!" I said, "Well, you ain't gettin' nothing here!" They didn't use this story in the movie. They want everyone to think we're all American boys!

The Germans had a big open field to get to us, and they'd come over with their tanks. They couldn't get through the forest where we were—the trees were too closely packed. So they drove the tanks to the edge of the trees and fired 88s, then they'd back off and come back with more. The shells would hit the trees, explode, and shoot shrapnel everywhere, lot of guys hit from one shell. Treebursts, we called them. Made the trees a good ally to the Germans. The trees acted as a coordinator with these shells. We might not have had as many wounded and dead if not for those trees. The forest started to get bare real fast, it started to look like a bunch of toothpicks.

After we got shelled one day, I ran over to the area that was hit and Sal Bellino was lying facedown not moving at all. This was before he got evacuated for trench foot. I asked, "What's the matter?" He said, "I'm hit, my back." I think the shell hit the trees, and a branch fell and hit him in the back. But he looked okay, so I smacked him, and he jumped up and there was nothing wrong with him. He got scared. He got whacked by a bunch of trees and it scared the hell out of him.

We had no Air Force with us. They couldn't fly until the weather cleared. If we had them, we would have kicked the Germans' asses and got the hell out of there. There wouldn't have been a Bulge. Hitler knew what he was doing. He knew there was nobody on the front lines, they were all going to Japan.

About a week in, we were almost out of ammo. We could see the German trucks bringing ammo and supplies to the Germans, we could see all the German activity over in Foy, but we couldn't do a damn thing about it. We were lucky, they thought we had more than we did, or they would have gone through us like a dash of salt. They had tanks, artillery, SS troops. Aggressive, cocky sons of bitches, those SS. All we could do was stay and fight and repulse them, and they'd run. We stood our ground, that's it.

Around that time, the cold, the chaos, the casualties, the exhaustion, the feeling like you're left there to fight the whole German army yourself, a couple guys here and there were starting to get fatigued, mentally. Not many, but a few. You could tell a guy had enough when he walked around in a daze.

Mentally, physically, we all felt bad. We were dirty, hungry, exhausted, weapons weren't up to par, you couldn't use them like you wanted to, we were living like animals. You thought, *Maybe I'll be lucky, maybe a shell will come in and hit me, and this will be over.* But you knew you had a job to do and you did it. Some guys, you saw a change in their demeanor. We all started to feel it. We felt pushed as far as we could go. You knew a guy was done when he had a blank stare. You couldn't say anything to him. He didn't pay attention to you. When the officers saw a guy that was gonna go, the only thing they could do was try and get him off the line. Winters was good about getting those kids off the line if he saw it. Sometimes they came back later and were okay. Then you had a lot of guys you just never saw, like an officer from Philly, a lead officer, I won't say who he was. I don't mean Dike. If he had a chance not to be out front, he wasn't, simple as that.

Bill and Frannie before he left for Europe, 1943.

Bill Guarnere's private collection

Babe, 1943. The paratrooper uniform showed you were the best of the best.

Babe Heffron's private collection

Posing with our hats on backward. (L to R): Joe Toye, John Sheehy, Don Malarkey, Bill, Skip Muck, J. B. Stokes, at Ft. Bragg, 1943.

Bill Guarnere's private collection

Capt. Sobel (3rd from right), overseeing a boxing match between Burt Christenson (facing camera) and Tom Burgess. Bill is far right, James Alley is 2nd from right. Camp Toccoa, 1942.
Robert Burr Smith's private collection

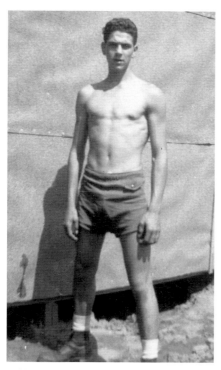

Bill, 1942. In typical physical training uniform, at Camp Toccoa.
Bill Guarnere's private collection

Bill, 1943, Ft. Bragg.
Bill Guarnere's private collection

Our buddies Alex Penkala (left) and Warren "Skip" Muck, at Camp Mackall, 1943. They were killed in action together in Bastogne on January 10, 1945.

Courtesy of Rudolph Tatay

Skip Muck (left), and Chuck Grant, 1943.

Robert Burr Smith's private collection

(L to R): Bill, Woodrow Robbins, Johnny Martin, 1943.

Bill Guarnere's private collection

Dick Winters (rear, facing camera), teaching his men to pack parachutes. Skip Muck (right, facing camera), Camp Mackall, 1942.

Robert Burr Smith's private collection

The 118-mile record-march from Toccoa to Atlanta, December 1942. That's George Luz with the towel around his neck.

Courtesy of Lana Luz Miller and Jim Benton

Babe's buddy, Easy Company medic Ralph Spina, in Saalfelden, Austria. One "practice" jump away from going home.

Ralph Spina's private collection

Henry Guarnere, Bill's brother, killed in action in Cassino, Italy, on January 7, 1944. Bill found out the day before he jumped into Normandy, D-day.

Bill Guarnere's private collection

Babe (right) and a buddy, at the Bama Club, where Babe won a jitterbug contest. Phoenix City, Alabama, 1943.

Babe Heffron's private collection

Lt. Lynn "Buck" Compton, an enlisted man's officer, 1943.

Courtesy of Lynn "Buck" Compton

Easy Company funny man, George Luz.

Courtesy of Lana Luz Miller

Carwood Lipton, 1945.

Bill Guarnere's private collection

Bill's right-hand man, Rod Bain (middle), and John Plesha (right) at Camp Toccoa, 1942.

Robert Burr Smith's private collection

Joe Toye, Columbus, GA, 1942.
Courtesy of Peter Toye

Don Malarkey (left) and Burr "Smitty" Smith, contemplative in Austria at war's end. *Courtesy of Don Malarkey*

The real heroes: Easy Company medics, Ralph Spina (left) and Eugene Roe. Berchtesgaden, just after the capture of Hitler's Eagle's Nest, May 1945. *The U.S. Army Military History Institute*

Dutch residents greet the 101st as they enter northern Eindhoven just after landing in Son. *Photo by Martina van de Gevel, courtesy of Peter van de Wal*

Bill (far left) and Babe with Honey and Mom Vermuelen, their hosts on their first visit back to Holland after the war. Eindhoven, 1954.

Babe Heffron's private collection

Life after war: Bill and Frannie, with sons Gene (left) and Billy Jr., 1949.

Bill Guarnere's private collection

Life after war. Babe with wife, Dolores, and daughter, Trisha, 1964.

Babe Heffron's private collection

Back together ten years after the war. (L to R, bottom): Bill, Chuck Grant, Harry Welsh, George Luz; (top, standing): Ken Baldwin, Dick Wright, Babe, Shifty Powers. *Bill Guarnere's private collection*

Bill and Babe with the cast of *Band of Brothers* and coproducer Tom Hanks (front) on the Hatfield, England, set, July 2000. *Babe Heffron's private collection*

Babe with Robin Laing, aka Babe Heffron, on the *Band of Brothers* set, Hatfield, England, July 2000.

Babe Heffron's private collection

At a dinner to honor Tom Brokaw, November 2002. Brokaw (far left) Forrest Guth (far right). *Bill Guarnere's private collection*

(L to R): Babe Heffron, Tom Hanks, Trisha Heffron Zavrel. November 2004, Los Angeles. *Babe Heffron's private collection*

Bill with Frank John Hughes on the Normandy site of the *Band of Brothers* set. Hatfield, England, July 2000.

Photo courtesy of Frank John Hughes
Babe Heffron's private collection

In the pasture at Brecourt manor in Normandy, 2006. Bill heads toward the trench where Easy Company took out a battery of four 105mm cannons pointed at Utah Beach. Behind Bill to the left is where German machine guns covered the 105s from across the field.

Photograph by Tracy Rhodes

Visiting graves of their buddies lost 55 years earlier in Holland. Margraten Cemetery, September 1999. *Bill Guarnere's private collection*

Bill and Babe visiting the graves of their war buddies, 1999. Margraten Cemetery. *Bill Guarnere's private collection*

In the Bois Jacques woods at Bastogne. The place is eerie, and brings back bad memories. *Babe Heffron's private collection*

Babe visiting the grave of his buddy John Julian, killed in action at Bastogne, January 1, 1945. Luxembourg Cemetery, 2004.

Babe Heffron's private collection

Best friends in Paris. Babe (left) and Bill, 2001.
Babe Heffron's private collection

Bill's sons Gene (left) and Billy Jr., stand in front of a photo that Frannie believed to be their dad, taken on D-day, in a Normandy Museum.
Bill Guarnere's private collection

All the time I put in the line with Easy Company, never saw him. There were a few like that. Top officers.

I never felt it. Fear was something that was with you all the time, but you ignore it. People all around you are getting killed and wounded; if you stop and think, you're not going to do your job, and you're dead. You walk through the fear, or it's going to be worse. I didn't think, I didn't analyze, I didn't let anything get to me. I did think, Jesus Christ almighty, how the hell am I going to hold off this German army? *I had days where I wanted to get the hell out, that's all. We all had them.*

A situation like Bastogne, you feel helpless. Where's the rest of the Army? Where's the ammunition, where's the food, where are the clothes, what the hell is going on? You felt like you were left there; if the enemy doesn't kill you, you'll freeze to death. We were angry at the Army. But we had no idea of the magnitude of what was going in, that up and down the line everybody's fighting, not only us. You don't know you're in the middle of the largest, bloodiest land battle in history. You find that out later.

War is, plain and simple, hell. Every move we made, we had no idea what was going to happen. But, as a sergeant, you had a responsibility over the men. My theory was this: I couldn't care less if they loved me or hated me, I did the best job I could do to get them out alive. Your actions speak for themselves.

The men who weren't in leadership positions, they could let their guard down, some cried. In Bastogne your tears would freeze. I did more praying then anything else. We saw a lot of bad things. There's nothing you could do to change the situation or bring people back to life. There's nothing, you feel helpless. You feel bad. You curse everything, and it makes you madder. I had my private thoughts about each and every man. But until you're not being chased by Germans, you don't have time to reflect. You just reflect on keeping the damn Germans out and killing the sons of bitches.

None of us wanted to be there. But some people can handle it better than others, whether it's a matter of sensitivity or emotional stability, I don't know. We had a 2nd lieutenant who was with us a few days, then he got his first taste of combat, and the next day he took a weapon and blew his hand off. Was he yellow? Some would say yes, but I don't think so. If you make it into the Airborne, how can you be? Men in the Airborne show a lot of courage just getting through training—they make many jumps at night, and it takes courage to go out of a plane at night. If they showed any signs of weakness, they wouldn't be there. Anyone who makes it into the paratroopers, you have to respect that man. I think that lieutenant couldn't handle that he sent some guys to their deaths even though he was only following orders. Seeing your buddies blown to pieces before your eyes can do something to your mind.

My younger brother Jack served on the *San Jacinto*, a small carrier in the Pacific. One of his fellow crewman turned and said to him, "Boy, it's hot up here," and then disappeared over the side of the ship. And this was after a battle. If he was a coward, he'd have done it before the battle or even during. The battle had been fierce and their sister ship, the *Princeton*, had just been sunk. I think the pressure got to him.

In our platoon, Bill would constantly make the rounds and tell us, "I'm here to get you guys home." He was no bullshitter. He meant what he said, and he was only my age, but he had that kind of knowledge and authority about him that we all trusted him. It gave you a little mental boost.

★　★　★

About two days before Christmas—at the time we didn't know what the hell day it was—the weather cleared, and our air force could get in. We knew the

German air force was practically wiped out. We learned before Normandy they couldn't concentrate in a way that was going to do you harm. It was the Allied air force that made the invasion so successful, so when you heard planes, 99 percent of the time you knew they were Allied. Well, when the weather cleared, the Allies got thousands of fighters and bombers ready to go. We were given panels—giant orange and red panels, about four-by-twenty feet, with stakes in them, and we put them out at nine in the morning, positioning them all around our lines so the air force can tell us apart from the Germans. We heard the first P-47s come in, we saw them overhead, and they started shooting at our panels, and by the count of ten, the panels were destroyed. When the next wave of planes came, and there were no panels to put out, we were scared as hell. We took cover. The planes came down shooting at us, strafing the woods, everything. They must have figured out where the Germans were pretty fast, because after that, they had a field day blasting the Germans.

Later more planes came, dropping supplies, food, ammo by parachute, in boxes and bags. The Germans started shooting at them, so the planes were going up, down, right, left, dodging the fire and dropping the supplies wherever they can. They got dropped all over—sometimes behind German lines, or right in front of you but you couldn't go out to get it or you'd get your head blown off.

We were so happy to see our planes flying overhead. They tried to find open fields for their drops, and if you happened to be near it—five yards, ten yards, a hundred yards away—you ran out to try and grab what you could. But there was always somebody that issued the rations; everybody got fed. If you were on outpost, they brought it out to you.

We hadn't eaten for about twenty-four hours, and each man got two boxes of rations. The K rations had brown crackers wrapped in in cellophane. I hated those crackers, so I asked Jim McMahon if he wanted them, and he didn't, so I threw them away. We all went back to the platoon area, and later on, news came over the walkie-talkie that we should go easy on the rations since we may not see more food for a while because of the weather. In the pitch dark, I walked back to look for those crackers. I found them in a shell hole and headed back to my squad. Those crackers weren't so bad after all.

Even after the drop we were still short of everything. They didn't give us enough ammo for the machine guns or the rifles. Nothing to keep us warm, at least I didn't get anything. Neither did Babe. Babe remembers getting K rations. I don't even know when I ate, how I ate, or what I ate. We were so damn cold and frozen that my priority after staying alive was keeping warm. Sometimes I'd realize, hey, I haven't eaten for a day or two, I'm hungry. I looked around and grabbed whatever I could. Somebody always had something and they shared it.

It was hard to find fresh water, everything was frozen, so you had to go looking—if we could've built a fire and melted the snow we would have had water, but we couldn't, we'd give our position away. One day I told Babe to grab a jerry can, and I grabbed one, and we went to look for water. We walked up to a stream, it wasn't frozen too bad, so we started chopping the ice to get to the water. After we filled our cans, I noticed down the bottom of the stream there were brains in the water. Men's brains. Heads with brains. Oh man, oh man! I said to Babe, "Don't say a damn word, just throw the goddamn water in the thing and let's get the hell out of here." You're in one hell of a mess, you can get killed any minute, you're gonna care about the water? You're gonna die any day, you're not worried about water.

I looked down at the bottom of the stream and thought, *Jesus Christ.* When we first came upon the stream, we saw a helmet laying in the snow, with a hole right through the center of it. A soldier nearby said it was a guy from I Company, he got hit when the planes were strafing us earlier. He said, "Yeah, a P-47 came down strafing and he thought this kid was a kraut and he opened fire." Sometimes the guys would wave at the planes figuring they're Allied planes, and they'd get shot at by friendly fire. The lines were never consolidated long enough. It wasn't the pilot's fault. My assistant machine gunner, Al Vittore, waved at them one time, I said, "You son of a bitch, get back here! You can't be waving at these guys! He said "It's a P-47." I said "I don't care!" The plane peeled off and gave us a burst. I dove into the hole, and he dove in on top of me. He ain't the only guy that was told and still did it. You feel so proud it's your planes, you want to wave to them. They don't know who the hell you are.

We got back to the platoon with the jerry cans; Bill said, "Line up, we got fresh water." What were we gonna do? We needed the water, and we got it before the stream was frozen over. After that, you weren't getting water anywhere. I never mentioned it. Nobody ever said, "Don't that water taste funny?" I drank mine. Bill kept hollering to the guys, "Put those goddamn pills in there so you don't get malaria from the water." We had sulfanilamide pills. We used them all over the European Theater.

The thing about lighting fires, little fires were smoldering everywhere, so it wasn't necessarily a telltale sign. During the day some small fires were lit, but not often. We were able to make coffee using Sternos. It's a little can about two to three inches deep, you take the top off and put a match to it, and it makes a little blue flame, so you could take some snow and make some coffee. Most of the time we drank the fluid in the Sterno, it had alcohol in it, so we took a swig. I don't know what the hell it was, but we drank it! It didn't kill us, did it? Funny, but true. So we didn't have to light fires, the Sterno would make whatever we wanted to cook. If you had a tea bag you could make tea, or we melted chocolate. That was a treat. And how!

We had no idea what day it was. It was just another day of trying to push back German patrols. Mike McMann said to me, "Hey, Heffron, ain't tonight Christmas Eve?" I said, "How the hell do I know?" He said, "Take a look in back of us." Here the krauts were bombing the city of Bastogne. We found out later they bombed one of the hospitals. Mike said, "Christmas Eve, ain't this nice?"

We got a message that day from Gen. Anthony McAuliffe, he was our acting division commander, he's the one Babe was next to at Mass in Mourmelon. The Germans sent McAuliffe a letter asking for the 101st to surrender because they had us surrounded. We knew we were surrounded. It was the same as if we jumped in there. We're always surrounded, you understand? So we can do the job. Any other infantry unit would have had to surrender, like those kids running scared when we came in. That's why we always said, "They got us surrounded, the poor bastards." They surrounded the wrong goddamn outfit.

McAuliffe was pissed and sent back a message: "Nuts!" The Germans didn't understand what "Nuts!" meant, so McAuliffe sent another message telling them, "It means go to hell!" The American colonel that delivered the message saluted the German general—that's the protocol—and he wished him luck. He should have said, "I hope we kill all you German SOBs," but he wished him luck. He regretted saying that, but it was proper under the circumstances.

If our general would have said, "Drop your weapons," I don't think a man in the 101st would have surrendered. Wouldn't have happened. I think they would have gone against his orders. As bad off as we were, as cold as we were, as hungry as we were, as sick as we were, I don't think an American Airborne soldier could throw down his gun.

True. To a man I don't think anyone would have surrendered. The Germans had more men than we had. They figured they'd blow Bastogne off the map. And we said, "Nuts!" They thought, These guys must be crazy.

I'd have thrown my gun down if I'd seen a broad there.

You wouldn't have shot her, I know that.

★ ★ ★

Every day you got a little smarter about covering your foxhole. We always put wood across the top, put all kinds of branches, heavy stuff. But when it got to the point where the shelling knocked that off, we started looking for dead Germans and put them on top of the foxholes. They were frozen like bricks. They were heavy and we would drag them to our foxholes, and help the other guys drag them. When the shells came in, the treebursts didn't hit you, they hit the bodies. It's true. We had to stay alive, that's all, you used everything you could get your hands on. No matter what it was you used it. Everything served a purpose.

We held our lines almost ten days. December 26, some of Patton's Third Army, from the south, under Gen. Creighton Abrams—he was lieutenant colonel at the time, they broke the German lines and came through. We were no longer surrounded. Trucks were able to bring up supplies. They were able to get the wounded out of Bastogne and back to England.

When they broke through, we hoped for some relief, but there was no time for them to get help to the troops. We still had to push the Germans back, so the battles got worse instead of better. Their goal, the higher-ups, was to get the Air Force in again and hit the Germans. Some supplies came in and that was a bonus.

The guys from the armored divisions are under the impression that they saved our asses when they got to Bastogne, that they relieved us. Let me tell you, anyone in the 101st or 82nd Airborne gets burned up when we hear that. It's absolutely wrong. The word isn't "relieved." We never got relieved. The armored forces can only say they broke the siege. They did break the siege, took the pressure off us, allowed some supplies to get through, but definitely no, they did not relieve us. We held the line before they came, and we stayed on the front lines during and after, and the fighting and casualties got worse. We lost so many men in the days following Patton's Army breaking the siege that you could never call it "relieved," or "saving our asses." In fact, Patton's tanks drew more fire for us. But we needed them. We went on to spearhead the Army all the way through to the 17th of January, for a full twenty-two days after we supposedly got "relieved." It ain't fair to read something that's not the truth. I hear these armored guys walking around telling people they relieved us, and I say, "Relieved who?" I'm ready to go fist city.

★ ★ ★

Communications were getting through, so we found out the 101st was famous back home. Imagine, no info was released like it is today. It was all censored. When the Germans broke through and created the bulge and surrounded us, they identified the 101st Airborne as the ones surrounded. They thought we were goners I guess, so it was news. The 101st is surrounded! That's not news for a paratrooper. But that's how the 101st Airborne got so famous, even though many other great outfits were fighting the war, too. The 82nd Airborne was to the north of us, they were fighting just as hard as we were. The reply "Nuts" got famous, too. Another reason people came to know the 101st. Now you're getting too educated!

After Christmas, General Taylor came back and took over as commander, but nobody wanted to see Taylor. Here, the guy's the commander of the 101st Airborne, and he took time off to go and have Christmas dinner in Virginia. When we found out he was in Virginia, we couldn't believe our general left us in a spot like that, and we didn't want to hear no excuses. The guys resented it. Oh, they did, too! Nobody liked Taylor after that.

A day or two later, Jim McMahon got hit with shrapnel. Roe sent him to get treated, and he came back a couple hours later, three or four in the morning. I was in my foxhole and he said, "I got something to make you laugh. When I was getting treated they brought a badly wounded kid in, a sergeant. He was lying on a homemade stretcher and he had a 45 on him, and the radio was on and Bing Crosby was singing "White Christmas." The wounded sergeant took out his 45 and blew the radio to pieces. He said, "Come over here, you son of a bitch, I'll give you a white Christmas!'"

As good as Bing Crosby was, that soldier was in no mood to listen to that. We had snow up to our eardrums. It was one hell of a Christmas. Jim's story made everyone's day. At least we all got a laugh.

Around that time, the officers had a lottery for a thirty-day leave. They gave it to Peacock because Nixon won, but turned it down. He wouldn't leave the men on the front line. That's the kind of officer Nixon was. Peacock was more than happy to take it. We all told him, "Couldn't happen to a better guy." He thought everyone was happy for him, but he took it the opposite of how we meant it. We meant good riddance! Lieutenant Foley took over the platoon. We all liked Foley. He was a good leader, a good soldier. One of the best in Easy Company. And a real Pennsylvanian. He was from Pittsburgh.

I told you about Shifty's observation skills, and how he could use a gun. The kid was a crack shot. In Bastogne, everything looked the same every day. One day, Shifty told Lipton, "I think that tree wasn't there yesterday." The tree he saw was a mile away, and there was a whole bunch of trees there. How the hell did he concentrate on one tree? You tried looking at what he was looking at and your eyes get cockeyed. Then the tree moved. It had Germans hiding behind it with artillery. The tree gradually moved up, up, up. Lipton had to look with binoculars. Shifty saw it with his own eyes. Finally Lipton saw it move, too, and they got the forward artillery observer on it. Shifty said, "It's going to be his last move." And it was.

Brad Freeman and Buck Taylor also had skills like that, they were also outdoorsmen, but not like Shifty. The kids who grew up in the mountains and farms with guns in their hands had talents we city slickers didn't have. All we knew was robbing, stealing, going to jail, wreaking havoc. But that came in handy, too! Each man had their individual talents. When you meshed them together, that's what made us good. A good sergeant utilized those talents, knew who's gonna get the job done.

When New Year's Eve came, I was in a foxhole with Joe Toye. We got a phone call. Joe picks up the phone, and whoever was on the other end said, "We're going to give the Germans a little New Year's Eve greeting." At exactly midnight, all our artillery up and down the line was getting together to blast the Germans with a ton of ammo. When the clock hit twelve, they let loose, except the shells started to fall short, short rounds, and they were hitting right in front of us! Toye got on the phone, "Get those shells up, get 'em up! Jesus Christ, they're hitting over here!" We almost bought the farm that night. They really did give the Germans a working over, but they almost gave us one, too.

The next day, the Germans beat the hell out of us with an air raid. The sky was filled with Luftwaffe, they were hitting everything. We were lucky we didn't get the worst of it. Joe Toye got hit in the arm with a piece of shrapnel and was sent to the aid station. That was his third time hit. Toye just couldn't catch a break.

We figured we were going to be relieved any day, since Patton broke through, at least get taken off the front line for a little while. We were exhausted. We were short of men. We needed a break, a warm room, a shower, hot food, then you can rearm us and we don't care what you give us. But that's not what the higher-ups had in mind. They took care of the other units instead. I guess they figured the Airborne can take it; we'll give the other guys the ammo, we'll give *them* the supplies.

Instead of relief, Eisenhower wanted us to launch an offensive on Foy and Noville. Everybody was looking at one another, saying, "Jesus Christ, they got to be kidding." I remember Johnny Martin saying, "We're staying here? Are they kidding?" Nobody could believe it. We looked at the foxholes, we thought, *Oh my God.* Nobody could believe it, nobody. It took a little bit out of us. Nobody needed to get out of the cold more than we did. And to get away from seventy-some days on the line in Holland, and to put up with this, and they knew it, and still they wouldn't take us off the line. The guys were really burned up. The problem was, they had nobody else to send. They had the best up there and they're gonna leave the best up there. Do you know in Holland, Montgomery wouldn't let Eisenhower take the 101st or 82nd off the line because he'd have to replenish with other troops, and he didn't want to lose the best he had? A lot of men died because of it; we were exhausted. It was a mistake from the beginning. Lots of mistakes were made by guys that never once heard a shot fired.

In Bastogne, we were lucky that the Germans didn't know what they were facing; they only knew they were facing airborne troops. It kind of slowed them down a bit. They didn't want to get too aggressive because they knew they'd have to fight to the finish, too. They didn't know what we had or didn't have. If they knew, we wouldn't be sitting here today, that's for sure.

No matter what we thought about our orders, we stayed focused on what we had to do. Everybody in the company gave 100 percent.

★ ★ ★

The same day, January 1, I was on my machine gun in the woods. I heard Johnny Martin hollering that John Julian got hit. I said, "No, not Julian." My best buddy from jump school. Guys in his squad came and told me about it, and they said nobody can get to him, the krauts got him zeroed in. I left my foxhole and my squad and went to where he was. I couldn't believe it. He was shot through the throat. The kids in his squad said, "Don't try to get him, we tried and we can't." I wanted to get him away from the Germans. I also wanted to get his class ring, his wallet, his wristwatch and get them back to his family. We'd made that pact with each other in jump school. We said, "Look, if anything happens to me, make sure you get my things back to my family, make sure you call them, and make sure you do this or that." I had that pact with Julian and Henderson. The three of us had a pact.

But anytime anyone tried to go near Julian, the Germans opened up. They had a machine gun nest there and they could easily throw mortars. You can't sacrifice three, four, five men to bring back one man you know is dead.

What happened was 1st Platoon had gone out on a patrol. It was a single patrol of seven to eight men, and they went out just to reconnoiter the position and see what was out there. It was routine, but it happened that the krauts were well dug in and they had a machine gun nest at the railroad tracks. Julian was the forward point for his squad—you had guys on the right and left flank and the point is front and center—and that's what he ran into.

I couldn't get to Julian. It was an ambush. We all tried to get him. We couldn't. I was lying behind a big rock and a big mound of dirt. I was trying to get him from all angles. Sure enough, every time I tried, they fired on me. Any movement toward him, they opened up. Later one of our platoons pushed the Germans back, and Julian's squad went back and got him. They came over to me and said, "We got John's body over there if you want to see him." I said, Nah, I couldn't handle that. I didn't want to see him that way. I was shaking, we were all shaking. It was nighttime, and we just lay there in our foxholes. I never thought it was gonna be him. I guess he thought the same thing about me. We didn't imagine we'd ever buy the farm. You never get over something like that. I'm only glad he didn't suffer long. I'm glad it happened that way instead of taking one in the belly or something. It could have been a lot worse. Julian was a good kid. We took care of each other, and I knew what I had to do when I got home.

The next day, Joe Toye came back from the aid station with a sling on his arm. Winters told him to go back, but he wouldn't. Now *he* was a hero. He had his ticket out, but he wouldn't leave the men. No matter how bad he got hurt, he just kept at it. A hell of a soldier. I had the utmost respect for him. He thanked me once for carrying him back to the aid station in Holland the day Campbell was killed, and it was one of the greatest compliments I ever got, because it came from

Joe Toye, one of the greatest soldiers I ever knew. (Bill adds: "Finest Irishman I ever knew." Babe adds: "Toughest SOB I ever knew.")

Our orders were to move out and get the Germans out of the Bois Jacques woods. We had over a foot of snow, you could barely move, you had no visibility, and the Germans knew we were there. We were still fighting from every side. The biggest challenge for the sergeants was keeping contact with each other in the snow. You couldn't see a damn thing. But if you didn't maintain contact, you were done. And once the krauts break through, they'll send everything they have right through. They tried like hell to push us back with mortars and 88s, but we stood our ground and had to dig new foxholes for the night. The sergeants didn't dig foxholes, I was sharing a foxhole with Bain, and he dug it for us. It wasn't an easy job. The ground was frozen solid. Your hands are frozen solid.

That night, I was leaning on a tree, waiting to go on outpost, talking to some of the guys. Don Hoobler was in a great mood. He killed four krauts that day and was bragging about killing a kraut on horseback and looting his Belgian 32 pistol. He was showing off his new souvenir to all the guys. It was just a little bigger than your hand, and they were arguing over whether it was a Belgian 32 or a Czechoslovakian 32. I said it was Czech; the other guys said it was a Belgian 32. It ended up it was a Belgian 32.

I continued on to outpost, and about two or three o'clock in the morning, in the pitch black, I heard some artillery and small-arms fire in the distance. Then I heard a shot less than three to four yards away. I walked back to the woods to check it out and saw Hoobler lying on the ground with some troopers frantically working on him. He was saturated in blood, yelling, "Help me, help me, I'm dying!" They were trying like hell to stop the bleeding, but it was too dark to see anything. One of the guys wanted to light a light, and somebody said, "You light a light, I'll blow your goddamn head off." You couldn't—there were German tanks all around they would have annihilated everyone. It's one man or the whole company.

What happened was that Hoobler and a few of the guys were standing around talking, holding canvas shelters over their heads because the snow was falling heavily. Hoobler went to shake the snow off his canvas and the gun went off in his pocket. This pistol didn't have a safety, and Hoobler didn't have a holster. The bullet hit his leg in the main artery, so he never had a chance. He knew he was dying. He kept saying it. Before they got him out of the woods he was gone.

Makes you realize how fragile life is. A lousy accident, and a good soldier gone. I thought about the telegram that would go home to Hoobler's family in Illinois, saying "Killed in Action," no explanation, no mention of some crazy accident. Hoobler was the most gung-ho out of all of us. Guess that kraut got his revenge all the way from hell.

The next day, January 3, after a few clear days, the sky turned white and it started snowing again. We came back to our old spots in the Bois Jacques woods, and just as we reached our old foxholes, they started shelling the hell out of us. There was another company, I think Fox Company, in our foxholes while we were gone and by the time they left, the woods looked like a bunch of toothpicks. The trees were shredded. The Germans must have been watching the area. They knew as soon as we got there, and had us zeroed in.

The Germans started pounding us with artillery. When you got an artillery bombardment, shells went screaming over your head, you dove into a foxhole and crouched down as low as you could. The shelling was unbearable. Never saw so many shells in my life. It was Boom! Boom! Boom! *The ground, dirt, snow, body parts, blood, goes shooting up all around you. The ground shook like an earthquake, worse than an earthquake. The noise made you deaf. You can't believe you're still alive. If you're a sergeant, you have to make sure the men are in their holes, and then you take cover. I can tell you this: When shells were flying over your head, and you didn't know where they would land, you started making promises to the man upstairs. I said, "God, if you get me out of this place alive, I'll do anything you want." I did that probably a million times. "Get me out of here, Lord, and I'll do this or that." You make all kinds of promises. We had a guy named Leo Matz, he prayed if he got out he was going to become a priest. He became a priest as soon as the war was over, made up for all us scallywags that didn't keep our promises.*

The Germans had us zeroed in. It was horrendous, there's no way to describe it. Shells were hitting all over the place and everybody was running to get into a foxhole, anybody's foxhole. Guys were getting hit, screaming, hollering for medics all over the woods, and there were very few medics around, you understand? Joe Toye was running around trying to get everyone to take cover. Next thing I know, Joe Toye is hollering, "I'm hit, I'm hit!" I looked up and he was lying on the ground about six to eight feet away from me. His leg was blown to bits, hanging off his body, all mangled, he was bleeding all over—from the chest, back, head, arms, legs. I thought he was dead. I ran out to try and get him to safety. As soon as I got to him, Wham! A treeburst exploded above our heads. I was hit. I fell next to Joe. I felt like I was on fire, like someone took a sizzling hot poker and was burning me. I thought I was dead. My right leg was blown off, and the snow was red from all the blood. I went from burning hot to freezing. Me and Joe lay there freezing in the snow, shivering, bleeding, both of us were full of shrapnel. He said, "Jesus Christ, what the hell do I have to do to die?!" It was Joe's fifth time hit. Lipton, Malarkey, and Babe came running over to help, I was half out of it. Doc Roe was right there, trying to patch us up. Without him, we wouldn't be alive. Roe was the best medic we ever had. He was born to be a medic. You could always depend on him. You hollered, "Medic!" he was right there come hell or high water, he knew what he was doing. He was compassionate, took care of you mentally, physically, every way. They put me on a stretcher before Joe, I said, "I told you I'd beat you back to the States," and then I passed out.

★ ★ ★

I was in my foxhole on my machine gun about twenty feet away. The krauts really gave us a laddering that time, and guys were running over from other companies hollering, "We need medics, get some medics!" We told them, "Jesus Christ, we ain't got no medics to spare!" When Joe Toye got hit and then Bill, Hank Hanson told me and Ed Joint to run to the other woods and try and get another medic. I said, "Hank, they're coming over to us trying to get medics!" The only medic around was Roe; he was running around trying to take care of everybody, and he got right in there with Bill and Joe to try and stop the bleeding. They were both in bad, bad shape. I didn't think they were going to make it. None of us did. If you saw them, you wouldn't have given two cents for them. Their legs were hanging off them. I can't describe it. They were in bad shape. But they were calm. They just lay there. I tried to get a cigarette to Bill. I didn't know what else to do. There was a lot of confusion. Everybody was shook up because it was Bill and Joe. Me and Malarkey helped get them onto stretchers, and as luck would have it, a kid on a Jeep came by taking 81mm mortars to his unit, an antitank company. One of our guys, Eugene Jackson from Arnold, Pennsylvania, stopped the driver and told him, "Get these men to the aid station." The kid said, "I've got ammo to take up front." Jackson pulled his gun out and said, "The hell with the ammo! Get these men back!" One of our guys—we called him Sad Sack, because he looked like the comic strip character, and his helmet was always falling off his head—he was crying like hell, and he jumped on the Jeep to see them off. He cried for four or five days, just sat in his foxhole sobbing.

Joe Toye and Bill were the noncoms who really took care of the men. They were two tough sons of bitches, very courageous men. Bill risking his own life to save Toye—that tells you the kind of guy Bill is. He puts others before himself, to his own detriment. Losing just one of them was a blow to the platoon and the company. Losing both of them together shook us all up. You can't help thinking, *There but for the grace of God go I.*

★ ★ ★

They took me to Bastogne and medics tried to get out the shrapnel as best they could and stop the bleeding. Thanks to the medics, I got out alive. I think the cold weather coagulated your blood, otherwise we both would have bled to death. I was in extreme pain from all the shrapnel dug into my body. Since I could use the upper part of my body but not the lower part, they put me next to a kid that could not use his upper body, but could use his lower body. So I guarded him, and we helped each other, and that's how they kept your mind up. They couldn't get the wounded out to hospitals, we were still surrounded. We were out in the open, on stretchers in a churchyard somewhere; we couldn't keep warm. I was sure I wasn't going to make it. I started thinking about my mother, father, Frannie, and my brothers and sisters. I wondered, Who's going to tell them I'm dead? So many thoughts go through your mind. I thought of Henry. Mom and Pop losing two sons. It was almost a year to the day Henry died. The next day I woke up and thought, Good, I'm still here. *It took three to four days before they were able to push the Germans away and get us out. I was sent to a hospital in Paris.*

None of us knew if Bill or Joe Toye was going to make it. It didn't look good. But that Jeep coming up when it did, and Eugene Jackson ordering the driver to take them back—that may have saved their lives. Jackson was a private in our platoon who joined the company in Holland. He was a good kid.

Right after it happened, Buck Compton was evacuated. The emotional impact of seeing two of his best buddies, Bill and Joe Toye, in such a bad way was too much. I was there when he rolled up his bedroll. He had it pressed against his chest. I said, "Buck, where are you going?" He had a blank stare, he had a bad look about him. He said, "I just lost my two best buddies." Then where he went, I don't know. He must have gone back to the aid station.

Some guys could handle more than others. Compton was one of Easy Company's best officers; he was willing to put his life on the line for his men and his country without a thought. How much personal loss each man can take is another story. I don't think any of us thought less of a man for losing his emotional strength after a while. Seeing your buddies die right before your eyes, day after day takes its toll, no matter who you are. And when you see two guys like Guarnere and Toye go down, it had to affect you mentally.

On the 10th of January, the krauts started bombarding us with 88s and mortars. Just blasting us. Everyone was running for cover. I was in my foxhole talking to Muck and Penkala, who were about ten feet away. George Luz went running by to get to his hole, and Muck and Penkala were yelling, "Luz! Jump in! Jump in!" They wanted him to take cover in their foxhole. Luz ran past and jumped into his own foxhole. Just then, a shell exploded on Muck and Penkala's foxhole. Luz ran over and looked down, and there was nothing left. He said,

"They're gone." I got out of my hole and looked down. They had vanished into thin air. We were in shock. I looked up into the trees. Usually when a tree burst exploded and someone was hit, body parts went flying, and since we were in the forest, they went flying up into the trees. There was nothing in the trees. There was nothing left. Nothing but a hole.

Even while you're mourning the loss of your buddies, you can't help thinking that it could have been you. You can't help being glad to be alive. I was right there. Instead of going a few feet to the left, the shell went a few feet to the right.

I thought back to the Mass Muck and I had been to a few weeks earlier, and Father Maloney saying, "The Catholic faith is the hardest to live by but the easiest to die by." I thought how sincere that was and how much it made sense. Muck died in a state of grace. I still think of Muck every time I take communion.

In mid-January, we were advancing toward Foy for an attack. The snow was at least a foot deep. You could barely move, between the snow and the equipment we had on us. The snow kept falling and we had been marching for what seemed like hours. My mind went back to a movie I'd seen a few years back called *The Fighting 69th*, with James Cagney and Pat O'Brien. There's a scene where Jeffrey Lynn, playing the poet Joyce Kilmer, is marching with his men through the snow, and he recites a poem. Of course, I couldn't recall the poem at the time.

I saw a dead trooper on the ground. He was from the 501st. His hands were up in front of his face in a catcher's stance, like he saw what was coming and tried to catch it. His helmet and bazooka lay beside him, and his black, wavy hair was blowing in the wind. Two dead kraut soldiers were lying next to him, frozen and twisted with pain on their faces. I thought, *Here's a kid who looks like any Italian American kid hanging out on the street corner in South Philly.*

In Foy, we had to go about a mile through an open field to get to the village, and we were advancing out in the open. We were crouched down in the snow waiting for an order, and Dike froze, he couldn't give an order. The Germans starting firing at us. Johnny Martin's platoon was up front and they were taking a licking. There were Germans all around, and they killed Frankie Mellett and Harold Webb. Perconte got shot in the ass. Winters sent Speirs in to relieve Dike. I was on my machine gun covering the platoon, right next to Dike, when Speirs came running over and told Dike he was taking over. That day Speirs took command of the company for the rest of the war. A couple of the German snipers were taken prisoner and killed. Shifty Powers took out a couple of them. He was the guy when you had snipers to take out.

Later we were exchanging fire with the krauts in the woods when a lost German patrol strayed into my path. I opened fire and really got my kills.

We dug in outside of town, freezing to death, some of us with our burlap bags still on our feet. It tested our endurance, taking the dirt and the filth, being so cold, with no relief, no way to warm yourself. You had to lay there and freeze and when your buddy got in the foxhole with you, you had a little body heat.

At one point I looked up and saw our battalion commander wearing fur-lined boots. I thought, *Where the hell did he get them from?!* Some of the officers took care of themselves first, even though the men on the front line were the ones in need. The higher the rank, the less you saw of them. Whether it was back on garrison or in combat, some of them were soldiers' soldiers, and others we considered outsiders. Winters was a soldiers' soldier. He took care of his men. He was the best leader Easy Company ever had. After him the best officers were Foley, Compton, and Welsh. And it was our NCOs that made the company what it was. The worst was Dike. I don't think he was a coward, I just think he just was a bad leader. He was scared to see men get killed. He was one of the guys who couldn't lead men, and some officers who *could* lead couldn't hold a glove to Bill and the rest of our noncoms.

★ ★ ★

I was transferred from Paris to a hospital in England, then Scotland, then back to the U.S. When I was in England, I wrote to Johnny Martin. He wasn't there when I got hit, and I wanted to tell him what happened, tell him I was alive, and to take care of the men. He wrote me back January 12, 1945: "Dear Bill, I received your letter today . . . Anything you asked me in the letter I'll do. You know that. As far as what went on after you left, you've probably read it in the papers . . . it was plenty rough . . . and I'll tell you later about who got it and who didn't. Well, Bill . . . I'm going to see you whether it be soon or a long time, but I'm going to see you no matter what . . . Bill, when I got your letter, I was at the Co. CP. Of course, everyone was interested to hear from you. Well, they said read it out loud. Well, the Co and the rest of company headquarters were there. I got halfway through and started to cry in front of all the guys. I just had to take off, Bill. Boy, I never felt so hollow inside in all my life. From now on when you write, please . . . leave anything about your leg out of my letters. Just do it as a favor for me. I guess I'm not near as good a man as I thought I was. Boy, for the first time, I never had any control of myself. When I heard you were hurt, I got all the poop I could, but you know where we were, and I couldn't possibly get to see you.

All the guys told me how you took it cooler than anybody yet. Laying there shooting the shit when you were hit like that. Some guys about shit when they get nicked with a bullet and you get hit like that and just shoot the shit. Well, I just want to tell you right now, you're so much better of a man than I am it isn't even funny. I don't mean only in combat either. You're better than any officer or EM I've ever seen or ever will. You're the first guy whom I've ever met I could hit it with and it's just because you're such a swell guy . . . For God's sake, Bill, don't let it get you down . . . I know you're the kind of guy who will see it through to the end . . . I expect to have a lot of fun when we get back to the States. Buddy, we'll rip her apart when I get back. When I go to bed tonight, I am going to pray that I get a furlough to England. I hear they are going to send them out . . . Well, I suppose you want to know what changes there are in the battalion. Our CO is now Lieutenant Speirs from D Company. I think he's the best one we've had yet. There is a new officer in charge of 2nd Platoon. Welsh is S-3 and we have a new S-2 officer. Nixon is Regiment S-3 . . . I'll close now, and if I don't get a couple of letters a week from you, I'll be disappointed . . . So long for now. Your pal, 'Jason' Martin."

When I read the letter, I couldn't believe it. That was a side of Johnny I never seen. We were in and out of trouble together, me and Johnny. He was a good soldier and a good friend. I guess it shook him up. I think we wrote a couple letters back and forth before I was transferred to Scotland.

In Paris and England, they just tried to get all the shrapnel out, keep me bandaged up, gave me medication to keep me alive. When I got to Scotland, they operated to take off whatever was left below the mid-thigh. You're wide awake when they do the operation, they numb you, but you're awake. When they were at the end of the operation, the doctor reached up to grab a saw, like we were in a butcher shop. I thought, Holy cow. They said they were going to trim the bone. I said to the nurse, "Put your hands on my skidonies, so they don't saw that off." Everybody laughed, but she did it. I never forgot her, a little nurse from Boston named Rose Kramer.

I felt lucky to be alive. What I saw in the hospitals was so horrible it can't be described. One thing I'll never get out my head is the smell of burned flesh. I get sick just thinking about it.

Most of the GIs went home by boat, but the more serious cases, they flew home. On the flight home from Scotland, we were supposed to land in New York, but they had engine trouble over Newfoundland. The props started sputtering, everybody was getting nervous, and I was lying there on a stretcher, and the plane was going up, it was going down, and you don't know what's going to happen. So I said to myself, I'll be damned if I'm going to go through this whole damn war to wind up going down in the ocean. I unstrapped myself from the stretcher and hopped out and I said to the nurse, "Give me a goddamn parachute. I'm going out the door." I figured if the plane goes down, I'm going down with a swan dive. I'll take my chance in the water. She told me to get back on the stretcher. I said, "I'll kick that door open and jump out of this plane." Finally the plane leveled off, and we did an emergency landing in Gander, Newfoundland.

★ ★ ★

One day in mid-January, just before we were going to advance and take Noville, which was just beyond Foy, I picked up my machine gun, and I couldn't move my hands. They were numb, and my wrist was in excruciating pain like I used to get playing football at home and throwing cases of whiskey at work. I started rubbing them and rubbing them with the ice that had formed on the machine gun to get them good and cold and loosen them up. I couldn't wear gloves, the gloves were soaking wet. So I put my hands in my pockets when

I wasn't carrying my gun. The pain was so severe, I couldn't even hold my machine gun. For days, I ignored pain in both my hands and feet, because I wasn't about to leave the line. But at this point, I wasn't worth a damn. I couldn't hold anything and my feet were turning black. I didn't want to tell anyone. You felt guilty about complaining when you saw what was going on around you. I ended up in the hospital for five days and four nights. The captain there told me he hadn't seen this condition since he treated pregnant women. I said, "Doctor, I assure you, I'm not pregnant!" He said my calcium was too low and sent me to a hospital in Liège, Belgium, quite a truck ride away. I have to say this: I never would have let them put a medical tag on me to go to Liège, Belgium, if Guarnere and Toye were still with us. I would have never left them. I didn't care how much pain I was in. When they were around, I stuck it out. I would have run right back to the unit. I put up with the pain in Holland and in jump school. I think I never would have made Toccoa, so I'm glad it worked out the way it did. I did what I wanted to do. I got to fight with the best unit in the Army, even with my hands the way they were.

The kid in the next bed, they were taking both his legs off in the morning. The nurse heard me talking and said, "You're from South Philly?" She knew the accent. She said, "You're a Two Streeter." Turned out she graduated Catholic school with a girl from Mifflin Street, who was a member of my parish. "You look like an old man," she said to me. Those six words really affected me. That's what war will do, turn a nineteen-year-old kid into an old man. She put my feet up on a pillow and gave me three big saucers of dehydrated milk. After four days the captain said, "There's nothing more we can do, you're a walking case." I had to go AWOL to get back to Easy Company. The nurse knew what I was doing and gave me a bottle of champagne for the trip. On the way out, I bumped into two kids from Fox Company, Farley and Green, and the three of us hitchhiked our way back. Sergeant Green was from Georgia, and he and I hit it off. We made a date to go to Paris as soon as we got off the line.

★ ★ ★

The Germans attacked Alsace-Lorraine on the France-Germany border, so the entire regiment was sent up to Hagenau to relieve another outfit and hold the line there. They knew they couldn't use us to do any more pushing, Jesus Christ, we didn't have anybody left. But they put us in a defensive position, to prevent the Germans from breaking through, and we set up at the edge of the Moder River. We were on one side of the river and the Germans were on the other. It was a big change from Bastogne, because we stayed in houses. Every platoon had their own house. We could even do OP duty sometimes from inside a house.

We switched off on outpost duty every couple hours and sent out patrols to keep an eye on the krauts and try and push them back. I was on outpost along the river one day, when a guy swam up and was climbing up on the bank carrying something. As soon as I saw him, I laid into him with my rifle. He had no business being there, and no one ever said a word to me about it.

We did some firing back and forth, but it wasn't constant. We shelled them, they shelled us. And let me tell you, they had this huge railroad gun behind their lines that had us on edge. It was a 205mm cannon attached to a railroad car. They didn't have many of them in operation—they were from World War I, and they weren't very mobile, but boy, oh, boy. Ooh! They'd fire one round of that railroad gun, and let me tell you, you could feel the ground shake, and then you looked up in the sky, because it was so heavy, it would go chug-chug-chug-chug over your head. No speed. You could hear it cutting the air. You couldn't see it but you could hear it, and it was so slow moving, and we thought, *Oh my God, where is this going to hit?* You knew it was going to be a hell of a shell. These shells could take out a whole house. Once it goes over your head, you know you're all right. There's a rule of thumb: You never hear the shell that hits you. Shells travel faster than sound, so by the time you do hear it, it's on you. Once they fired a round of that gun, they had to move their position, because all we had to do was go look for the railroad. Once a day, twice a day, they fired that damn gun.

I stayed in a house along the riverbank. One day I wrote my friend Tony Cirigilo a letter. I couldn't say where I was because our mail was being censored, but the officer was kind enough not to decode our letters if we promised not to put our location. So I wrote, "As I am writing this letter I hear shrapnel hitting the back door." I got a letter back from Tony a few weeks later that said, "Babe, as you are hearing shrapnel hitting the back door, all I hear while sitting in my parlor is the Number Five trolley going up Third Street." Boy, that hit home. I thought of my dad, who got that trolley every morning to go to work up in Holmesburg, Pennsylvania. I knew that sound of the Number Five trolley going up Third Street. But also, I felt bad for Tony. He wanted to fight the war like the rest of us—the guy could street fight like a son of a bitch, but he was 4F, meaning he got a medical discharge for his perforated eardrums.

One night when I was in the house, there was a bang on the door. You know it's not a kraut knocking on the door. They'd throw a grenade and blow the house apart, like we did. Someone hollered, "Is Heffron in there?" and it wasn't familiar. It was a kid from Fox

Company. He said Sergeant Green won't be able make that date to Paris. I said, "Did he get wounded?" He said, "No, he was killed last night. He stepped on a land mine." Green had told this kid, "If anything happens to me, go see Heffron in Easy Company, Tell him I won't be able to make that date in Paris."

A week after we got there, regiment wanted a night patrol across the river to get some prisoners. Every platoon was involved. Ken Mercier, one of our best sergeants, led one of the patrols. Mercier was a professional soldier. He was in the Army before the war; he knew his job, you didn't have to tell him anything. One Lung McClung was lead scout. I was on my machine gun to provide covering fire, we had our guns aimed at the German outpost. Once they got the prisoners, they signaled us, and we started firing everything we had— rifles, machine guns, mortars, artillery, everything, and the Germans started firing back. It was a hell of a fight. When they got back, Eugene Jackson, who was on the patrol—he was the one who helped save Bill and Joe Toye—had been hit by a grenade. A German dropped a grenade from the third floor of a building, and it hit Jackson in the brain. He was screaming in pain, hollering, "Where's Mercier! Get me Mercier! I want Mercier!" He knew he was dying. Mercier walked over and held his hand while they were carrying him away, and right after Mercier got to him, he died.

The patrol brought back a couple good prisoners, so Sink wanted another patrol to go out the next night. Winters told Sink he'd take care of it, then told the men he wasn't sending anyone out, but they'd report they went out and couldn't get any prisoners. Winters knew what he was doing. The krauts would have been ready for us. It would have been a disaster. He led by common sense, not standard operating procedure. He could have got himself in big trouble defying orders, but he was willing to take that chance to save a few lives. No one ever said another word about it.

After a few weeks, we were finally relieved. We had two and a half months of fighting, and we were sent back to Mourmelon by train, on forty-and-eights, these old World War I jobs, it had boxcars that were open at the top. When we got back, we were in a different section of Mourmelon than before, we were billeted in tents, but we got showers and new uniforms. We were beat the hell up but we felt like a million bucks. You really appreciate the simple things, like clean clothes and showers, when they're taken away for a while.

We spent most of the time on training exercises with the replacements that came in. A couple weeks after we got there, we had a division parade. Nobody liked a parade, regardless of who was coming. You put a new tie on, you shine your wings and your boots, and you're out there and it can be a hundred degrees or thirty degrees, and nobody wants to hear officers talk and talk and don't say nothin'. But we were all hepped up because Ike was coming. The entire 101st was being awarded the Presidential Distinguished Unit Citation for our defense at Bastogne. We were happy we were getting the citation because we deserved that, I'll tell ya, for our stand at Bastogne. We were the first division ever to get so honored. But we didn't mind standing out there, not for the medal, not for the decoration, but for Ike. He was the coolest. All the guys loved him. (He got my vote twice when he ran for president; I think he might be the last guy Bill ever voted for.) We opened ranks, and we were all at attention—you looked straight ahead—and Ike walked down the line and congratulated some of the guys personally. He stopped and asked me where

I was from. I said Pennsylvania. He said "What city?" I told him Philadelphia. He said, "That's a beautiful city." He wished me good luck, and walked on and spoke to a few more of the men.

At the end of March, we got orders that we were moving out. We had a Mass with Father Maloney, and we went up on trucks into Germany.

8

---⭐---

GERMANY: NOW I KNOW WHY WE'RE HERE

Spring and Summer 1945

BABE

We took up positions in the Ruhr pocket near Düsseldorf, guarding the bank of the Rhine River. The platoons took turns on outpost duty by the river, or went out on patrols. We stayed in houses, which was a nice change from a frozen foxhole. But the town was in shambles, it was heavily bombed by Allied forces because it was an industrial town. They produced a lot of steel, and it was one of their major seaports.

When we got into Germany, the Allied troops started finding forced labor camps the Germans had. The krauts had imprisoned people from Russia, Poland, Hungary, Czechoslovakia, most of Eastern Europe. The Allied soldiers set them free and put them in camps for displaced persons until they could get them situated. Part of our job, in addition to guarding the Rhine, was to guard the DPs.

When we weren't on outpost, we were searching house to house, flushing out the Germans, killing who we had to. Four of us were in a rural area and we came upon a house with a German farmer inside, and he must have seen us coming because he ran over to his pot-bellied stove and was trying to burn a book. I grabbed it from him. The book was *Mein Kampf*, which means "my struggle," by Hitler. I took it; I still have it, and you can see the edges of it are frayed, and the German farmer had his name in it, too—Schmidt. He was defi-ant. You could see he must have been a veteran from WWI, because he was that old. We left him there because he didn't try anything. If he had—and he was thinking about it believe me, he was going on about how great Hitler was, how wonderful Germany was, he was saying, *"Heil Hitler!"*—we would have killed him. But he was an old man. He was a loser. Let him dream.

Those Germans, they loved Hitler, boy. A German peasant said to me when we took over Düsseldorf, he said "Why shouldn't we be good to Hitler when he gives us all this?" And he waved his hand to show me how beautiful the land was. And it was. The beauty of Germany was breathtaking. It was the most beautiful place I'd ever seen. But I knew some of it was at the expense of the people in France, Holland, Belgium, and Norway. The Germans were bringing in baby farm animals, produce, and slave labor from those countries. These people had to have known it was coming from somewhere.

One thing that happened in Düsseldorf, I've had nightmares about it for sixty-three years. About what could've happened, not about what *did* happen. I was leading a patrol with three guys from my squad. Our orders were to clean out one side of town. We were going house to house when we came across a bomb shelter. Standard operating procedure was to throw a grenade into the bunker, then kick open the door. A voice in my head told me *Don't throw that grenade!* I told one of the guys I was with, a kid from North Carolina, to hold his grenade, and I held mine. I had a Tommy gun in one hand and a grenade in the other. I took a risk and kicked open the door.

What we saw took our breath away. A young girl about twenty years old was standing there, with two little toddlers holding on to her dress and an old couple standing behind her. They were scared to death. The mother was talking to the children in German trying to calm them. They must have heard us coming, and when I kicked the door open, they thought they'd be killed. We looked at them, and we didn't say a word, but we threw some candy and chocolate from our pockets onto the ground, and we left. If we had followed orders and thrown the grenade, an innocent family would have been killed. Innocent children would have been killed. I have nightmares that I *did* throw the grenade.

Outside, me and the other troopers looked at each other. One of the guys said to me, "Jigger, what in the hell made you hold that grenade?" I said, "With the look on your faces, I know I did the right thing." It left me wondering for days, *What would I have been? What would have happened to me? Would I have become a vegetable?* I know I couldn't have lasted, I couldn't have lived, after killing little children. Later that day, another Easy Company man said, "Aaaah, it's war, what's the difference, they're krauts. If you did it, it was an accident." I said, "No. No, not the children. I was told since I was a little boy that you can't blame the children for the sins of a father." I learned that from the nuns, and how true it is. He said, "You know, my parents used to say that, too." I saw these babies and it didn't matter who or what their fathers were. Even Bill said to me when I told him this story, "I couldn't picture you being around after that, Babe."

I didn't even want to talk about this experience, but Bill wanted me to. Talking about what could have been. But you want people to know the hell and reality of this and how it affects you for the rest of your life. I hope the woman's husband lived through the war and knew that an American soldier refused to follow orders and didn't kill his children.

Bill and I talk about what made a good leader, and I was not a leader. Maybe I shouldn't have been leading men, taking a squad. Winters said, "Babe, you went against the book, but I'm glad you did." Luckily it all worked out.

Another day, Ralph Spina and I went out on a patrol, and we saw a house and went to check it out. Inside, a group of men, maybe eight or ten, were cooking and setting food out, and we hit the place, got them against the wall, searched them, and took whatever we found. They said "Please don't take the food, this is the only food we have." Spina spied a metal box, like you throw change in, and he said "What do you think's in there, Babe?" and it was full of German marks, and I mean full, too. And this guy was trying to tell me it was the payroll for the people that worked there. We didn't care about that. We told them to shut the hell up. We said, "You ought to be glad we don't shoot you." They were in civilian clothes. I don't know if they were soldiers, but we didn't have any trouble with them. We searched the whole house, went into the cellar—infantry procedure—and there was nothing there. So we assumed they were maybe ex-soldiers.

We took the payroll and went back to our quarters and sat on our beds and had a drink and tried to figure out what to do with the money. The next day was a Sunday, and we went over to the church in town and gave the money out to people coming out of church. We knew them, they were DPs that had just been liberated. We figured they deserved it. Of course we kept half of it for ourselves.

Things started to quiet down in the area, because the Germans started surrendering, about a few hundred thousand of them in the Ruhr pocket. But we had to be careful, because they were still fighting, there was still some machine-gun and sniper fire going back and forth. We continued daily patrols and outpost duty there for about a month, until the end of April. Then we got on forty-and-eights, and headed up to Bavaria, where Hitler's Eagle's Nest was. After a few days on the train, we boarded DUKWs, amphibious vehicles that move in water like boats, and then wheels come out and they can drive on land. They look like boats with wheels and they go about forty miles an hour. We went up to Bavaria on the autobahn. It was the most beautiful road I ever saw. Four lanes. Well paved. Very pristine. The men couldn't get over it. The scenery, especially around Heidelberg, was breathtaking—winding mountain roads, beautiful villages, deep green forests and lush greenery everywhere, snowcapped mountains in the background. Everything was beautiful. I couldn't believe how clean and pristine everything was. The Germans and the Dutch are the cleanest people I ever saw. Even during a firefight, you'd see them out sweeping their pavements.

We stopped for a couple days in the area of Landsberg. Somebody told us there was a concentration camp up there. We went up, and the scene was devastating. All we could do was look at each other with our mouths open. We couldn't believe what we were seeing. It was bad. Hundreds of prisoners in black-and-white-striped uniforms. They were like skeletons. They could barely stand. There were piles of burned bodies all over the camp. The odor made us all sick. A couple guys were puking, some were crying.

This camp didn't have ovens and gas chambers. Their death was to be starved and burned and buried alive in mass graves. Eddie Stein, he was my assistant machine gunner and my friend, he broke down next to me. He said, "Babe, can you believe what man can do to man?" He said, "They're my people." I said, "Ed, I know." He had me crying. None of us had any idea. How the hell they endured that I'll never know. I grew up with Jewish kids. I thought of them when I seen this—the Jewish people at home, and how lucky they were to live in America.

Ralph hollered, "Come over here." We walked a few feet away from the camp, and there was an abandoned train. You could smell it before you got to it. The smell was overwhelming, sickening. Ralph slid the train door open and the inside it was stacked full of dead bodies. I said, "Why the hell did you have to show me that." It was a sight I'll never get out of my head. We knew it was all Jews from the concentration camp. We walked back to the camp. If any of the guys didn't know why we were fighting the war, they knew then.

We had to wait for someone to come up and delouse the camp before they could open the metal gates and let us make body contact with them. The gates were locked. Before we got there, the Germans found out we were coming, locked them, and ran away. Eddie kept saying, "I'd like to kill those bastards." Eddie wasn't the kind of guy to look for a fight. A good guy. He was old for the paratroopers; he was twenty-four. We called him Dad and Pop, because we were eighteen, nineteen. I joined when Eddie did, but he was in a different barracks in jump school. He wasn't as close to me as Julian and J. D., but we got closer in Germany when he became my assistant machine gunner.

There was a young Hungarian Jewish girl, she had her hands on the bars, and she was looking through at us. She was crying, and she kept saying, "You are my heroes, my angels, my God, we're free, we're free at last." She had naturally curly, red hair down to her shoulders. She was beautiful. About nineteen years old. She should have looked fifty with what she'd been through. I couldn't stop looking at her. I said to one of the guys, "Boy, she's *shayna*" (German or Jewish for beautiful). A Polish slave laborer from a nearby farm heard me, and he looked at me and said, "*Shayna*, huh?" I said, "Yes, a beautiful girl." He said, "She was the German officers' favorite." Oh, boy, that hit me. *The German officers' favorite.* It got me sick. And Eddie, too, he started crying more. I thought to myself, imagine if that was your own sister, or your daughter. I can see her clearly today. She didn't have the striped garb the other prisoners had. She had women's clothes. She got treated differently.

That young girl really affected me, I never forgot her. Maybe because she reminded me of a beautiful redhead back home named Claire Wilhelm who I was in love with and would have liked to marry. I wrote to her during the war. I don't even know if she would have had me—there were a lot of guys after her—but she died just after I got home. I didn't realize it until later, but that might be one of the reasons I never forgot that beautiful Hungarian girl.

If anyone ever tells you the Holocaust didn't happen, or that it wasn't as bad as they say, no, it was worse than they say. What we saw, what these Germans did, it was worse than you can possibly imagine. It burns me up when I think about it, because lots of countries knew about it and let it happen. Jewish people tried to escape by boat, thirty-five-hundred of them, and they were turned away from every country they went to, even the United States, and ended up back in Germany and were killed. Everyone in America, their families immigrated here so they could have better lives. It wasn't fair.

★ ★ ★

We left there and headed south to Berchtesgaden, where Hitler's Eagle's Nest was. All Hitler's top officers, the Nazi leaders and the top SS officials, lived there. We were all talking about outflanking the British and French to get there first. Everyone was trying to outrun each other.

I can't imagine what the residents of the towns must have been thinking as we drove past them on DUKWs, and their own German soldiers were surrendering and walking down the middle of the road, just looking at us as we drove past. But this gives you an idea: At a town where we stopped for the night—I think it was Bad Reichenhall—a soldier from the 101st came running over hollering, "Get a medic! We need a medic!" We asked if one of our guys was hit; we weren't encountering much resistance. He told us the *Bürger-meister*—the town's mayor—killed himself, his wife, and their three children. He found them all dead on the couch. As we got closer to Bertchesgaden, thousands more German soldiers surrendered and were walking the streets. You saw a dead SS soldier here and there, and as we drove by a wooded area to our left, on the edge of the woods, we saw a bunch of SS on their knees, and the French soldiers were giving them each a bullet to the head. The French hated the Germans, even though they let the Germans have their country without firing a shot. They had every right to kill them. The SS were Hitler's loyalists. They were Nazis. They started training to serve Hitler from ten years old. They loved him, they would rather die than surrender. We all looked over and said, "Kill the bastards!" We didn't have to fire a shot, the French were doing it for us. The entire way up, we saw dead SS in their black uniforms lying on the ground. They fought right to the end.

May 5th, Easy Company took Berchtesgaden. We were the first ones in, with the rest of 2nd Battalion following us. French forces came in after us, along with other American units. We had no resistance. The place was crawling with SS, so we had to be careful of any radicals. But most of the resistance we got was from the residents when we looked for houses to stay in. Winters had to order the people out.

There were a lot of beautiful homes in Berchtesgaden, especially the Nazi officials', with wine cellars and luxuries. I can tell you there was a lot of looting and drinking going on. The Eagle's Nest, Hitler's home, was very beautiful. It was right on the border of Austria in the Alps. The scenery was the most beautiful I've ever seen. When we got to the Eagle's Nest, we had to secure it, and then we went in, and everybody took what they wanted. The house was elevated, and the room where all the booze was—downstairs—was where all the guys wanted to go. We could have stayed there for twenty years. Hitler had enough food and booze to last twenty years. We did some drinking there. I didn't drink much, it was all wine and champagne, which I don't drink, but I had some champagne on Hitler. The one who really took advantage of the booze was one of our lieutenants, Lewis Nixon. The guys called him Blue Beard, he needed to shave two times a day, but he never did. There's a picture of him in *Band of Brothers* that shows him the morning after he got ahold of Hitler's wine.

We were only in Berchtesgaden a couple days, but we had a lot of work to do. We set up a main line of resistance and put guards out. Thousands of Germans were surrendering and we had to direct them to POW points, get their weapons, and keep order. The German soldiers were all in step, they tried to stay in step, they were proud. They went in as soldiers and they were going out as soldiers. Most of them didn't look at us. They kept their heads down. But a couple looked over and gave a weak smile. They were glad it was over. They were going home to their families. We were hoping that was really the end of it.

I was guarding a crossroads, on roadblock, directing vehicles and prisoners of war where to go when a big, black new model German car pulled right up next to me, with a German colonel in the passenger side. There were no women, no other cars. He said, "I have a general here, General Tolsdorf, he wants to surrender to someone of equal rank, and we would appreciate it if you would get someone." I thought it was strange that the general was driving the colonel. I said, "Tell him to get out of the car." The general was a big, strapping guy. I said, *"Kommen Sie hier!"* He got out, and he came up and saluted me, and I did not return the salute. That made him mad. But I didn't care about him. I lost buddies. I ain't hand-saluting that son of a bitch. I found out later it was General Theodor Tolsdorf, commander of the army we were fighting in the Bois Jacques woods.

I said, "You want to see someone of equal rank? Good." I wanted to get my hands on the keys and clean the car out, see what was in there. One of our lieutenants was across the way. I called him over, and said, "I have a German general who wants to surrender," and he took him to Colonel Sink. They walked away, and I got in the car and stripped everything out that I thought was valuable. There were maps, a German Luger, Iron Crosses, and five hundred obscene photographs. It wasn't your ordinary pornography. It was human sexual organs shaped into furniture. Dirty pictures of furniture! Couches, chairs, beds. The couch arms were carved into the shape of a penis, the middle of the couch was shaped like a vagina. Five hundred pictures like that. I heisted most of the stuff I found and took it home, the Luger, the pictures, and the Iron Crosses. Afterward, I leaned against the car and thought, *Wow. A kid from South Philly, a private first class from South Philly, having a German general surrender to him. Not bad.*

That happened May 7. On May 8, the war was over. Second Battalion was sent to Zell am See, while the other battalions waited back at Berchtesgaden to be relieved. We stopped at Saalfelden, and stayed there at least a week, overseeing thousands of DPs from all over Europe.

We needed places to stay and the Austrians didn't want to give up their houses. They were meaner to us than the Germans were. They were big into Adolf. Winters went around and ordered them to get out of their houses. He said, "These men aren't going to sleep in the ground again. You will get out, or we'll take further measures." He'd have thrown them all in prison. Winters was laid back, but if you got him burned up, he was something to see. You didn't mess with him. If you didn't take care of his men, he'd see that it happened.

The Austrians all had swastikas in their houses, and we really did some looting there. That's where I got some good stuff. I took a gold sword with a swastika on it, it was encrusted with stones. I figured it was worth something.

After about five or six days, we got transferred to Kaprun, where we stayed for a few months. Our job was to go house to house flushing out German soldiers, and taking over homes. You had to watch yourself. Every night we had guard duty. That the war was over didn't mean nothing. You had the radicals. Austria was SS country. The whole time in Germany and Austria, I never saw one SS surrender. I seen them getting killed—they were defiant. Every ten to fifteen feet the SS were lying dead. We assumed the French got to them.

The entire 506th occupied the northern part of the country—in Saalfelden, Kaprun, and Zell am See. Headquarters was in Zell am See. We stayed on occupational duty, guarding and overseeing the displaced persons who were freed from work camps, and guarding weapons depots where all the German guns and vehicles were being stored. You had to guard them so the SS didn't break in and take them; we kept them under lock and key. We never knew when something was going to start up again. We had more trouble with the Austrians than anyone else. They didn't want us there. They treated us worse than the Germans did. But we had no sympathy for them.

As soon as we got there, I took some men on a patrol, and Ralph Spina tagged along in case some SS troopers were still in the mood for a fight and we needed a medic. My patrol hit a house, and an elderly man greeted us at the door and told us he needed help, because his wife was very sick. Ralph went upstairs with the man and I took the rest of the men to the back of the house and the cellar to check the place out. Ralph hollered for me to come upstairs, and when I got there, he was holding the woman by the wrist. I made a bad joke; I said to Ralph, "Are you running with that broad already?" He said, "What's the matter with you, Heffron. The woman is dead." The man wanted a priest to give his wife last rites. His son was saying in German, "We need a priest, we need to get a priest!" I told the man he had to take his wife out back and bury her. We didn't know what she died of, we couldn't take any chances, and I wasn't going to let anyone go running around to find a priest. My orders were that dead bodies had to be buried immediately. I made like I was shoveling, I said, "You bury her." We didn't stay to see if they buried her, we assume they did. Being a Catholic myself, I felt awful, I felt like a louse, but orders outranked my personal feelings. I told him he could do what he wanted when the war was over. I imagine later he gave her a proper burial.

I spent my twenty-second birthday, May 16, on occupational duty. I didn't even know it was my birthday, every day goes into the next. In war, you don't know what day it is, or where you are most of the time. But like that girl back in the hospital in Belgium said, I was old. I felt old. That's what a year and a half of combat will do to you. I also had a relapse of something around that time. My throat was all inflamed, and they traced it to my tonsils. I felt like I was on fire. So they took care of it as best they could and told me to get my tonsils taken out when I got home, which I never did.

The DPs in Kaprun were mostly Polish, French, Hungarian, and Russian Jews, and they thought we were the greatest thing since the wheel. We had a nonfraternization policy with the German and Austrian civilians, but we could go with the DPs, so we spent a lot of time with them. Talk about happy people. They had potato booze buried in the ground. They called it schnapps, and it was good stuff. We stayed in Kaprun for a few months. We helped them get situated in Austrian houses, but a lot of them wanted to just sleep outside on the ground. "No more locks and beatings," a little Polish girl named Annie said to me. She was cute as a button, short, with blond hair and big blue eyes. "We are free like butterflies," she said. Boy, there were some beautiful girls in that camp, and once they got cleaned up, you had the best companions in the world. Many of the troopers found women to be with, a couple of guys married them. I ended up lying with Annie, and we would spend hours talking and laughing. She was only eighteen. We were both young and both had seen death and destruction all around us. She said to me, "Eddie, it's been a long time since I laughed," and it made me wish I could drop her and the other DPs in the center of the good old U.S. to show them how great it is to live in a free country. They loved hearing stories about Philly, New York, and Chicago. The French DPs were moody and stuck to themselves, but the Russians and the Polish people loved to drink and dance. We held dances in the village many nights, and these people were so joyous, it was the most fun I ever had in my life. Funny thing was, you never saw the Austrians around. They resented the way we catered to the slave laborers. We wanted to give them some joy after all they had been through.

We got a lot of downtime in Austria, some peace of mind, a bed. They had indoor plumbing—you didn't find that in Holland, or Belgium, or France. The scenery was beautiful, the mountains, and the lakes, and the forests. Some of the guys went hunting. A fella named Lampis, who was sergeant of the mortar squad, he took me hunting with them one day. I saw a mountain goat, I said, "What the hell is that?" It had big curved horns on it. They were all over the place. I said, "Well, I'm not going to kill the son of a bitch, but I ain't letting him near me, either!" I never went hunting again.

We were there two and a half months when the Austrians started coming around and talking to us. They started to like us. We never hurt nobody. We gave the kids candy. Like I said, you can't blame the children for the sins of the father.

Things were pretty peaceful until one night, we got word that Chuck Grant got shot in the head by a crazed, drunk American soldier. Right away, we all went up to the area to try and track down the guy who shot him. Sure enough, one of the squads got him. We all wanted to string the son of a bitch up. Nobody wanted him to get back to the States because he'd get twenty years or something and be let go. When I saw the guy, he was half drunk, pleading innocent. They took him into a room, and everybody was trying to crowd in. They were going to kill him on the spot. One of the troopers said, "We're going to shoot him or hang him." Then an officer killed the whole thing. He said, "We got to make sure it's the right man." That's the American justice system. No one seen him shoot Grant, so they had no proof. This guy was a crazy son of a bitch. Raped a German girl, killed an English major to take his Jeep, and shot Grant.

Chuck's squad got him to an Austrian doctor, who did a hell of a job on him, saved his life. But he was left with some brain damage. It was terrible, one of those strange things that happens. Chuck was one of the best guys and one of the best soldiers in the platoon. Loved life. Loved women. Sharp as a tack, too. But that all changed after he got shot. He was in the hospital for a while, and they sent him home. He came to a couple of our reunions, but life was hard for him, it was tough to see him like that. For that to happen after the war was over was hard to take.

Our training schedule started up again because it was assumed we were heading to the Pacific. Rumor was that we were getting a thirty-day leave, and then heading over there. None of us were happy about it. At the end of July, we boarded a train for Joigny, France. It was a forty-and-eight, so it was open at the top, didn't move very fast. Annie got there when the train was leaving, she had a little suitcase with her, and she started chasing the train down the tracks, yelling, "Eddie, Eddie!" Ralph Spina and a couple of the guys grabbed me and hung me upside down out the boxcar by my ankles. Someone had me by the belt buckle, and Ralph had me by the boots, and was yelling, "Here's Eddie! Here he is!" She ran after us for a while, and then she gave up. I kind of missed her for a year or so. She was cute as a button.

We were on garrison duty in France for about a month, and in August, we got great news: we weren't going to the Pacific. The U.S. dropped a bomb on Hiroshima, the Japanese surrendered, and the war was over. We were so relieved. It was the greatest thing that could have happened. Somebody once said to me that the bomb was the worst thing that ever happened, that the U.S. could have found other ways. I said, "Yeah, like what? Me and all my buddies jumping in Tokyo, and the Allied forces going in, and all of us getting killed? Millions more Allied soldiers getting killed?" When the Japanese bombed Pearl Harbor were they concerned about how many lives they took? We should have dropped eighteen bombs as far as I'm concerned. The Japanese should have stayed out of it if they didn't want bombs dropped. The end of the war was good news to us. We knew we were going home soon.

We were in Joigny, and I just got back from a ten-day leave to London. Dick Davenport, Eddie Stein, and me were playing Jew Pinochle on a cot, and Ralph Spina said "Babe, did you see the bulletin board?" We all went out to look. On the board it said that to stay on jump pay, we had to jump one more time. You didn't have to jump, but if you didn't, it said you'd be taken off jump pay by October the 5th. This was the latter part of September. I walked back in to talk to Stein and Davenport. They didn't know if they were going to jump. Ralph decided he wasn't. I said, "I'm doing it because I want to, I'm not letting them get the best of me." After all we had been through, and after all of the kids we left behind on the battlefield, they're going to take away our jump pay for not doing one last jump for posterity with only a couple months left to go? The guys who didn't want to jump but needed the money to send home to their families, those are the ones I felt bad for. They earned the right never to jump again. But that's the Army. All for fifty dollars a month jump pay. I get burned up just thinking about it. But I also liked jumping. I came in a jumper, I was leaving a jumper. A couple hours later, we were lying on a bunk in our quarters and Ralph said, "Hey, Babe, I changed my mind." He said, "It's my birthday, I'm jumping." I said to the guys, "If Bill Guarnere would see that bulletin board, he'd have torn that paper off, walked in the barracks, and said, 'Every goddamn one of you guys are gonna jump! This is Easy Company! If the Army can be that lousy, we can fight right back.'" All the time, I thought of Bill, and what Bill would say or do in different situations. He always came through.

It was a day jump, the last jump I ever made. We were jumping at two-thousand feet, so if the chute had any trouble, we'd have time to open our reserve. I was concerned about my hands going on me. I just hoped everything went well. I was number seven in the stick, and the guy in front of me froze in the door. When you freeze, you're gonna hold the whole stick up and go over the drop zone. I drove my static line and drove both my arms under his and I got him out the door. But that put me in a bad body position. When I left the plane, I thought, *I'm in trouble.* I was facing the motor, instead of the tail. My neck was pushed down to my chest and my lines were tangled. I started saying Hail Marys. Then I twisted my feet, and suddenly my chute popped. That was a relief. When I got on the ground, there was a truck waiting for us, and I told the guy who hesitated that he gave me a bad time. He said, "Did I hesitate?" I said, "You had time to paint the goddamn door!" We kind of laughed it off, but I was still a little shaken. I was just glad I didn't have to use the reserve. After that Ralph and I went out and celebrated his birthday with a few beers.

I got discharged from the Army in December 1945 and left for home on a troop ship. Oh, that ride was bad. The waves were forty feet high, nobody was allowed on deck. A couple guys had their rosary beads out and were saying prayers. We all said, "Hell, all the shit we went through and we're going to die on the boat ride home!" We were sick as dogs for the entire ten days, but the ship made it safely to New York, and we were happy as hell to be home.

9

★

BACK HOME IN
SOUTH PHILLY

BILL

We landed in Presque Isle, Maine. It was a holding place for the men before going home. They gave you anything your heart desired. *Who wants oranges, who wants fries, who wants ice cream?* They asked me what I wanted and I told them, "I'm just happy to be alive, happy to be home, I don't need anything." Everybody's eating ice cream, steaks, hoagies. The Andrews Sisters were on the radio singing "Rum and Coca-Cola," and I'm lying there, and I said, "What the hell, give me some rum and Coca-Cola." They brought me six of them. I drank two or three and poured the rest all over my body, and passed out.

There were five or six hospitals on the Atlantic City boardwalk where veterans were sent. I went to Haddon Hall, where Resorts International Casino is now. I was there about a year with Joe Toye.

Joe had his leg amputated below the knee in England, and when he got to the States, they amputated above the knee. Poor Joe had holes and scars all over his body. Tough as nails, Joe. He never complained.

My sister, and Frannie, and Mom and Pop came to see me. They had no idea about my leg. Just before I got home, Mom got an Army postcard—I still have it, a yellow postcard dated February 3, 1945— that said, "I am pleased to inform you that on 25 January 1945 your son Sgt. William J. Guarnere 13113070 was making normal improvement. Diagnosis: Fracture of the left leg, condition not serious." It said, "not serious," so that was all they knew. They were absolutely stunned when they saw me. They were crying, they couldn't believe it. It was just a year since they lost Henry, too. I told them, "I'll be fine, I'll be okay, they'll give me a wooden leg, I'll be fine." I knew I would be fine. I had it in me, I knew what I had to do. I never once thought otherwise.

As soon as I saw Frannie, I felt different, I felt stronger, I felt lucky to be home, and lucky to be alive. I wanted to marry her right away. I wasn't the same kid as when I left. I came home really skinny, minus a leg. But she didn't care. What do you think was the first thing she wanted? To give me some cigarettes! Overseas, cigarettes were rationed. You couldn't find them. So when you were in the hospital you got all the cigarettes you wanted.

I had more operations and rehabilitation, but I was able to move around in a wheelchair or on crutches. As soon as I could, I started running around in the wheelchair, *get the hell out of my way*, I felt like a million dollars. Me and Joe, we raised hell in that hospital. We got in our wheelchairs and raised hell. We'd go up and down the boardwalk, up and down ramps, shouting. We'd stop in bars, get drunk, go down the steps to the beach, and drop in the sand headfirst. We'd get stuck in the sand. We were young kids! We were lucky we didn't kill ourselves. But we were having fun, everyone knew we were there, just home from war. Complete strangers came up to talk to us.

I went back and forth between home and the hospital for about a year. The healing process happened at home, not in the hospital. Being with family. So they sent you home for thirty days, back to the hospital for a few days, a week, and back home for thirty days. They eased you into civilian life. At the hospital, they had to operate, do rehab, and get you physically fit. When I got to the States, I looked like a skeleton. They had to build you back up. I had three operations, rehabilitation, and they put me on an artificial leg.

While I was in the hospital, I met a boy about my age, his name was John Nocarato. He was kind of shy and he took to me real fast. He never told me why he was in the hospital. He was in the 1st or 4th Infantry Division, and when he came back to the States, he didn't know anybody. I talked to him for a few days, and when I came back from visiting my family, he was still there. I said, "You didn't go home?" He said, "No." For as long as I was there, he never went home. One day he said, "Would you do me a favor?" I could see he was scared. He said, "I want to go see my family, but I want you to come with me." They lived in a little town called Spotswood, New Jersey. So the doctor and nurse said I could take him home. We got to Spotswood, and when he got out of the car, I saw his pants started swinging. When his parents saw him, they hit the ceiling. He had gotten his leg blown off. No one knew. They screamed and hollered and cried—it was just turmoil for an hour or two. He didn't tell nobody. In the hospital, when he had his leg off, he wore his pants hanging down to his shoe. So when he's walking, looked like he had a leg with a shoe. The other people tucked their pants up, you could see they had one leg. That's why he wanted me to go back with him. He was crying. It was very emotional. I tried to ease things. I told him there were a lot of us like this, he wasn't alone. By the end of the night, his parents began to accept it. I brought him back to the hospital that night and stayed with him. He was having a hard time. He was trying to hide everything. You can't hide it, kid. You have to face it, and make the most of what you got. There's living to do. I kept in touch with him for about twenty years, then he got married and had kids and he died young.

When I came home, I just wanted to get married, have a family, forget about the war. I didn't say nothing about the war to nobody. I got out of uniform, people saw me on crutches, I said a shark bit my leg off. No one asked questions. No one at home knew about the war, they only knew you went. You were the only one who knew what you went through. It was good, because you wanted to be left alone to get on with your life.

I thought of Henry every day. I went out and got a tattoo in his memory—a cross with a wreath under it, and his nickname "Dunk," because he used to dunk everything in milk or coffee. Two guys from New York came down to see me and Mom, they served with Henry. They told us how he died trying to help save somebody and he got the Silver Star and lots of medals. He was a tech 5. I just read in *World War II* magazine about the war he was in, the Battle of Monte Porchia. They lost a lot of Germans and Americans in that battle. I went to visit Henry's grave in Italy. I went on my own quietly. Just once. I still talk to him when I'm alone in the house.

Frannie and I wanted to get married right away, but our families tried to talk us out of it. They didn't want Frannie to marry a cripple. They gave us a lot of trouble. They told Frannie, "You're going to have to take care of him. The older he gets, the worse it's going to get." But that wasn't me. I knew I'd live a normal life. I never believed in saying "I can't." If someone else can do something, I can do it. I may do it different, it may be awkward, but I'll do it. If you climb a ladder, I'll climb a ladder. I may go up every rung on my ass, but I'll do it. I have done it.

April 23, 1945, Frannie and I ran away to Elkton, Maryland, and eloped. Not a penny between us, just each other. When you got something good you don't let it get away. I married an angel. She put up with me and my crazy ways. Calmed me down. She understood me, helped me, never stopped me from doing anything I wanted to do. She was my leg, she was everything. Gotta give the gal credit.

We went on our honeymoon in Columbus, Ohio. Drove to Johnny Martin's house. Where were we gonna go, Hawaii? We didn't have a damn dime. Johnny got discharged early for medical reasons, so we went to see him and Pat. We did things simple, but we had fun.

BABE

When the boat got to Pier III in New York, it was raining cats and dogs. The Red Cross was inside the building on the pier giving out coffee and donuts, and the Salvation Army stood outside in the rain to greet us. I'll never forget that.

I took a train from New York to 30th Street Station in Philly, and took the bus to 2nd and Morris. I came upon the bar where everybody in the neighborhood always had a few beers. During training, when I came home on the weekends we would go in there, or the Republican Club at 3rd and Wilder. That day, hardly anybody was around. I was discharged earlier than most of the guys. A lot were discharged in 1946. When I got near the bar, my uncle, Charlie Chew—he was a number writer—saw me coming down the street, and I gave him the watch I promised him, a watch I got off a kraut. He told me my dad and brothers were inside the bar. My brothers Joe and Jimmy came up and hugged me. My dad was at the end of the bar. He walked over and said, "Hey, son, welcome home," then he went back to his seat at the bar. My dad wasn't into the emotional scene. I think he was glad to see us home but he would never come out and say it. He was a man's man, he would never hug you, none of that. I went home and talked to my mother before going to bed. My dad came home and went straight to bed. He never said, "Was it tough over there?" or "You must have gone through hell." Never even asked about the war. I had some decorations, the Presidential Distinguished Unit Citation for our defense at Bastogne, the Bronze Star for Holland, two Purple Hearts, and a star on my wings. But I never discussed them with my dad, or anyone in my family.

The first breakfast my whole family had together was about a year after the war was over. It was a Sunday morning after Mass, and me and all my brothers were at the table. My father must have had a late night at the Republican Club, and he finally came downstairs. He took a bite of his eggs and hollered into the kitchen, "Anne, these eggs are cold." She knew he was late coming down, and she came out and looked at him and said, "Joe, go shit in your hat." He turned to my brother Jake and said, "Did you hear what your mother said to me? She never talked to me like that." Jake said, "Dad, it's getting-even time! Her boys are home!" We said, "Way to go, Mom!" and Dad got mad as hell. Mom smiled and took the eggs and heated them anyhow. She felt so good about her boys being home. She had suffered a heart attack while we were gone, probably from the stress, and now we were all home safe. Not even my father bothered her. But my father never got over my mom telling him that. He brought it up for years. He'd say, "Do you remember that morning . . . ?" I'd say, "Yeah, Dad, you deserved it." He'd say, "I know."

Dad softened as he got older. Many years later, he sat my brothers and me down in the kitchen for a few beers. Jimmy and Jake were there, and Joe came over—he lived across the street. My father said, "You guys never talk about the war. None of you tell me anything." We all looked at each other. My brothers didn't have any stories to tell, so my dad asked me if I had any, and my brothers said, "Don't ask Babe! Christ, he'll go into a long story!" I said, "Well, one time I had a German general surrender to me." My brother jumped ten feet off the chair. "Dad, we told you he'd come up with stories!"

I went right to work when I got home, as a foreman in the shipping department at Publickers Industries, a whiskey distillery plant on Delaware Avenue, at the old Pennsylvania Railroad building. When the company moved to Linfield, Pennsylvania, I quit and got a job at the waterfront as a cargo checker and clerk. I stayed there for twenty-seven years, and retired in 1993. They were the only two jobs I had in my life. I also got back to playing football every weekend with the kids I grew up with. We played semipro football, then Pop Warner conference, then with the church team, Corsack. Then we played for Adelstein Bulldogs, the guy who owned the bar at 2nd Street. All the guys had fought in the war. We had a few Marines, Bill met one of them, Elmer Beach, he was our halfback. And Dampy Galloway played quarterback, he lost a brother in Italy, and Georgie Adams, he got killed in Italy, he was our tackle, and the whole list goes like that, guys that got killed and wounded in the Navy, Army, every family had something.

I played football until I was thirty-two, and at thirty-seven, I married Dolores Kessler. She had three children—Dolly, Harry, and Bobby, and two years later, we had another daughter, Trisha. Being married was all right with me. I went to work, gave my wife my paycheck, and she gave me my spending money. I was very happy with that.

I got back to my hobby of betting on horses. I was running numbers before the war when I was helping out my parents. But I started going to the tracks and betting with my dad and my brothers. I still do it. I recently found out there's a horse named after me in Ireland. Yep. It's named Babe Heffron. The trainer's name is Murphy. Of all things, the horse is a jumper! Jumps hurdles. The Irish love their racing.

BILL

Everyone was starting to come home from the war, and there were celebrations almost every night. Frannie thought I was a drunk because for six to eight months, every time someone came home we celebrated and got drunk. I had to explain I wasn't a drunk! Johnny and Pat came down, and something crazy always happened when we were together. Me and Johnny went to the bar, one of the neighborhood kids just got back from war, so we got drunk, and were walking home, and Johnny starts puking in the street. We get home and Pat says to him, "What happened to your teeth?" Johnny had about five artificial teeth in the front and they were gone. So we had to backtrack a few blocks and pick through the puke, and the teeth were in the puke on Mifflin Street. Every time I go down Mifflin, I think of Johnny's teeth.

We drove out to Johnny's house a couple times, too. Nobody in

South Philly had cars, but I got a car because a senator from Connecticut put in legislation for the president to sign that all amputees from the war got a free automobile. I belonged to a club of amputees, and we got a letter from the senator. So we go to the White House to meet Truman. We're in line and the kid in front of me starts blabbing away with Truman about the Yankees. I said, "We're not here to talk about baseball, we want you to sign legislation for an automobile." He said, "Kid, you got it." And we all got free cars. I shook his hand and thanked him. I got a brand-new black 1946 Pontiac, a model they didn't start selling until 1947. One new car in South Philly! It stood out like a sore thumb. So I gave it to Frannie's father, and he gave me an old junk car he had. I never regretted doing it. He was so good to us. He had nothing, and he gave us a lot. He gave us the home I own right now. He wanted to give it to me for free, but I wouldn't take it for free. I paid him two thousand bucks for it. That's what it cost in 1947. I paid twelve dollars a month for fourteen or fifteen years. They were lean days, but good days. I look back and it's crazy. How the hell we done it, I'll never know. No money, no credit cards, somehow everything worked out. People helped each other in those days.

When the men were back from war, quite a few came to visit me. Winters, Lipton, and five or six others came to see me. That's the kind of friendship we had. I got in touch with Babe right after he got home. He took a walk down and found me on the street playing craps, and I never got rid of him! The dirty rat!

As soon as I was out of the hospital for good and we got settled, I started college to get a degree in engineering at Spring Garden Institute in Philadelphia. When you go to war, your life changes. There are no guarantees. If I came back with two good legs, I might have pursued a career in sports—football or basketball. I thought I was good enough that I could make it. I was on the basketball team at home, and played a lot of football, too. It was in my mind that that's what I wanted to do. Buck Compton was an All-American catcher and an All-American guard for UCLA. But he decided to go into law. You never knew until you got back. You made the best of it.

When I was in school, my discharge from the Army came through. The records caught up with me from the court-martial. You find out your decorations, too: I got the Silver Star for Normandy, which I knew. Me and Buck Compton were the only ones in Easy Company who got the Silver Star. I got three Bronze Stars, for Normandy, Holland, and Belgium; two Purple Hearts; two combat jump stars; two Presidential Distinguished Unit Citations, one for Normandy, and one for Bastogne. The one for Bastogne was a special one. It was the first and only time in Army history that an entire division won the award. The 10th Armored Division's Team Cherry and Team Desiree got the award with us. The bad news was I was discharged a private because of the court-martial, and they said I owed them money, I was being paid as a sergeant, so they withheld my comp payments. I had to drop out of school, I could only afford to go for six months. I was so pissed at the Army, I didn't care what they did with my discharge, but Frannie pursued it. She talked to Joe Toye, Babe, Winters—got letters from everyone verifying I was a sergeant. She got it straightened out, but it took five years.

We had a baby on the way, and no money; I had to take various jobs for survival. Very few people were going to hire an amputee, they were afraid you could fall. I got a job at an insurance company, worked as a VA clerk, sold rugs for a friend, worked for U.S. Gypsum, worked as a printer for a while. I was trying to figure out what I wanted to do.

Our son Gene was born in March of 1946, and then Billy Jr. in August, 1949. We moved from Broad Street to Winton Street to raise our family. Family life was peaceful and quiet. I took the kids to the parks; we had a nice normal family life. Every night we sat down and had dinner. No hamburgers, no McDonald's. Frannie could cook—she almost killed me a couple times, too—but I was a better cook. I was cooking since I was two, kid! Whoever got home first did the cooking.

Desk work wasn't for me. I figured out what I really wanted to do was use my hands, build. I started working for myself, doing construction, building houses. I did cement work, plumbing, electric. I remodeled homes. I bought my first house on Broad Street, where Frannie and I lived, and I built a second home in New Jersey and sold it. I could always make a dollar. I was adept at anything. I read up on things I wanted to do, schooled myself at it. Like when I wanted to take a job with my friend in the printing business, Nick Cortez from F Company, I bluffed my way through the interview like I knew everything about printing, and of course, I knew nothing at all! But I got the job, so I read up on it, looked in the book for places that will school you, took some classes. I did that with everything. I did it in the war. I did it with construction, too. So I did okay. I stayed with construction twenty years. I still had my artificial leg then. In 1967, they had to remove it, because I was having too many problems. I was a maniac on the leg, but it kept flaring up, and the flare-ups started affecting the other leg. The more they tried to get it right, the worse it got. The doctors finally took it off, and I had to learn to live on crutches. It made things a little harder because it takes away the use of your arms, they become your legs in a way. I did mostly desk work after that. But I still climbed scaffolding, did brick and concrete work. I was younger then. When I got older, I got smarter—let other guys do it for you! When my two boys got old enough, I put them to work, too. Old enough to eat, old enough to work!

BABE

I was home near a year when I looked up Bill. After all you had your own troubles to straighten out when you got home. I took a walk out to 17th and McKean to see if he was there, and sure enough he was in the street shooting dice with all the guys. I was so happy to see him alive. I jumped on his back and said, "You son of a bitch!" I got so excited to see him I forgot about his leg. He had a prosthetic leg on. He grabbed me and hugged me, and said, "Goddamn, I thought you were a cop." We went and had a beer and I met his wife, Frannie, and then he said, "Come on, I'll drive you home."

After that day, we got together or talked on the phone almost every day. We go to our favorite places. We have breakfast at Cousins, or a beer and a sandwich at the Irish Pub, or dinner at Popi's. We go to E Company reunions together. We've been back to Europe together many times. Bill was the best man at my wedding to Dolores, and he's my daughter Trisha's godfather. She calls him Uncle Bill. Bill settled down a lot after he got married. He wasn't out raising too much hell anymore. That shows you, raising a family, he had a lot to do, he can't be worrying about running around.

BILL

Me and Babe became like family. He was at my house, or I was at his house. We did construction projects on each other's houses. We did some work at Babe's house, and he helped me remodel my kitchen. I made him do the hard work. I had him mixing cement! I thought, *I need help, and there's only one nut that don't know what he's doing, I'll call Babe!* We go out a lot, too. Partying and socializing. I drive and he doesn't—he takes the bus everywhere—so I always pick him up when we go out. We went back to Europe in 1954 and 1959 and about fifteen times since then. We have a good time. Even though Babe's nickname is "Grumpy." That's his nature. Babe is not flexible. He won't bend for nothing. No way. He lives by his watch. Don't be a minute late. Don't even be on time, that's too late. But Babe is a good guy. A very loyal friend. He'll give you anything he has. He'll give you the shirt off his back. Our friendship has meant everything. Just like with any of the E Company men, when you spend all that time so close together trying to survive, you got something you can't explain. If I could explain it, I'd be a genius. It means something your whole life. Like every Christmas, the memories that time of year brings back are very sad. A lot of our buddies were killed. So there's somebody there that understands.

BABE

In 1949 Bill and I were invited to the premier of the movie *Battleground* at the Boyd Theater in Philly. The movie was about the 101st Airborne at Bastogne, so they invited us to talk about our experience. Before we got on stage they asked us about broads during the war. I said, "We didn't see girls in Belgium!" Bill said, "We'd rather have had a heater than a broad!" The guy told us we couldn't say those things on stage because they were trying to push Denise Darcel, make her a star. They wanted it to be a sexy show, so they told us they were passing us by!

Bill and I worked together at Publickers Industries after Bill retired from construction. He worked down where they fermented the whiskey; he bottled it. We worked in different departments but went to a few union meetings together. You had to be a member of the union to work there, and every week, it seemed, the union went on strike. One time we formed a picket line along the railroad, and they were going to drive the train into our building. Bill was there, I was there, there were about forty to fifty of us. The engineer was married to my sister-in-law, and he got off the train and wouldn't cross the line. So one of the bigwigs, a guy in a three-piece suit, gets on the train, and we knew he'd run us all over. So Bill gets the idea to lay down on his back and put his leg across the tracks. They didn't know it was an artificial leg. So the engineer started the train up and was moving down the tracks toward Bill, and he was gonna defy Bill, and Bill was gonna defy him, and we're all rooting for Bill. Well, the engineer stopped a couple feet from Bill, but they called the cops. They came in with dogs and threw us in the paddy wagon. We went to the police station, sat down on the benches, and waited for a lawyer to get us out. When I got to work after the strike was settled, they told me I can no longer be the foreman since I was one of the forerunners of the strike. I said, "You might as well fire me, then." One of the fellas came in and said, "You're not gonna fire him for something like that, everybody was there." Bill was the troublemaker, but he didn't get fired. They knew he was a goofy bastard. I lost my job and had to wait for an opening, and I was put into inventory. I can say one thing about Bill, though. He has a way of getting things done.

After Publickers, we worked down at the waterfront. I started 1968, Bill started a year or two after that. We both checked cargo. We worked with South Philly's longshoreman. They're the best in the country. As rough as cops. They work in gangs of thirteen to fifteen men to unload cargo from ships. Then checkers count and check what comes off to make sure it's right. Everyone moves fast because the ship is usually expected at another pier. Bill had to leave the water-front because of the chisels and the forklifts—it was a dangerous sit-uation for him. He couldn't get out of the way of them fast enough.

BILL

When they started drafting for Vietnam in the late sixties, my son Gene was about twenty. He enlisted in the Army to go to the 101st Airborne like his pop. By that time the 101st Airborne changed from paratroopers to an air mobile division. They were trained as para-troopers, too, but instead of being jumpers they were used to fly and rappel down from helicopters. I got my son Billy exempt from duty. I knew what it was all about, and I wasn't about to send both sons. I told them Billy had to stay home and take care of me. I lied, but I'm glad I did it. That conflict was a mess, just like Iraq. Decisions are made with no common sense, and our kids go, they give their all, and they give their lives. Thank God Gene came back alive. He came home, and we never talked about it. You never talked about it in those days. He said, "How in the hell you done it, Pop, I'll never know." He got married and had six children. Billy had three children. Today I have nineteen grandchildren and great-grandchildren. With Vietnam, I finally understood what my parents went through. My wife and I worried every minute, it was hard keeping Frannie calm. When you lose a kid, that stays with you forever.

At that time, America was an entirely different country from what it was during WWII. When I went to war, we had good government, good leaders. They had common sense. Today, nobody has common sense. You mix politics and religion, you got trouble. America gets worse, not better. No common sense, no patriotism. Everybody was trying to get their kids out of going to Vietnam, trying everything. They sent them to live in Canada. They laughed at you because you sent your kids. An entirely different generation.

The one thing I can say about war is that the winners lose and the losers lose. But I'm proud that I fought for my country, and that my son did, too. And proud that we fought with the 101st Airborne. I wear the eagle on my hat, on my jacket. I have eagles all over my house. If you go upstairs, your eyeballs will come out. I've got a whole room full of eagles. Four shelves of eagles and plaques. My wife used to say, "You like the eagles so much, go sleep with them in the back room." You know what they call us today? The old buzzards! We're a bunch of old geezers.

The division is still active today. After World War II, they were in the Korean War, and then nothing until the fifties when they formed the air mobile division. When they needed a mobile division, the 101st was the first one formed and it's still the only one today like that. They fought in Korea and Vietnam. They are now in Iraq. Any hotspot in the world, the 101st can be ready within a day. The 82nd Airborne is still paratroops. A year or two from now, the helicopters will be history and they'll have rockets, who knows? That's technology today. Now you're getting too smart!

★ ★ ★

I stayed close friends with Johnny Martin until he died about a year ago. I flew out to bury him, and his son Billy said he had a gun I gave his father. I said, "Billy, you're nuttier than a fruitcake, I never gave him a gun." "Yeah," he said, "I have the note you wrote that you got it right after D-day and you gave one to him." I didn't remember. Took me about a week. Beating my brains out trying to think about D-day and everything that happened. I went to every man in the company until I got to George Luz. He spent a lot of time with me and Johnny on pass in London. *Bang*, it hit me like a brick. I captured two German SS, and they surrendered, gave me their guns, and I shot 'em. I gave one gun to George Luz and one to Johnny.

Another story about a gun and Johnny Martin. His brother Billy was in the Merchant Marines and they delivered stuff by boat—all the supplies to England and all over the world. So one time he came to England, and me and Johnny went to meet him. I grabbed a Thompson submachine gun, wrapped it up, and gave it to Billy. I don't know whose gun it was. There was stuff lying around all over the place. If somebody noticed a gun missing, I probably blamed Smitty. I always blamed Smitty.

I told Billy, "Take this back to the United States if you can. If anyone tries to steal it, throw it in the ocean, don't give it to nobody. If you get it back, and I don't make it back, keep it as a souvenir." When I got home and went to see Johnny Martin, sure enough Billy was there and gave me the gun. When I took it home, Frannie was scared to death of it. After all that, I ended up giving it to a neighbor to get rid of it!

(Babe adds: "Bill's still the troublemaker that he was. Wait till you hear stories about Europe.")

BABE

A friend came up one day and gave me a box of chocolates, and we went to take a box to Bill. I said to him in the car, "I'm gonna put a five-dollar bill here and tell you verbatim what Bill's going to say to you when you hand him the chocolates." Bill opens the door, my friend hands him the chocolates. And Bill says, "What are you trying to do, give me diabetes?!" My friend handed me a five and we laughed like hell. I know what Bill's going to say before he says it.

If you ever hear Bill's sayings, he copies them from me. If you offer him something to eat, he says, "No, thanks, I just had a peanut." Well, he got that from me. It's supposed to be funny, but he says it constantly, so it gets on my nerves. Bill says, "I'm sorry you ever told me that one."

I can't say enough about our friendship over the years. Anytime we go anywhere we have a good time. We've never had an argument or dispute, or a bad word. Never. We're there for each other. We give each other encouragement. If he's ever broke, I got it. Same with me; if I was broke, I wouldn't hesitate to ask him. Bill was good to my daughter while I was sick. I was lying in a hospital bed for almost a year, and the doctors didn't expect me to walk again. Bill took care of us. He came to see me every day.

(Bill adds: "You owe me for parking. Sixteen dollars a day for a year! He was on so many drugs, he was nuttier than a fruitcake. Coco loco!")

They had me on all kinds of drugs, and when I came home, I wouldn't take any more pills. I'm supposed to take three of them—high blood pressure, iron, and high cholesterol. But I don't care if I'm healthy or not, no more pills. I can't get myself to put foreign things in my body. Since I was a kid I never cried cop, and I don't believe in crying cop. Bill don't take any pills either. We're eighty-four. Doctors get all worked up when we tell them. You'd think the doctor was the one whose body it is. Joe Toye said to me one time, "You guys from South Philly are tough sons of bitches." It's true. I never worry about death, because I know there's something good on the other side.

As for the problem with my hands, after I got out of the hospital in Belgium, I did my duty. I didn't say a word, I led patrols and carried the machine gun and never said a word. I was home about twenty years before it finally left me. The doctor, when I come home, said you have to drink a lot of milk. Twenty-three years later it was gone, and it never came back. I remember, it was my first year on the waterfront when I realized I hadn't had any pain, it just went away. No doctor ever told me what the hell condition it was, but I must have been lacking something, and my body got what it needed after a while.

The 101st Airborne had a reunion the year after the war was over. It was great seeing the men again, especially off the battlefield! I can't say enough about the men I fought with. They were all just good, top-shelf guys. Bill started getting the men together for the reunions in 1947, after he got out of the hospital, and ran them almost sixty years. He made it so the men didn't have to lift a finger. He did everything, and no one helped. I made phone calls to the guys in my platoon, but Bill did the rest. It's because of Bill that we've all stayed so close.

The reunions have always been more fun than serious. When you're with the guys, you're eighteen years old again. The guys still kid each other. At the first reunion Bill went to Walter Gordon and said to him, "I didn't know they let guys with one leg in the paratroopers!" There were so many crazy stories. I can't say anything without getting someone in trouble with their family. Their families will say, "Well, I didn't know *that*, you son of a bitch!" Bill and I try to have fun. When Bill was still wearing an artificial leg, he tattooed a giant eagle on it, and wore his pant leg up so everyone could see, and he danced all night. One year, we dressed up in zoot suits. Me, Bill, and Ralph Spina. We looked like the Three Stooges. Pin-striped suits with the big shoulders and peg legs, and hats. When the elevator opened and I saw Bill in his zoot suit, I took such a laughing fit, everyone thought I was gonna drop dead. The guys couldn't believe what they were looking at. Colonel Strayer said to his wife, "Now I've seen everything." I thought, *Well, he's the president of an insurance company, so he just thinks we're nuts.* We always try to make the guys laugh, make everyone feel at home.

My jump school buddy, J. D. Henderson, went to a couple reunions with us. He was a farmer, never had much. Many of the guys didn't have much. I've had it pretty good, so did Bill, we got no complaints. We've traveled all over. Bill would call me and say "Babe, we're going here and there." We went to reunions in different states, or to Europe. We used the governor's plane to go to St. Louis in 1951. I got a photo in my parlor of that trip in 1951, sitting with Eddie Stein. He died in 2000, he was a good guy. He took Landsberg (the concentration camp Easy liberated) pretty hard. I liked Eddie; he owned an entire block, he had a big company selling eggs and poultry, he had fifty people plucking chickens. Bill and I visited him there and met his wife, Vernelle.

We were so happy to see some of the guys become millionaires, they made their way in the world, and they worked hard to get there.

Walter Gordon did well, Winters did well with his own company in Pennsylvania. Compton did well; he graduated UCLA, played football and baseball, worked for the DA, became a lawyer and a federal judge. He sent Sirhan Sirhan away, life in prison. He's the one who shot Robert Kennedy. Compton wanted to give him the death penalty, but the jury voted against it.

Other guys in E Company had it tough, but we all did well overall. We all lived and had children and grandchildren, and when you think of the guys that never got the chance, right there, we all made out well. But we can't forget the kids who came home and had to struggle through life with their physical wounds, like Chuck Grant. He had a hell of a time. When he got shot, the war was over, and this crazy bastard shot him in the head. He lived with brain damage. That was the toughest part of the whole thing, that he made it through the whole war, and then that happened.

I never forgot my promise to John Julian, the pact he and I and J. D. Henderson made. It took me about twelve years to get up the guts to contact his mother. I wrote her a letter and she called me and said, "Babe, you don't have to travel to Sispy, Alabama." I thought she didn't want me bringing up old wounds. But instead, she was coming to me. Her daughter was having a baby in Camden, New Jersey, right over the bridge, I could have walked there. I visited her at her daughter's home. It was tough. I was all broken down. She was a better soldier than I was. Stiff upper lip. Didn't show emotion. I gave her our regimental scrapbook. I only had one but I thought she deserved it. I said, "I know your son would love you to have this." She was so grateful that I came. My cousin went with me, and afterward, we stopped at a local bar; let's be honest, I needed a drink. It gets to me just repeating it. But I had to do it because I gave Julian my word. J. D.

couldn't do it, he had no money. He said, "Babe, I'm proud of you." I know Julian was looking down on me saying "Good job, well done." You hear people say, "The veterans are full of hooey, how can they keep these things in mind for sixty years?" But we do.

I hear Vietnam vets say they suffer from flashbacks and I think, *Hey, I've been having them since 1944, I have seniority!* Any soldier who lived through combat, whether it was in 1776, 1861, 1918, 1942, any war, will never be entirely free of the war he fought. Some are just able to brush it off better than others. Bill doesn't think about the war. He thinks about the men. I think about the war every day, only because reminders are all around. During a thunderstorm, when the sky lights up after the booms, it sounds and looks like the recoil of the big German guns. It always makes me happy to be standing exactly where I am, and not back in 1944 Europe. In September and October, I'm thinking of Holland and everything I experienced there. In December I think of Bastogne. With Christmas comes very bad memories. January 1st, New Year's Day, I always think of John Julian. I never, never enjoy a New Year, and never cared about Christmas. I just like to be left alone. Bill says, "Humbug on Christmas, humbug on New Year's." I say, "You're right, Bill. Humbug!" Most of the guys can't handle it, because of the Bulge and the friends we lost. It's part of living.

Stephen Ambrose called around 1990 and started interviewing all the members of Easy Company to write a book about us. Bill met with him and some of the Toccoa guys. Ambrose called me on the phone. When *Band of Brothers* came out in 1992, people wanted to talk about the war. As hard as it is for all of us, I think we all believe it's important for people today to know about the war. Kids today see these movies and they think it's a fairy tale. They don't understand this was real; this was no fairy tale. Kids today are different than we were. Today, they're spoiled rotten, and they don't have the same respect for their country or even their parents. We were raised to be self-supporting. When we made money we brought it home to our mother. And they don't want to hear nothing of fighting for your country. It's unpatriotic to fight for your country! A kid at the neighborhood bar said, "I ain't fighting any wars for this country, my parents should have stayed in Bolivia." He was talking to someone else. I said, "Your parents *should* have stayed in Bolivia." He said, "I wasn't talking to you." I said, "That's right, I just wanted to agree with you." I said, "What if a German had a bayonet up your ass, are you gonna fight then?" I didn't want to get locked up, so I finished my beer and left. It seems to me a lot of kids today are like that. I hope we never have to prove it, I mean on a large scale—not like Iraq, and they can't get them to volunteer for Iraq. I hope I'm wrong.

One of the problems is they fight wars differently today. They tell the enemy what their plans are. The media gets hold of it. How can you fight a war like that? It's on the news, on the Internet. They're letting these kids use cell phones from a goddamn foxhole. The time Ronald Reagan jumped into Panama with the troops, and he went to the microphone and announced the troops captured the president of Panama, and everything was secured, it was a success, one of the guys from the media said, "You never told us the troops were going in to invade Panama." Reagan said, "If I would have told you, I would have told the enemy. They're my troops, they're my men." He was right. We all loved him when he said that, and we weren't even in the Army then.

★ ★ ★

When the book came out, people started calling us heroes. We're not heroes. It burns me up how people use the word "hero" today. The heroes are the kids who gave 100 percent; they gave their lives. The heroes are the mothers who gave up a son, who carried him for nine months, and raised him to do right, and he does right, and at eighteen, he goes to fight for his country, and he dies doing right. That's a hero. When they call a baseball or a football player a hero, that player is playing a game they love, and getting well paid for it. How is that a hero? You can call him the star of the game, but he's not a hero. The word is misused. Bill and I get furious when we hear it used in the wrong context. We know we're not heroes. The kid who went to war and never walked back through his mother's front door, he's the hero.

The book got more veterans to talk about the war, not just us, but all veterans, from the Navy, Marines, Army, Air Force. And if telling the stories makes people think about it, then we're doing something good.

I get on the bus sometimes with a woman who was in Auschwitz. She started talking to me one day. She knew me because she saw *Band of Brothers.* She showed me her tattoo, and she said, "Thank you, you did so much for my people." Her husband tended bar in the city, and he showed me his tattoo. It amazes me how they lived through these things, and went on to move forward, try and forgive the past, and to make productive lives for themselves.

Recently there was a Holocaust Memorial Dinner to honor survivors, and me and Bill were invited as guests, because they knew Easy Company liberated the Landsberg concentration camp. We were told there were going to be survivors from Landsberg there, and I wanted to talk to them. I know it's far-fetched, but one thing I wanted to ask them was about the Hungarian girl with the reddish hair. Did they know her? I imagine they did. They were from the same camp. I never got to talk to them, they left too quickly. But over the years, I've thought about her, and I hope she did well.

I hear about these idiots like a well-known movie star's father who said there was no such thing as the Holocaust. He don't even believe a man went to the moon. I'm disappointed in him. That's why I call up newspapers to set things straight. You need to speak up about people like that. They weren't there, but they think they can tell you the way it was.

The people who saw the things we saw, it affects you for life. You remember things, and they affect you emotionally and physically. Nothing that makes you take a turn for the worst or anything, it just affects you for a few minutes. That's why I couldn't tell my stories for a long time. I never told my wife or my daughter anything about the war. I started telling them to my son-in-law Ed in the last twenty years. He wanted to know everything. It was very hard. The Greeks have a saying: If you keep a hero's name in the public's eye, the person never dies. That's why I started telling certain stories. Like about Jim Campbell and John Julian. I couldn't get myself to express them before. I didn't even tell Stephen Ambrose when he interviewed me for *Band of Brothers.*

One funny thing happened after the book came out: My brother Shad called me and said, "I want to apologize. I just read the book. You did have a German general surrender to you!" He said, "We thought you were full of shit!"

I feel good to be able to say things worked out exactly as they have in my life. That I didn't wait to get drafted, that I didn't tell anyone of my hand condition—because if I waited to get drafted I might have—and that I didn't go into any other outfit. As bad as it was—and you paid a heavy price for being a paratrooper, believe me, always put on the front lines under bad conditions—and even with the emotional scars you live with, I'm glad I did it. All goodness came out of it. I would never have had the opportunity to meet guys like Winters, Guarnere, Toye, Ed Joint and Joe Lesniewksi, Malarkey, J. D. Henderson, Shifty Powers, Chuck Grant, One Lung McClung, Compton, Jim McMahon, and most important, Muck, Penkala, Campbell, and Julian, who never came back. Guarnere, I don't have to mention, he's nuts, he always let's me know *he's* around! It makes you feel good that you were with these guys all over Europe in some tough spots, guys you shared a hole with, and guys who saved your life, like Sheehy. He saved my life in Holland. When someone mentions that a guy named Dick Winters wrote a book, I get proud as hell. I'm too happy to say he was my company commander. To call these men my friends is a privilege.

BILL

Right after the war, the 101st Airborne had a reunion in 1946 in Indianapolis. I couldn't go, I was in the hospital, but I went to the next one in New York. For the first couple years, the towns we went to were up in arms that we were coming, they were scared. We were just fresh from war. They figured we were killers, we were savages, we were going to turn the town upside down. They must have heard what we did to London after Normandy! But when the men got there, we were like pussycats. After combat, you don't even want to kill a bug.

About ten or so Easy Company men came to the first couple reunions, and I started calling the men every year trying to get them to go. When enough of us were going, I suggested we have our own yearly reunion. Just Easy Company. So that's what we did. Frannie helped me organize and run the reunions for fifty years. About forty or fifty men came to the first one, and it grew to eighty-three one year—when we went to San Diego. We had a core group that always came—Babe, George Luz, Walter Gordon, Gordon Carson, Joe Toye, Bill Wingett, Burt Christenson, Lewis Nixon, Buck Compton, Don Malarkey, Rod Bain, Johnny Martin, Gene Roe, Ralph Spina, Herb Suerth, Popeye Wynn, Carwood Lipton, Buck Taylor—that's just a few. Dick Winters came to two or three reunions, too.

The first reunion Rod Bain came to, I saw him coming in, so I stood behind a column, and jumped out and hollered, "Bain!" Figured I'd do it one last time for posterity. He said, "What do you want, Sarge?" I said, "Get me a Seven and Seven." So he brought me seven Seven and Sevens, and said, "There you go, don't bother me anymore!" He's a great guy, God bless him. We were together a lot during the war.

Like Babe said, we mostly have fun, drink, dance, laugh. But when we see each other it's emotional, too, just nobody talks about it. The first year I convinced Malarkey to come—now Malarkey's sentimental anyway, cries like a baby when he sees us—he got so overwhelmed, he started drinking and went for a walk, and come nighttime, he went missing. We all got in cabs and went looking for him, even the police went looking. The next morning, someone found him sleeping at the back entrance of a store. He was drunk, got lost, and fell asleep. We gave him holy hell. He's come every year since.

I tried to get Captain Sobel to come to the reunions. He lived in Chicago. I paid his Airborne dues for him and I sent him a card. I said, "Come, the men want to see you." The war was over. He was another man in E Company. You don't carry grudges. We disliked him, but never hated him. What he put us through was almost as bad as being in combat. We didn't know he was doing something good for us. He got us ready for the worst of the worst. We have to give him credit for what he did. But he never came to any reunions. His sister contacted me in 1988 to tell me he died. He tried to commit suicide before that. That was sad news. It didn't matter what we'd been through, or how we felt. After *Band of Brothers* came out, she came to our reunion in Valley Forge. She was furious about what the book said about her brother, but it was all true. She wanted to kill me and Malarkey. She was crying. She gave me a letter she wrote to us. It was scathing. I said to her, "Sit down and talk to us. Any question you have, we'll tell you the truth as it was, but I can't change it." She got the full story, she understood a little more, and apologized to everyone. She died right after that.

People can't believe we've been together every year. Some others do it but it's very, very rare. It was important to me to keep in touch with the men. Beside the reunions, I stayed active in the 506th, I was on the board of governors for thirty years. When I think about the war—I think about it every day of my life—I think about the men, not the war. Thoughts of the men from the beginning of the war, from Toccoa, to the end. Easy Company lost sixty to seventy men in the war. I can tell you what happened to each one, from Alley to Zimmerman. No one else could do that. It's not something I'm bragging about, it's just that I made it my business, that's all. I cared about each and every one. When I go on the tours with Babe or go back to

Europe, I think of what happened there and who was killed. I never had nightmares. That post-traumatic stress disorder, quite a few people got it, but I didn't. I just have good, fond memories of the men. Whenever I think of someone, I pick up the phone and call him, or his family, because a lot of the men are gone today. This goes way back, from the time the war was over until today, and my phone bills were sometimes two hundred dollars a month. I just gave up doing the reunions two years ago, now my phone bill is twenty-one dollars a month. I'm saving money!

When the men get together, nobody talks much about the war. We talk about our families, what we've been doing. If something comes up that has to do with the war, we look at each other and we don't have to say a word. You give a guy a hug or squeeze. It's understood. You were both there, and you both know. If you're a combat veteran, war never leaves you. Every Christmas you spend, you spend at Bastogne. Whether you know it or not, you spend it there. It's in your mind, body, and soul. In September you think of Holland, too, but it's not got the same charge as Bastogne, that was the most haunting part of the war. What happened there remains inside every one of us.

Strange things from the war still happen today. In 1989, they found the C-47 that went down on D-day with Captain Meehan and head-quarters. They found some of the men with crickets still in their pockets, they found dog tags, knives, a static line hook, English money. All still there from forty-five years before. Real strange and eerie!

There's nothing that's changed my life so dramatically as the Army. Being associated with these guys from Easy Company has been the most important part of my life after my own family. It's a love and brotherhood you can't explain. I've kept them together. I always give them hell. Always have. It's because you love them, but you don't tell them you love them. You just give them hell. And they say, "Oh, there he goes again. Gonorrhea giving everyone hell." I just keep after them, that's all.

People ask if the war changes you. The war changes you in lots of ways. Damn right. You get home and say, "I'm lucky to be alive." Everything is incidental. There are no big problems in life. Everything is incidental when nobody is trying to kill you. Nothing bothers me. I couldn't care less if we have forty feet of snow, nineteen inches of rain. Thunder, hurricanes. Nothing can compare to being in the war. No matter what you say or do today, nothing can compare to the experiences in the war. Everything is minor. You got a headache? Foot bothering you? Get the hell out of here! Minor detail. During the war, you never know if tomorrow will come. Every day, you lived like it was your last day. I still live that way. War gives you a different perspective on life. It's true. You can't understand it unless you been there.

Life is more treasured, too. You appreciate every day and live every day to the fullest. You think, "I might not be here tomorrow." You appreciate everything you have. I always did, because we didn't have nothing growing up, but war magnifies it, makes you appreciate it even more.

Another thing is, I was always good at figuring people out. I think it's something you're born with. But during the war, leading forty-eight men, you become an expert at it. I knew inside out the personalities of my men. I knew who was capable of what, I knew how to push buttons. Some people didn't do what you asked. I kept that in mind, too. I knew who goofed off, who was goldbricking. For those people it was fist city, *bing-bang-boom!* They knew you meant business. When it's war, it's not a game. Since the war, I've met thousands and thousands of people, I talk to someone for a few minutes, I get a feel for them right away. I can tell their nature right away. Most of the time I'm correct. I can tell who to put my time into and who not to bother with.

The world's changed a lot, too, since the war. Today, TV is fighting the war for you. And the politicians fight the war. When I hear the computers and the cell phones and the e-mails and the answering machines, it depresses me more than the war. It's a different generation, kid. Back then, people interacted with each other, they were patriotic, they cared about their community, shared what little they had. Today everybody's separate. Families don't help each other. Everybody wants more and more, nobody's satisfied with what they got. The more people have the more they want. Back then life was simple, families were closer, people were happier. I wouldn't trade those days for all the money in the world. It's funny, how your memory goes way, way back. Do you remember the song "Seven-Twenty in the Book"? When I was a little kid, we had a man in Philly, before the big bands of the early twenties, and his name was Jan Savit, and he had a band like Glenn Miller. I liked his records, and the most famous song was "Seven-Twenty in the Book." Every time I hear it on the radio, I can still sing it now. That's how things carry on all through your life. Today's music is all noise. You can get away with anything. You can burn the flag, too, if you want. That's America.

I still feel like I did when I was twenty years old. Me and Babe still feel like kids. We can still stay out partying all night! Still chasing the broads, just can't catch them. Age is just a number, kid. If you start thinking of the numbers, you think you're going to die. I say, "Get the hell out of here!" Just run! I just keep running.

When the phone rings, I say nineteen prayers. I am afraid for bad news. Because I know everyone in the company, they call me. They don't call Winters, they don't call Babe, just me and me alone, because I have been the one trying to keep everyone together. I do it to keep Easy Company alive and the memories of the men alive.

Stephen Ambrose came to our reunion in New Orleans around 1989. He was interviewing veterans, he wasn't planning on writing a book about Easy Company. When he saw he had forty to fifty men from one company, he was very interested in how we stayed together for almost fifty years. He knew he had gold. I feel like if me and Frannie didn't put in all that work, it wouldn't have happened. We put our lives into it. Try doing it once. I don't know how we did it, but it got done.

When Ambrose decided to write the book, he got most of his information from Walter Gordon, Winters, and Lipton. Winters especially, because he had a diary, and then he got Ambrose in touch with the key men in the company, and Ambrose contacted me. I met him at Winters's farm in Hershey, Pennsylvania, and I stayed there for a few days for interviews. Then I spent two days with Ambrose at Lipton's house in Southern Pines, North Carolina. For most of us, that was the first time we talked about the war since we came home. At the time, I thought Ambrose was nuts. I couldn't imagine who would want to hear about it. I thought, *We're no heroes.* It took everyone to win that war. It took the Army, Navy, Air Force, Marines, Merchant Marine, and the people on the home front—the moms, the pops, the kids, everyone. It was a concerted effort by everyone in America. No matter what they done, we needed everybody. Easy Company was different from other companies in a way. The bond the men had. No other company had this. No other regiment trained together and went into combat together. So we were bonded different right from the beginning. Then we had Sobel. He beat the crap out of us, and it made us closer. Made us better fighters, too. We were a hell of a company. We had street smarts. Made us natural killers on the battlefield. We were pussycats off the battlefield! But it was the bond that was special. How else can you explain staying together every year from 1942 until today? I talk to veterans all over the world and I ask them, "Do you guys see each other?" They forgot the names of the men they fought with. So when I say we've been together since 1942 until today, that speaks for what we are.

10

★

BACK TO THE PLACES
WE FOUGHT

(Bill's Stories in Italics)

When you go back to these places where you barely survived, and you lost buddies, and you saw terrible things, you have no feeling. It makes me feel worn out and old. It all comes back to you, and physically and mentally, we just don't believe we went through it. I look around and hide tears sometimes. You can't believe you survived it, you can't believe what you seen, and you can't believe what you did. And then you remember the faces of the people you liberated, and then you know why you were there.

Bill and I have our private moments when we go there, but the people really welcome us, especially in Holland, and we have a lot of fun with them.

The first time, we went back to Eindhoven, Holland, in 1954 for the tenth anniversary of the drop. The Dutch government was celebrating the liberation and invited the 101st Airborne. We marched through there September 17, 1944, as paratroopers and liberators, and went ten years later as civilians. Oh, the Dutch love the American soldiers. They couldn't do enough for us. For twenty-one days we lived in Dutch homes. They had parades. The children put wreaths on the graves of the soldiers. So you see it was a foreign government that celebrated the Allied forces first, and they still do it every year. A man named Mathew van Luyt created a group called the Dutch Airborne Friends. They invite the 101st back to Europe every year. They call it Remember September. They have a big parade. Later, they started doing it in France and Belgium, too. They have schoolchildren put flowers on the graves there, too. It's carried on until today.

That first year, they were putting us up in Dutch homes, and we had to wait in line to go up on stage and get a family to stay with. There was a pretty young Dutch girl there—and Bill was married, but I was single—and she and I are both next in line to get paired up, and I'm all excited to end up staying with this girl. Next thing I know, Bill's telling the director, "I would like my buddy, Babe, to stay with the Dutch people I'm staying with." He was staying with an old couple in their late seventies! I wanted to kill him that day, but they ended up being like family to us. We called them Mom and Pop Vermuelen. They had a fourteen-year-old granddaughter; we called her Honey because we couldn't pronounce her name. They lived at 402 Hoogstraat, which means High Street in Dutch. There were bars every six feet, and I had a hell of a job getting Bill home. He had to stop in every bar. Mom, the old lady, walked into the pub, grabbed Bill by the ear and pulled him out saying, "You had plenty beer, plenty beer!" We were thirty-one years old, old enough to know better!

They gave us a bed that was maybe three feet by three feet. Bill fell out of bed. But that wasn't the worst of it. The bathroom was outside, and we were drinking a lot of beer. The first night, we were in our bedroom with the door shut, discussing, "How are we gonna keep going outside? We drank all this beer?!" Mom and Pop must have heard us anguishing over it, because she came knocking on the door and handed me a bucket. She said, "You go here, you had plenty beer today." My God, I am still embarrassed today. So in the morning, Bill says to me, "Babe, my leg is starting to bother me, I wonder if it could be from the beer." I said, "You never complain about your leg! Are you too goddamn embarrassed to carry the goddamn bucket down? I'll take the bucket down!" We're arguing about who's going to take the bucket down and in walks the old lady, and she looks at the bucket and she says, "Oh my! Plenty beer!" It had a head on it! I looked at Bill. We were so worried about being embarrassed, and she didn't care at all! Right, Bill?

Why, certainly! To her, it was just a bucket of beer! Are you telling this story for everyone?

It shows how broadminded the Dutch are. We really enjoyed ourselves with them. They just loved being with the guys that dropped there. We used to take them out, we'd buy food for them in the market. We bought Honey a bicycle. We loved doing things for them.

We loved our time there. It was beautiful, nobody thought of the war. They were just happy and free.

We went back five years later, and visited a few times after that, and around 1970, Mom and Pop passed away. But we got to know a lot of people by then. Before *Band of Brothers*, if Bill and I were sitting in Eindhoven, they would come right over and know our names. They knew we were from the 101st and that we liberated them. Their newspaper, the *Dagblad*, always had us in there. In Son, they had an article on us. They've recognized us every year. Since *Band of Brothers* came out, now everyone knows us. When we go to Holland, my job the first morning is to get postcards and stamps while Bill waits in the room. One morning, two guys started hollering out to me, they must have seen the eagle on my jacket, and next thing I know, they picked me up bodily and took me into a pub. Everyone in the bar started clapping and hitting their glasses on the bar. They wanted me to drink. It was ten in the morning! I may have had one. And then another. And then another.

I never got my postcards! When he came back I said, "You're a fine-looking specimen." He was drunk as a skunk.

We also became friends with a Dutch man who saw us come down from the sky. He loves us like brothers. Today, he's the head of the Van Gogh Museum.

That first trip back, I met a Dutchman who said, "Let me show you something." He pulled out a photo of himself on a motorcycle with a trooper behind him. I thought, Jesus, I hope this ain't the guy whose motorcycle I stole! He's caught up to me after all these years and now he wants me to pay for it! But it wasn't him—thank Christ for that. He just wanted me to sign the back of the photo. I was nervous there for a minute.

We went back to Holland again in 1959. Everything looked newer and cleaner, and well taken care of like they were proud to be a free country. During the war it was downtrodden. It didn't look like the beauty that you knew Holland could be.

It was all farms. Now there are roads and houses. No more open farmland that it was when we were there. Most of the places we knew disappeared.

Everything changed so much, where we fought, the center of the city is all changed. When we go today we don't recognize it—skyscrapers, airports. Time marches on. Every year we go back, it changes more and more. New buildings and homes and condominiums, same as any city. It's always in your mind what it once looked like. Secondary roads, dirt roads, grass and plants not being cared for. Nothing was like it was when I got there ten years later. The look on the people's faces there was different, too. They're free. The Dutch are fun. They like to talk and they like to sing, and they love their beer.

We wanted to go to a certain few places, and they told us these things weren't there. We know there was a church in Uden and they say it wasn't there. I know it was there. It was the one where J. B. Stokes and I went up the belfry to look for our platoon.

The field where we dropped in Holland, there was a man who had a farmhouse in the field. I guess he owned the field. The farmhouse is still there and we went back to visit. Everybody visits. He has a plaque on his property commemorating us. I think Easy Company gave him a plaque, too.

Today, a lot of the people we liberated are gone, but their children, who were ten or twelve years old at the time remember us. They passed on to their children the stories of the sacrifices made for their freedom, so even the little children are so grateful. They still thank us. It's sixty-some years later, and when we walk down the street, people run out of their houses to thank us. They know the eagle on our jackets.

When we dropped into Holland in 1944, there was a woman shoving an autograph book in our faces while we were trying to fight the war. Well, about twenty-five years ago, the woman found us. Yes, she did. Babe and I, and other Easy Company men went to Eindhoven and this woman came up and introduced herself. Her name was Sylvia. I said, "Bring the book tomorrow and we'll sign our real names," and she did. We're friends with her now, and with her son, who was born twenty years after the war.

We have fifty or so people who call us regularly. We meet more and more people we liberated, and then they introduce us to people. One man, Theo Staal, he lives north of Eindhoven, his sister was a young girl of fifteen,

sixteen, when we liberated Eindhoven, and we met Theo and his family when
we went back. He sent us a plaque, which is hanging up in my house. It says:

> *You fought and bought us freedom in Eindhoven on September 18,*
> *1944.*
> *Thanks For Ever [sic]*
> *Your Dutch friends*
> *Family Theo Staal,*
> *Roosendaal—the Netherlands*

When the book Band of Brothers *came out, we got lots of letters; some*
of the Dutch were trying to retrace our steps, figure out where everything
happened. I got a photo in the mail of a green pasture and a ditch filled with
water, looked so peaceful, and on the back it said, "Is this the dike where
Dukeman was killed (p. 149)?" It's their history, too. They research. They
know more than we do.

The Dutch people started coming to the States to visit us, too.
They come to Philly, or E Company reunions, or meet us in Vegas.
They're fun people.

John van Kooijk from the Dutch resistance came and spent a couple weeks
here. John became an American citizen after the war and died soon after. His
son Eddie van Kooijk joined the 101st Airborne and fought in 2nd Battalion
just like us, under our Colonel Strayer. He lives with his wife, Maggie, in
Tennessee. Eddie said to me: "I'll tell you why the Dutch love the American
soldiers. When I was eight years old, I rode on a bike with my mother down
the street in Neunen. We stopped at a corner and a German soldier grabbed
my mother by her neck and threw her on the ground. He got on the bike and
took off. That's not living. Not when a German soldier can do that to my
mother."

On our trip back in 1959, a guy named Eddie Posnick, who was in the 501st, was on a tour with us. He got wounded in Veghel, but before he got wounded, he was in a Catholic school where there had been some heavy fighting, and on the ground, he found a statue of the blessed mother with the head blown off. He was Catholic, so he picked it up, said a few prayers, and put the head in his musette bag. He kept it all through the war. So the tour stopped at the Catholic school, and Eddie laid his musette bag on a desk. The mother superior came down to see us, and when Eddie took the head of the blessed mother out of his bag, the mother superior got all excited and started to scream, "I knew it would come back, I knew it would come back!" She ran up some steps and came down with the rest of the statue, and the head fit right on. She said they had kept it all these years and prayed that the head was going to return. She said people thought they were nuts. All forty of us were in disbelief. We couldn't believe what we saw, the pieces were back together all those years later.

In Aldbourne, everything and everybody we saw during the war is all gone. There are a few pubs that are still there. No horse stables. No barracks. The horse stables were taken apart and relocated to Camp Toccoa, Georgia. Today they don't know who we are. Me and Babe went over there and they threw us out of the pub. They close it from two to four p.m. What kind of joints are these? I think it was the Blue Boar. They're young kids. They have no idea who we are. They're still limeys. They're nice people. but they're still limeys.

We always stop at a pub in London called the Coal Hole. They used to run barges from the Thames River up to the cafe, and they took coal off the barges there. It was a very ritzy place until we got in there! We were on a tour one year, and we were supposed to give a talk, and I don't remember giving a talk, and Bill don't remember giving a talk, but they said we made a nice speech! Even the bobbies come over. They had me outside directing traffic. Bill yelled outside, "Get in here before you get hit in the ass with a bus, no one can see you!" I said, "They can see me!"

Bill and I went to a Mass one Sunday morning in London at a church named Corpus Christi, on Maiden Lane across from the Strand Palace Hotel. The Strand Palace had the Cove and the Gardens, where a lot of us hung out during the war for dances and beer. After the Mass was over, Bill and I were walking out and he said, "Babe, guess who I just got done talking to." He said, "Joe Toye and Chuck Grant." They had since passed away. I looked at him and I said, "Bill, you've got to be kidding me. I just got done talking to both of them, too." We just looked at each other. It was eerie.

I told the story about going back to Aldbourne, to where we ate, slept, and trained, and how I could hear the Easy Company men counting cadence, double-timing, rifle bolts being pulled back, the guys shouting and kidding each other. Bill heard it, too. Is it all in the mind? These kinds of things, they sound strange, but they happen a lot.

We went all the way up into France and they were not as friendly as the Dutch. They wanted no parts of us. What we encountered, someone else may have encountered something different. You see, you can't compare the Dutch with anybody else in Europe. The American troops loved them. They stand out in their minds better than any.

Some of the men go back to Normandy and they remember where they been. Nothing looks the same to me. Nothing's familiar. We've been back to Brecourt Manor a few times, and everything's changed. They try to keep it the same, the trees are there, but they're a lot bigger—it's been sixty years! When I go there, I think about what we did there, the men I was with, how I felt when I was there. Most of the GIs don't like the French, they weren't friendly during the war.

About a year ago, I was contacted by a teacher in France, Christelle Zuccolotto. She lives near Normandy. She was collecting all kinds of documents and photos from the Normandy invasion, she has a big collection. She started the Band of Brothers Project to teach children about the war and the liberation of France. A few of the Easy Company men volunteer time to answer questions from the students—me, Malarkey, Perconte, and one or two others do it. They send us letters and we answer. I never mind helping the kids. They should know their history's no fairy tale.

The first time we went back to Bastogne, thank God it wasn't winter. The foxholes are still there. There's some debris lying in the holes. The outline from the baseplate of the mortar is still there, where Malarkey had it set up. Occasionally they find cartridges or pieces of webbing from soldiers' belts or pieces of weapons. During the war the shelling took all the bark off the trees. The trees grew back. You always get that creepy feeling in Bastogne. There's something about those woods. You always get that feeling a shell's going to come in. You feel very unsettled, very uncomfortable. Being there brings back a lot of memories, none of them good. You don't know how the hell you lived through it.

We think of all kinds of things when we're there. Each soldier has his own personal thoughts about what he experienced there. You think of what happened there, who was where, who was hit, who died where, you look for foxholes. Some of them are graves of our buddies. You barely survived there.

No place has the same charge as Bastogne. It looks like it did in 1944. The woods are there, the foxholes are there. The place is eerie.

We were in Bastogne in 1994 and a little Belgian boy about six years old was with his father, and he was pointing at Bill's leg and saying something to his father in French. I imagine he must have been saying, "What is that, Papa, the man has only one leg?" His father answered him and must have been trying to explain. I said to Bill, "The boy is looking at your leg," and Bill said, "Yeah, I know, he's been looking at my leg since we've been here." So Bill walked over and said to the man, "Tell your son I lost my leg here in these woods, and if he can find it, I'll give him some francs." And the little boy got a big smile on his face, and he took off and came back crying. He told his papa he couldn't find the leg. We gave them both a lot of francs, and the little boy was happy again. It was eerie that it happened in the very place Bill lost his leg.

People often look at Bill's leg and Bill tries to have some humor about it and make people feel better. It shows you mentally how he's carried on with his leg, how he can make light of it himself. Other guys don't fare as well, but Bill accepts life as it is and tries to make the best of everything and enjoy himself at all times. His jokes aren't funny, but he tries.

In Bastogne, there's a monument to Easy Company. It's to all the men that were killed in Bastogne. Everyone goes there to see it. So many that the area's become a tourist attraction, and they hit you up for everything.

We were with a tour group going through the museum, and a bunch of us had to take a pee. So we're in a line, and the line is moving through, Babe is in the back of the line, and a big broad came and told us, "You can't go in there unless you pay." We were all looking through our pockets and bags and nobody had the money we needed to take a pee. So Babe yells from the back of the line, "Go ahead, the piss is on me!" and he paid for everybody. I still laugh at Babe hollering, "The piss is on me!"

It was twenty francs each, one hundred forty francs for everyone. I said to her, "You see those woods over there?" She said, "Yes." I said, "I took about five thousand pisses over there in those woods during the war and you didn't charge me a damn dime!"

★   ★   ★

The main reason we go to Europe is to visit the graves of our buddies, all the men we fought with and left behind. We've been back about fifteen times now. We go to the cemetery in Normandy, Margraten in Holland, Chapelle in Belgium, and Hamm, Luxembourg, where all the kids killed in the Bulge are buried. The cemeteries are beautiful, lush green grass with white crosses about four feet high, as far as the eye can see. Some Stars of David, too. It's sad, but beautiful. It takes your breath away. Especially with snow on the ground and snow in the trees, against the white crosses, what a beautiful picture. It's a very somber place. It affects you. I don't care how hard-boiled you are. It's a very hard thing to do, but it's something we have to do. We lost a lot of kids in Belgium. I'd say Belgium is the hardest. Every time I go there, I visit John Julian's grave, and say a prayer and leave flowers. And I visit Muck and Penkala, and the rest of the guys. They were all just kids.

General Patton is buried there, too. He died right after the war was over; he was killed in an automobile accident and they buried him in Luxembourg.

Once you go to one cemetery, you start thinking of all the guys that were killed, not just the ones that are there. I think of all the guys I fought with from Alley to Zimmerman, alive or dead, I think about all of them. You're there, but you're not there. Anytime you take a veteran that's been in combat to a cemetery, his mind goes back. Now or later he is going to cry. He might cry to himself, but he's going to cry. If they start playing taps, forget about it. It happened to us recently in Normandy. We were with all of the Easy Company men, and they started playing taps. You can't compose. And there was a broad after me, too, that day!

One day we were paying our respects to our buddies buried at Margraten, when the man who drives the tour said, "Hey, Babe, come over here." He was looking at one of the white crosses. There was a kid, Private Lucky, he was killed May the 7th, the day before the war was over. I have a picture of his grave. He wasn't a jumper. He wasn't in the 101st. But the fact that his name was Lucky, and he got it a day before it was over, that was very hard to take. I said to the driver, "How lucky was he." He said, "In name only, Babe."

11

★

"Babe, Meet Babe": *Band of Brothers* Goes to Hollywood

(Bill's Stories in Italics)

Nobody knew Band of Brothers *outside the military community. Then Tom Hanks read it and Steven Spielberg, and from one paragraph about Fritz Niland, a kid in the 501st who had three brothers in the war, came* Saving Private Ryan. *Skip Muck, who we lost in Bastogne, was childhood friends with Fritz Niland, and right after Normandy, Joe Toye, Malarkey, and Muck met Fritz in London. I never met him, but I met his sister in New Orleans after the war. Four Niland brothers were in the war, two were killed in less than a month. The third was missing in action, shot down by a bomber. The Army sent Fritz home after Normandy; he was the only one left. Later, the brother who was MIA was found in a POW camp in Japan. He was rescued* by the British. In the movie, three brothers are killed, they try to get the last kid out of combat and send him home.

That became a hit, and they decided to make another movie about the whole book. I thought they were all nuts. We didn't feel like no heroes. At first, it made me feel bad that we're the only ones that got attention. Everyone won the war. The 501st, the 82nd, the Brits, the Canadians, all the Allies, everyone, not just Easy Company. The whole Army is a band of brothers. The whole military is a band of brothers. I felt like, who the hell am I to be in a book and a movie? I was just a GI from South Philly who did his duty. A lot of vets get mad. They think because we have this book we think we won the war. But we didn't write the book. We got the publicity not because of what we done—a lot of units done great work—but because of the bond of the Easy Company men. We been together sixty-five years. How many can say that?

Tom Hanks and Steven Spielberg came to our reunion in New Orleans in June 1999, and that's when we found out about the movie. They brought a crew from HBO with them. They were shooting it already in London, they just wanted to meet us, and invite us all to the premiere in Normandy on June 6, 2001, D-day. Tom Hanks asked me if I wanted his autograph. I said, "Only if it's on a big fat check!" I told him he should be asking for my autograph. Tom Hanks is a hell of a nice guy. Down to earth. You would never know he was a Hollywood movie star. Spielberg, too. All the men liked them. Spielberg's a local kid. Came from Haddonfield, New Jersey.

They sent documentary crews to our houses, and they asked us questions for seven hours. Lots of questions. Trick questions, too, to see if our memories were intact. They were trying to make the movie as accurate as possible. I told them, "If you can capture what we were, you're going to have a goddamn good movie."

We started getting calls from the kids who were playing us, and we told them no question was off limits. Robin Laing was playing me, a redheaded actor from Scotland. A real nice kid. He has a thick Scottish accent. I didn't know how he was gonna play a guy from South Philly, but let me tell you, he did a fine job! Frank John Hughes was playing Bill. He called Bill every week, and he called me to ask questions also.

While they were making the movie in London, Tom Hanks flew me and Babe to the set to meet the actors. I was so excited to see what they done. Where could you live your life over again and meet these great people? It's an opportunity of a lifetime. We were thinking, How nuts are they to make a movie about us?

When we got to Heathrow Airport in London and got off the plane, a kid came toward us in a paratrooper uniform. It was Frank Hughes. He had the paratrooper uniform on because he didn't have time to change, he had to come right from the set to meet us. Bill shook his hand, and said, "I know who *you* are." He looked just like Bill as a young man. Frank said, "Boy, oh, boy, if you guys ain't got it made when you were kids—I got all the broads coming up to me. You guys must have had a picnic. The uniform draws 'em like flies." I said, "Christ, you even sound like Bill!" He said, "I have to stay in character." He had to stay in character!

When we got to the set in Hatfield, England, they were rehearsing for the Holland scenes. They had a little Dutch village constructed, it looked just like Eindhoven when we jumped there, very authentic. News got around that we were there, and everyone came out to greet us. About a hundred people came out. The actors started introducing themselves by their character names. They were saying, "I'm Popeye Wynn!" "I'm Ralph Spina." One kid said, "I'm Skip Muck." I said,

"I was there when you got it, kid." I said to another kid, "You got a short career, you're not gonna make it." A tall blond kid said, "I wasn't very well liked in the platoon, was I?" I said, "No, you weren't." It was so strange—they were naming our buddies. And they looked and acted like them, even talked like them. It was like being back in time. When I heard "I'm Babe Heffron," I had to do a double take. Robin Laing had the South Philly accent. He sounded like me. Robin unbuttoned his shirt to show me he had on rosary beads and scapular, just like I did all through the war. That really affected me. There were a couple times Bill or I had to walk away for a minute to stay composed. The kids all asked questions about their characters—what were they like, did we have any stories, they wanted to know everything. Donnie Wahlberg, who played Carwood Lipton, said, "You know, meeting you guys inspired us one hundred percent." A fella playing Chuck Grant said, "No, Lip, one hundred fifty percent." What was strange was when Frank Hughes or the other actors would talk to Robin Laing, and he'd say, "Hey, Babe," or "Hey, Heffron." It made me stop and look around.

★　★　★

We got a tour of the set, and they asked us, "Where are we now?" The place was all mud and construction. I said, "Camp Toccoa." I was right. I knew England, France, and Holland. Everything was right on, authentic. For the snow at Bastogne, they cut up little pieces of paper. Even up close, it looked like snow in the forest. And they made what looked like the woods of Bastogne inside of an airplane hangar!

This is funny—I'm still laughing over it: We were on the set and it was supposed to be Upottery Field where we took off for Normandy. I was told the planes were cardboard; you see, they have computers do a lot of work these days to make things look authentic. So me and the Babe are walking and in the distance we see maybe six airplanes. I know these are not real airplanes, but Babe don't know it. So he says, "Let's go take pictures of the airplane; I'll stand in the doorway and you take a picture." So we're about fifty yards away and still he don't know. He's all excited these are the airplanes we jumped out of! So we get to them and he looks at me. He sees they're all cardboard. I start laughing. They did look real. That's Hollywood, kid.

They took us into the editing room and showed us some footage of our D-day drop. Planes all over the sky, paratroopers coming down in the dark. My first combat jump. I'll never forget it. Adrenaline pumping, going into the unknown. That scene made me want to relive that jump in the worst way. Those dirty sons of beetles.

They showed Captain Meehan's plane getting hit, and crashing down on fire with eighteen Easy Company men on board. Me and Bill looked at each other and our eyes filled up. That was rough. Tom Hanks came over to us. We didn't even know he was there. He said, "We just wanted to get your reaction."

They showed more footage of D-day, and I thought, Mother of God, wait until those people see me. They're gonna know why they called me Wild Bill.

Another day on the set we were brought into the room where they replayed the dailies. While me and Bill were watching the monitor, Tom Hanks come up from behind and said, "Bill, Babe, don't turn around yet." When we did, he was dressed in an English officer's uniform. He said, "They gave me a cameo role. I'm going to be an English officer." I said, "Good, Tom, you could use the work." I told Tom Hanks he could use the work! I forgot he was Tom Hanks. He's such a regular guy. I'll tell you, I'd like to put a medal on him. Couldn't do enough for us. He kept telling people, "Take care of Bill and Babe. Take care of my boys from South Philly." Tom Hanks is top shelf.

We went around trying things on at the movie set. We looked ridiculous. The uniforms were heavy. I picked up an M1, I said, "Jesus Christ, it feels like thirty pounds!" When you're young you can pick them up, spin them around, throw them over your head.

I don't think Babe can pick up a machine gun today. We wore helmets, too. Now we put a helmet on, your neck will break.

Babe got his five minutes of fame—he was an extra in the Holland episode, a scene of Eindhoven. He's sitting at a table with a hat on, watching the action. He thinks he's a big shot now. I want to get in one of those Al Capone movies. Or be in Godfather Ten.

★ ★ ★

The first night, the actors came back to the hotel with us for drinks in the lobby bar. HBO gave us an open tab and twenty-four-hour limo service. We hung out with the guys every night. We wanted to see if they could hold their booze—they couldn't. They couldn't even stay up as late as us. Bill said to Frank, "How the hell you gonna play me going home this early?!" At the end of the week, we had a five-thousand-dollar liquor bill. Orange soda and vodka, twenty-two bucks a pop. We hardly slept in seven days, but we had a hell of a good time. Ivan Schwartz, from HBO, looked after us in London the entire two weeks we were there—he became like a son to us, and he visits us in Philly sometimes. What a wonderful guy he is, a credit to HBO.

Every day in London, we would end up giving things away as a memento, including our shirts. The kids would ask for them. I didn't want to end up without a shirt, so I went upstairs, I put three shirts on, and I said to Bill, "I know they ain't gonna get me this time; I put three shirts on." So we're sitting at the bar, and Bill is giving everything away, so he starts on me: "Come on, Babe, give 'em that one.

Give 'em that one, too." I ended up shirtless again, sitting there at the bar. I ended up giving my pants away, too. We were in the best hotel in London, and I was sitting there in my undershorts!

★ ★ ★

We couldn't believe the things the kids told us. They weren't allowed to use their real names the entire year they were shooting the movie. They called Robin Laing "Babe Heffron" and Frank "Bill Guarnere." They lived in foxholes at night, they stayed in character, talked liked us, went to basic training, and lived like we did. Tom Hanks told them right up front, "Anybody that don't want to do what these men did, you may as well quit now, nothing will be said, just go." He said, "You're going to go through what they went through." I never heard of anything like that before. None of them quit, they all stayed. Every one of them was dedicated. Robin Laing, the actor who played me, wore the rosary beads every day during filming, and he opened his shirt in one scene so that I would see them in the movie. He said he hung the rosary and scapular on his bedroom wall and looks at them every morning. Things like that mean a lot.

A couple days after I met Richard Speight, who played our buddy Skip Muck, he said, "Babe, have you seen the cuts?" I said, "No." He said, "Well, do you remember the other day you told me about you and Muck receiving communion up in the woods in the snow in Bastogne, and what you said to Muck—that if you died, you would die in a state of grace?" He said to me, "Babe, I never forgot you telling me that. So when we shot that scene with Father Maloney giving communion, I put that in myself. I turned to the character Babe, and said, 'Well, Heffron, if we die, we'll die in a state of grace.'" Richard Speight did that on his own. That really affected me. I often think of what I said to Muck lying in bed at night. I think, *Well, I'm going to Mass tomorrow. I'm going to say a prayer for Muck and the guys.* Because after communion, you think about dying in a state of grace, and I always think of Muck.

I can't say enough about the actors in *Band of Brothers*. They had the utmost respect for the men, they were dedicated, and they did it the way it was supposed to be done. Colin Hanks, Tom Hanks's son—he played Lieutenant Hank Jones—he's so humble, a real nice guy, like his dad. He told us he enjoyed our company. People don't know this, but Tom Hanks is related to Abraham Lincoln. Abe Lincoln married a Hanks.

★ ★ ★

The first premier was in Normandy on June 6, 2001, on D-day. All the guys were there from E Company. When we saw the movie, we would look at each other at different parts of the action. Seeing it again was a moving experience. You relived the war again all by yourself. It was very personal. Every man had his own thoughts. The parts where any of our buddies got killed were very hard to watch. Lots and lots of memories. I thought about how I had a lot going through my mind then. You're there, but you're not there. Only someone who's been in combat could understand. I only wish Frannie could have been there. She died in 1997. But I know the old gal was with me, looking down on me.

I watched the movie on TV with sixteen of my grandchildren. I cried. They cried. Frank Hughes portrayed me exactly right. He's from the Bronx. He looked like me. They watched Frank and said, "That's Grandpop." So you knew he done a good job. What made the movie good was the casting of the men. The casting was excellent. When I saw the men, I could tell you who they were even before they said who they were. Then I knew they got it right. I could tell where they were in every scene. They added some artistic stuff to the story, but the important stuff was exactly as it was. I think they cursed a little more than we did. But everything was authentic. I give Hanks and Spielberg a lot of credit. They done a wonderful job. Tom Hanks took good care of us. He still keeps in touch. He's done a lot for Easy Company. I can't say enough good things about him.

I didn't watch most of the movie. It's too hard for me, I get too emotional. But I wanted to see what they did with my story about the family in the bunker in Düsseldorf. That affected me more than anything else in the war, because of the children. In the movie, a trooper kicks the door open and there's a woman with two kids standing there, so they leave. Nothing else happens. Tony To, the director, told me they used my story but they changed it to Normandy. I said, "But you didn't say how I felt, you didn't say how I felt for sixty years." It didn't have any context or meaning to it. It was just another scene.

The movie made people want to know more about World War II. People got interested in the Navy and Marine Corps and other units in the military; hopefully, everyone got recognition for their part. If people are learning about history and the importance of freedom, I'll be happy as a lark. Remember, the past is a prelude to the future. Teaches you how to go forward.

Me and Babe have visited schools all over the country and all over the world, and we talk to the kids and we make sure they understand we played a small part in the war, that we done our job, but it took everyone to win the war: the Army, the Navy, the Air Force, the Coast Guard, the Marines, the families, everybody worked together during the war. Without the U.S. Navy, we never would have won the war. How do you think we got overseas? They supplied us. Everyone should get credit.

Since the movie, people in Holland, France Belgium, Luxembourg, every state in the U.S., they write. People send money—ten- and twenty-dollar bills. I send it right back. I get letters from kids ten years old. They're the only letters I answer, letters from kids. I stopped sending autographs to adults that asked for them because I saw they were selling them. So this little kid sent a picture and wrote, "I can't wait to do what you guys in E Company did." So I wrote him a letter, I told him: "You should not even *think* of doing what we did. You kids think war is a heroic thing. Well, let me tell you something: There are no brass bands playing, no flag waving. All you do is worry about staying alive along with the kid that's in the foxhole with you." I get filled up just talking about it. How foolish can these kids be? But I guess I was the same way when I was a teenager. You think it's all glory, and you're going to be a hero, and then you find out what it's really about.

When we were visiting the London set, the documentary crew followed us as we visited the cemetery in Margraten, where seven or eight of our buddies are buried. It was a beautiful day, and we walked ahead of the cameras to have our private moments. Bill was standing near the grave of one of the kids that we knew pretty good, and all of a sudden he just broke down. The worst I've ever seen him. He was crying so hard his body was convulsing, and he held on to the cross. I ran over to him, and the cameraman was putting the camera right in his face, and I said to the director, Mark, "Get him away from Bill! Get that goddamn camera away from Bill! That scene better not be on TV!" Mark agreed, and he stopped rolling. All of a sudden, it hit me, too, and I got bad and Bill said to me, "It's awful, ain't it?" I cried more for Bill crying than I did for anything else. I know he was thinking about his brother along with the kids we soldiered with. Bill's always been the one who keeps it together better than anyone. Now as we get older, Bill's gotten a little bit softer, and if he breaks, I break. It gets harder and harder for us to visit the graves of our war buddies.

★ ★ ★

Me and Bill sometimes go to the Irish pub in Philly at 11th and Walnut to get a sandwich and a beer. One Saturday afternoon Bill said, "Babe, let's take a walk to Chestnut Street to see the Liberty Bell."

I love living in a patriotic city like Philadelphia. People come from all over the world to see this place which is full of our country's history. It's a great feeling walking past the Liberty Bell, Betsy Ross House, and Independence Hall. These are all symbols of our freedom. The cost in blood is never counted, but places like these are reminders. I get goose bumps when I see them.

Bill and I walked a few blocks and sat on a bench across from Independence Hall to watch the tourists coming in and out of the Liberty Bell. The place was mobbed. People of all ages—grandparents and little children, families and couples. I often come to see the Liberty Bell by myself. I take the bus to 3rd Street and walk down to 5th and Chestnut. For a combat veteran, these things get you in the gut. You hope they're more than just tourist attractions. You hope they stand for something important for all these people.

Bill and I just sat there in silence, watching people go in and out.

He said, "You know, Babe, I can't help wonder if Henry's death in Italy, and the kids we got to know and love who didn't come back—I wonder if their sacrifice was worth it."

Bill never gets introspective. Only when he misses Henry. Not a day has gone by in sixty-three years that he hasn't thought about him. He won't tell you, but he gets tears in his eyes when he thinks about him. He wants to go to Italy and see the grave, and we haven't made it over, but he thinks of Henry in any cemetery we go to. Sometimes he's okay and sometimes he breaks down, and I walk over to him and put my arm around him, and say, "Everything's fine, come on." And he says, "I'm okay."

Believe me, I know the sacrifices made by those who fought and lived, and the complete sacrifice made by the kids who never came home. But I saw the faces of the people we set free from their occupiers—from France to Holland to Belgium, and I saw the people in the concentration camp—and I saw the life, and even joy, return to people who'd been starved and beaten close to death, who'd seen their family members die horrible deaths. Even *they* could find joy again once they were free. At least they had the choice.

Even if the people visiting the Liberty Bell don't understand what it symbolizes, it doesn't change what we accomplished. I put my hand on Bill's shoulder and told him, yeah, the sacrifice was worth it. He said, "Yeah, I think so, too."

EPILOGUE

BY *BAND OF BROTHERS* ACTORS FRANK JOHN HUGHES AND ROBIN LAING

BABE (ROBIN LAING)

I first heard the name Heffron when I was asked to read for the part during the casting of *Band of Brothers*. It seemed like a pretty good part and I was very excited even to be considered for such a project. When I arrived, I distinctly remember the casting director, Meg Liberman, talking about Babe—how fantastic a guy he was, how everybody loved him because he was so nice and funny, how inseparable he and Bill were. This was the first inkling I had of the regard in which he was held. The same thing happened when I was recalled to read for Tom Hanks. He must be some guy, I thought. Little did I know.

It was when I met voice coach Jessica Drake that I was to see and hear Babe for the first time. On video he was absolutely captivating. He brought home the random cruelty of war, recounting the simplicity of Jim Campbell telling him, "You stay with your gun Babe, I'll go on up," before the unimaginable happened. He sang songs—"little lambs eat ivy" always has me in stitches! He told lighter stories, too, like the time Al Vittore was asleep next to him in their foxhole. Seemingly Al was dreaming of his wife and slung his leg over Babe, only to be rebuffed with a dig in the ribs and the news, "Hey! I can't help ya!" I was fascinated. I took the audiocassette away with me and listened to it again and again.

It was on this day that I first met Frank (John Hughes). Filming had started and I went for a costume fitting. Joe Hobbs showed me into the changing tent where everyone was watching *Saving Private Ryan* (and getting very excited whenever anyone with the Screaming Eagle patch appeared!). He introduced me and went off to get something. Everyone's interest was piqued by my arrival and I remember hearing, "Babe's here! Get Bill!" being bandied about—fame by association. Frank appeared and we sat and chatted briefly about these two men we were representing. I remember he seemed keen to reassure me that I would have a good time on the project. When I returned to film I realised this was because of the bonds between the "boot camp" guys—the cast who had been together from day one, filmed the scenes of Toccoa, and were actually put through boot camp—and the distance they initially maintained between themselves and the replacements, the new recruits like me who arrived later. This behaviour stemmed from what had really happened during the war and the actors were keen to faithfully mirror it. I learned later from the veterans that this was partly because every new guy reminded them of someone who wasn't around anymore. However, the fact that I was Babe lessened it for me. I felt as if Frank was keeping an eye out for me even when we weren't working together directly, a lot like Bill making sure Babe was in Joe Toye's squad so that he knew he'd be okay.

I was able to get in touch with Bill before I got to talk to Babe, and found it was just as useful as speaking to Babe, as he was much more honest than Babe could be about himself. He told me if I wanted to talk to Babe I'd have to be up early or stay up late because he was never in, he enjoyed life too much. Up at seven in the morning and out until bedtime. As Babe used to say, "You ain't gonna find me dead in bed." I did get him eventually and what a blether (Scottish chat) we had. I didn't get off the phone until well after one in the morning! We talked about many things. General war-talk—what it was like to be involved in such a mammoth war—as well as more specific, personal things. He was amazingly frank and forthcoming about almost everything I asked of him and could recall events with a brilliant clarity. I enjoyed a story about him bumping into a guy who grew up one street over who he'd gone to elementary school with, who had also ended up in the 506th. They were just about to head for Bastogne and he hears a guy shout, "Turn around, touch the ground, eat rabbit shit, and howl at the moon if you're from South Philly!"

I also discovered that while at war Babe carried nothing with him whatsoever, barring his dog tags, rosary, and scapula. I wore all three throughout the entire filming. The daily ritual of putting them on instilled in me the importance of what I was doing. It wasn't just a case of me as an actor looking good; I was playing a living person, something I'd never done before. Once I had the seal of approval from Babe I was able to relax into the responsibility of realising this period of his life. I began to really think about how Babe would react to a situation or whether I thought a scripted line could credibly have come from his mouth. That filled me with an overwhelming sense of pride and satisfaction. I suppose I was lucky that we are quite similar people in our outlook on life. We like to laugh, keep things light, help lift other people when they're a bit down. This was important during filming, not only during the occasional moments of boredom but also when things became tough emotionally. One episode, for example, followed Easy Company as they liberated a concentration camp. The isolation of the set, coupled with the supporting cast of emaciated detainees, made these days very challenging. I made a conscious effort to stay upbeat, not to get too introspective. What it must have been like for the veterans is unimaginable. It was hard enough seeing the re-creation.

Bill and Babe came to visit while we were filming, and the excitement on set that day was palpable—Babe and Bill were coming! By the time I arrived there was a huge semicircle of people listening to them chat with Tom Hanks. I introduced myself to Babe and he did likewise before looking me up and down. Then he asked how I was getting on with the accent. "Fine," I replied. "Let me hear it," he said, and so I took a deep breath and did my best Philly accent. "No, your Philly accent," Babe said. He must have seen the disappointment on my face because he didn't let it hang in the air too long before breaking into a laugh and giving me a slap on the back. "I'm only messing witcha, you did fine." That moment has to rank among the proudest in my life.

Babe gave me his scapula—the one given to him by his mother before he left America, the one he kept through the entire war. He casually passed it on to me one day saying, "You're gonna need it now, kid, you're the one at war!" I still treasure it. That is probably the best illustration I can ever give of Babe's generosity and humility, coupled with his sense of humour.

That first night, we all went to the hotel where he and Bill were staying and talked, laughed, and drank until a ridiculous hour. Bill and Babe stopped taking meds they were on just so that they could drink. That's dedication for you. By the end of the night Babe was sitting in his vest having given his shirt and T-shirt away to guys who had offhandedly admired them. Everyone who came that night was made to feel special, another of the unique things about those men.

We kept in touch throughout filming but I didn't get to see Babe again until 2001 when I was invited by HBO, with my partner Pauline, to go to Philadelphia for the premiere of *Band of Brothers*. Babe was in the hospital at the time, and I went to visit him. It was such a shame that he couldn't be at the premiere to be recognised by the city and the country. I know he already has been in many ways but there was something specific about that night, whether it was the presentations by [then Pennsylvania Governor] Tom Ridge, the reception, or just the chance to see himself on the big screen. We did our best to represent him in the only way he'd want us to, by enjoying the evening and having fun.

The rest of our time spent in Philly was indicative of the esteem in which Babe is held. Everywhere we went, whether it was the Irish Pub—Babe sent us to see Jimmy and eat cheesesteaks—or at Cousins for breakfast, everyone knew who he was, and in his absence I got his respect. I must say Bill was fantastic that week, driving us all over Philadelphia to see where he and Babe had grown up. Telling us about what they had done to survive the Depression. Taking us to Popi's to experience broccoli rabe for the first time. The welcome we got by Bill's and Babe's families is something we'll never forget.

Just the fact that a laddie from Arbroath, Scotland, could end up playing this most Philadelphian of men is an indication of how incredible my relationship with him has been (although in truth the places aren't that different; the Declaration of Arbroath, pronouncing Scotland's independence from England, is said to be the template for the American one, which was, of course, signed in Philadelphia).

My wife and I often brag of the huge, extended family we've got in Philly. I'd bet that we see each other just as much as any family who lives continents apart—not as much as we'd like, but savoring it when we do.

Robin Laing
Edinburgh, Scotland
February 2007

BILL (FRANK JOHN HUGHES)

June 2000, London, England. It is unusually warm outside the Heathrow International terminal. I'm perspiring in my Army dress greens. They are standard 1944 issue, olive drab wool and they itch like a suit of poison ivy.

I have been wearing the uniform for almost three months now during the production of *Band of Brothers*—and everything about these clothes reflects the hard-earned pride and unshakable confidence of the American paratrooper. From the cocky angle of my "overseas cap" to the bloused trouser tucked inside my Corcoran jump boots and the Screaming Eagle patch on my left shoulder—everything emotes poise and swagger and I'm doing my best to look the part.

Up until this point I have never worn my dress greens in public and the experience is fascinating. To the average Brit who is not an expert in World War II uniforms, I am a modern-day American soldier—and heads are turning. It seems the women have become flirtatious, the men have become defensive, and the children are in awe.

I am intensely aware that it is not me, an actor full of untested courage due to my peacetime life, that generates this respect and curiosity. It is the 101st Airborne uniform that is doing all the work and many a good men have given their lives to infuse it with those qualities.

And it is two of these men that I have come to meet—Babe Heffron and his best friend—the man I am portraying in *Band of Brothers*—"Wild Bill" Guarnere, the Silver Star–winning legend of Easy Company. Although we have never met in person, we have been talking for a few hours every day for about six months and I'm eager to shake his hand and buy him a drink.

I first made contact with Bill on November 18, 1999—the night before my fourth and final audition for the miniseries. It was a gig I wanted more than anything in my life and I was hoping that a last-minute call would give me some kind of good luck—some edge that would make the difference.

I had read the book a few months before our first chat and had spent every waking moment since becoming an expert on all things Easy Company and all things Guarnere. The more I learned about him the more superhuman he became to me. From his rough-and-tumble childhood on the streets of Depression-era South Philly to his losing a leg in Bastogne to save the life of his friend—it all added up to a man unlike any other I had ever known. A hero. A legend, and I needed to hear his voice to make him "real" to me.

I dialed and hoped there was something he could say or share with me, some intimate inside knowledge of who he was, that I could use to set me apart from the other actors auditioning the next day.

At the end of the first ring he picked up and shouted, "Yowza!" in a raspy voice still full of Dead End Kid.

"Mr. Guarnere . . . it's a real honor to talk with you, sir. My name is Frank John Hughes and I am one of the actors who will be auditioning tomorrow to play you in *Band of Brothers*."

"Well, I don't think you'll get it. An actor came by my house last night and he seemed real right for it. But good luck with it."

I was taken aback. *Other actors had been to his house!?* So much for my "edge." "Where ya from, kiddo?"

"The South Bronx, but I live in Los Angeles now."

"What can I do for ya?"

"Any words of advice?"

"Yeah. Just be the devil. Cause I was a devil over there. A paid killer. Got it?"

They were chilling words.

"Anything else I can help you wit'?"

"No, sir, that's all."

I dug down and found some paratrooper swagger and added, "I'll call you when I get the job. I'll have a lot of questions for you then." Bill liked that and gave a hearty "sure ya will" laugh.

"Okay, kid, we'll see."

Well, I did get the job and I did call him. From that moment on Bill did what he and most of the men that served in WWII hated doing most—he talked about his war experiences. To do so was always akin to committing an act of blasphemy. To talk about what you did was perceived as bragging—a high crime to these noble, humble men. To his credit Bill intrinsically knew that in many ways his legacy—and more important the legacy of Easy Company—depended on the men's recollections to fill out Ambrose's wonderful book. So Bill did what he always did—he took the courageous route and emptied everything he had to give. His memory was impeccable and searing in its brutal honesty, failing only when it came to describing his own acts of heroism—which I found was the same for every Easy man.

It was through Bill's mouth, in vivid detail, that I came to know the leadership of Winters, the healing hands of Roe, and the wisdom of Lipton. From him I came to know intimately the courage and toughness of Heffron, Martin, Randleman, Compton, Malarkey, and Toye. All of these conversations ran through my mind as I waited for him and Babe to land on that June day.

Finally they emerged. Babe, strong as an ox, shuffling toward me as he carried and pushed *both* men's luggage. He gave me a wink and a smile as I walked up to them only to have Bill blow past on his crutches at a speed faster than any man on two legs could move. A blur of blue shirt, hat, and bolo tie. "Hiya, kid!" he said as he shot past me and was gone.

Babe shook his head and looked at me with his seen-it-all eyes. "That's Wild Bill, Frank. Needs to have a cigarette and flirt with the girls!"

When we did catch up to him we found Bill propped against the wall, hat on a jaunty angle, an unfiltered Pall Mall on his lips, winking at the passing ladies—throwing out "Hiya, ssshhweetheart!" in a voice like Bogart's. I took a moment to admire the men—full of energy and fire this late in a life that would have crushed most men. Still he oozed paratrooper guts and swagger. My God, what he must have been like at eighteen!

Since then I have had the honor of traveling the world with these two amazing men. Across the globe they have drank men fifty years younger than them under the table and stayed up later than everyone else. They remain unbreakable. Forged with materials men of my generation will never have or even know. Their unshakable commitment to each other through times of bliss and horror has taught me so much about friendship—a term they do not use lightly. Over the years Bill has taught me so much about being a better father, husband, citizen, and man. He has become like a grandfather to me and my wife and a great-grandfather to my son who has been fortunate enough to learn his history from the mouths of the men who made it. Bill is fond of the phrase, "A man is never bigger than when he bends to help a child." He lives that quote. Not only with my son but with the thousands of school-age children he and Babe visit around the world. I am honored to call him and Babe my friends.

With boundless love and respect I cheer *"Currahee!"* to both of them.

Your grateful friend,
Frank John Hughes
New York City, 2007

ACKNOWLEDGMENTS

Many thanks to our agent, Scott Miller, of Trident Media Group and to Natalee Rosenstein, our editor at the Berkley Publishing Group. Special thanks to Tom Hanks, Frank John Hughes, and Robin Laing. We'd also like to thank Michelle Vega at Berkley, Emma Stockton, Sooki Raphael, Trisha Heffron Zavrel, Arlene Guarnere, Fred Post, Michael Boone, Sara Shay, William F. Keller, Lorraine Dispalgo, Rod Bain, Don Malarkey, Ralph Spina, Susan Smith Finn, Lana Luz Miller, Pete Toye, Eileen O'Hara, Rudolph Tatay, Tracy Compton, Peter van de Wal, Tracy Rhodes, and last but not least, our families.

INDEX

INDEX

INDEX

INDEX

INDEX